ONLY COPY.

Roots of Jamaican Culture

Roots of Jamaican Culture

MERVYN C. ALLEYNE

PLUTO  PRESS

First published 1988 by Pluto Press
345 Archway Road, London N6 5AA

This edition published 1989

Distributed in the USA by Unwin Hyman Inc
8 Winchester Place, Winchester MA 01890, USA

Copyright © Mervyn C. Alleyne 1988, 1989

Printed and bound in the United Kingdom by
Billing & Sons Ltd, Worcester

British Library Cataloguing in Publication Data

Alleyne, Mervyn
  Roots of Jamaican culture
  1. Jamaica—Civilization
  I. Title
  972.92   F1874

ISBN 0-7453-0369-2

972.92
ALLE

Contents

List of Tables and Figures

Tables I, II and III are taken from Philip Curtin, *The Atlantic Slave Trade (1969)*. Copyright © University of Wisconsin Press. Reproduced with permission.

Preface

"A People without the knowledge of their past history, origin and culture is like a tree without roots."

Marcus Mosiah Garvey

This book explores the African contribution to the culture of Jamaica. It does so from two different, but integrated perspectives. It examines those aspects of contemporary Jamaican culture that may have parallels in Africa; and, more importantly, it looks at the transmission of what I shall call an African culture to Jamaica and the evolution of that culture in Jamaica. This process therefore entails both continuities and discontinuities. These and other key concepts will be defined and clarified in Chapter 1. But it is essential to begin by discussing the larger political issues that this book inevitably raises. To leave these issues unattended would cloud the real purpose of the book, which is to assemble under one cover, for the information of Jamaicans in general and as a resource for teachers and students of Jamaican history, facts, analyses, and interpretations concerning major aspects of the cultural development of the Jamaican people.

A group of history teachers has publicly made a call for such a study of the cultural history of Jamaica, about which virtually nothing has been written (but see Brathwaite 1971, 1981; Higman 1976; Baxter 1970; Alleyne and Hall, forthcoming).

We need to know about all the various ethnic groups that have contributed to the Jamaican cultural mosaic. We also need a major work of synthesis that would show the cultural outcome of the social, political, and economic interaction of these different groups in different periods of our history, culminating in what many people now refer to as "Jamaican culture" (in keeping with the national motto "Out of many, one people").

However, one group in particular – descendants of the African slaves brought here from the sixteenth century onwards – played a central role in this creative process. This group is demographically the largest, and it is the reservoir and agent of what is most distinctive and defining about Jamaican culture. It is therefore fitting that such a study should begin with the history of this group.

Interpretations of the cultural history and cultural affinities of the Jamaican people are inevitably strongly influenced by political considerations, and will be used for political ends. The earliest interpretations of the culture of Africa-derived New World peoples were based on racist beliefs about the physical and intellectual inferiority of the "Negro".

Later, new liberal interpretations emerged in North America, where White reformists explained Black culture as a deviant offshoot of White European culture, created by the abject social conditions (poverty, unemployment, and lack of education) in which Black people had to live. These reformists believed that once programmes for the social and economic uplift of the "Negro" were put into effect, Blacks would become culturally identical with Whites. In more recent times, Black ideologues seeking to establish autonomous Black nations in the Americas or to repatriate Blacks to Africa have stressed that Blacks are culturally distinct from Whites. Anthropological studies of Black culture are differently interpreted and put to widely different uses by thinkers of different political persuasions. Studies showing that New World Blacks have retained the essential characteristics, however veiled, of their ancestral African culture are welcomed by Black nationalists, both in the USA and in the Caribbean, where radical political movements stress the need to defend Black economic interests and to promote Black culture. But these same studies are used by rightwing extremists to back their calls for racial segregation, on the grounds that Blacks are intellectually incapable of assimilating White culture in spite of 300 years of contact and intense formal schooling in English.

There are three main theories about what became of African culture(s) in the New World. According to one view, Africans were stripped of their culture because of the brutalising effects of slavery and the deliberate mixing together of slaves of different ethnolinguistic origins. Others, for example Mintz and Price (1976), agree that Africans were unable to maintain their traditional culture, but believe that slaves created an original new culture in the New World. I myself have argued, along with other scholars, that Afro-American culture is largely an extension of African culture, though African influence is greater in some parts of the New World than in others (Alleyne 1980, Abrahams and Szwed 1983).

In trying to evaluate the merits of these different theories, we need to address a number of questions. For example, was the harshness of slavery an insurmountable barrier to the continuation of African culture(s) in the New World? Were slaves deliberately and effectively mixed to prevent interaction by members of the same ethnolinguistic group, or did the ethnolinguistic distribution of slaves – especially in the crucial early period – simply reflect the geographic development of the slave trade? How culturally diverse were Africans brought to the New World? Did the slaves quickly "orient their allegiances in New World rather than African directions" (Price 1980: p. 194), or did they continue throughout the history of the New World to see Africa as their ancestral home? [1] Did slaves of different nations (or ethnic groups) tend at first to isolate themselves from one another and pursue their own ethnic activities (Schuler 1979: p. 66) [2], or were new cross-ethnic bonds created, for example bonds between "shipmates"? (See pp. 71–2 below.)

The theories of "culture-stripping" and "original creation" both deny or minimise the importance of African cultural continuities, while the "original creation" and the "African continuities" theories both agree that Afro-American culture is not a mere parasite on "mainstream" culture, but is autonomous and distinctive. For the purposes of argument, we can narrow the debate down into a confrontation between the "deficit" and the "difference" hypotheses, in which case this study comes down unequivocally on the side of "difference". However, unlike Mintz and Price, I emphasise rather than minimise the importance of African influences, though I recognise that they are not everywhere equally strong at the present time.

This study of the fate of African culture in Jamaica does not necessarily assume that Jamaica is typical of Afro-America. Common features in the Afro-American experience have attracted the attention of anthropologists and linguists alike, but each region of Afro-America and each segment and layer of the Afro-American population remains different and distinctive. In some important ways Jamaica is not typical of the rest of Afro-America. In Jamaica one African ethnic group (the Twi) provided political and cultural leadership (as did the Ewe-Fon in Haiti); throughout the post-Columbian history of Jamaica a number of Maroon communities have served as custodians of African culture (as they also have in Suriname); after the cessation of hostilities with the British, some of these Jamaican Maroon communities developed close relations with the general Afro-American population, especially in St Thomas, Portland, St Mary, and St Andrew); finally, after emancipation, small peasant communities grew up in the remote hilly areas of Jamaica creating pockets of isolation and conservatism. Though none of these features is unique to Jamaica, their combination is unique, and helps to explain the distinctive course of Afro-American culture on the island.

I would like to think that this book does not set out to "prove" anything, but assertions of objectivity and scholarly detachment are in themselves meaningless and unconvincing. In any case, this book was not written from a position of indifference. I have been, at different times, a Marxist and a Black nationalist; I have come close to Rastafarianism, and I have tried to reconcile all three of these positions. I have never stood aloof from the struggles of Black peoples against racism and oppression and I believe that these struggles must continue, on several fronts. Imperialism in the twentieth century has been and continues to be inextricably bound up with racism, so that the struggle against oppression has not only a "class" but also a "race" aspect. I wrote this book both because of my academic interest in anthropology and linguistics and because I want to deepen Black self-awareness (and the awareness of others of Blacks). This does not inevitably condemn the book to partiality and bias. But for authors simply to assert that they are not subject to bias is pointless. More sensible is to allow the book to speak for itself.

I should like to thank the University of the West Indies and the ZWO of Holland for their support in the final stages of this book. Beverley Hall, Ena Campbell, Waldo Heilbrun, and Chris de Beet also helped with their valuable comments. Without Greg Benton's brilliant hand, the final version would never have seen the light of day.

Glossary

abeng   wind instrument made from a cowhorn and used by the Maroons in rituals and to give warning of the approach of outsiders.

anansi   in Akan and Jamaican tradition, a spider folk hero, often an anti-hero, the central character of folk tales.

asiento   import licence or patent which carried with it the privilege of controlling the slave traffic to the Spanish colonies in the New World.

bozal   term used to refer to slaves born in Africa, in contrast with slaves born in the New World (creole).

code switch   the use of elements from more than one language system within the same utterance. It is assumed that social and contextual factors trigger the switch from one code to another.

creole   originally meant of European origin, but born in the colonies, and referred to persons, animals, trees, plants. It then came to designate persons of African descent born in the New World, and from there, the language related by vocabulary to the European language, and which was spoken by African creoles in the colonies in the New World and on the West African coast.

dreadlocks   special way of arranging hair into locks practised by Rastafarians.

driver   category of occupation on a slave plantation. Head of a gang of slaves responsible for seeing that the tasks for the day were completed.

dundus   albino, African person lacking in black skin pigmentation. It may also mean freak, someone who is not physically normal.

duppy   spirit or ghost in Jamaica. More or less synonymous with *jumbi* (s.v.).

ginal   tricky or crafty person, a con-man. The word is derived from "general".

griot   person or member of caste whose responsibilities were to act as musician or praisesinger (in Senegal and Gambia).

interloper   unauthorised slave trader.

ital   probably derived from "vital". Adjective describing vegetarian food or food prepared without salt.

xii Roots of Jamaican Culture

jonkunu   band of masqueraders and musicians who parade through streets at Christmas time.

jumbi   (also *zombi, nzambi, mvumbi*). In Bantu religion and in the New World, deity or spirit.

Maroon   name given to slaves who fled into interior and set up independent communities. Three such communities exist today in Jamaica: Accompong, Scott's Hall, Moore Town.

mento   best known traditional song and rhythm of Jamaica. Also, type of dance associated with it.

myal   spirit; a form of religious music counteracting the evil of obeah.

obeah   the practice of "black" magic in Jamaica and the English-speaking West Indies.

obeahman   sorcerer

pidgin   a jargon, usually for trade, formed by contact between a European language and a non-European one during the age of colonialist expansion.

piezas de India   measure of potential labour used in *asiento* contracts. A young adult male was one *pieza*; the very young, the old, and the females were defined as fractions of a *pieza*.

quadroon   offspring of a white person and a mulatto, i.e. who has a quarter of African blood.

sabir   trade language of the Mediterranean in the Middle Ages. Also known as *lingua franca*.

vodoun   (also *vodu, vodun*). In the Ewe-Fon language and culture (of Benin), a lesser deity in the polytheistic system of religion. In Haiti, it refers to the whole religion based on the syncretism of Roman Catholic and African elements.

Introduction

The issues presented and discussed in this book do not lend themselves to final solution. Cultural forms are so complex that we can never be quite sure that we have grasped them in their fullness. Apart from the content and function of the form, there is the total structure into which it fits. The form may point in one historical direction and the content or function in another. Take for example the Jamaican Creole word *ben* (and its variants such as *min*, *en*, and *wen*). The outer form points in the direction of the English word "been"; the meaning of *ben* is "past time", either anterior to another past time (cf. English *had* + verb) or simple past time combinable with non-perfective aspect (*mi en a iit* "I was eating"). This makes it somewhat but not altogether like English "been". *Ben* functions as a preverbal invariable particle quite unlike anything in English; and it fits into a verb phrase structure that is very similar to the verb structure of some West African languages.

Cultural forms can become so transformed across the generations that they sometimes appear as imperfect or pathological manifestations of forms belonging to some other culture. Herskovits (1947: p. 26) understood this when he said of Trinidadian rural family structure that "we are faced with a retention of African custom that has been reinterpreted so drastically as to make the resulting institutions not only susceptible of description as pathological manifestations of the European family but ones which have been frequently so described". It is well known that Jamaican language is generally viewed as "corrupt" or "bad" or "broken" English. But, as I will show later, it is more plausible to derive Jamaican language forms from West African forebears, with languages like Saramaccan and Sranan (spoken in Suriname) representing intermediary stages of this evolution. Even within Jamaica the same linguistic form may appear to be dysfunctional and "corrupt" in one context, e.g. in juxtaposition to standard English) but not in another (say a rural village). Another example is the concept of time. In a rural environment, time is not represented by precise points on a chronometer, but relates to the slow gradual movement of geophysical phenomena and the behaviour of nature. Similarly, Jamaican language does not express tense as fixed categories of past time, past in relation to another past ("pluperfect"), present time, and future time, but shows whether an action is completed or not, whether it is in the process of unfolding, whether it is habitual, or whether it is prospective. In an urban industrialised context, this view of time appears

1

pathological and dysfunctional.

Finally there is the question of "proof" and what would constitute proof. The anthropological "sciences" cannot and do not approach the question of proof and evidence in the same way as the natural sciences or even the legal sciences. Within anthropology different disciplines have developed analytical methodologies of differing degrees of formal scientific rigour. Linguistics is an anthropological science that has developed rigorous methodologies of analysis. Linguists do not approach the "solution" of the historical problem of the origin and evolution of words, language structures, and languages in the same way as social anthropologists approach the problem of, say, the origin of family structure. Though social anthropologists are bound by the universal demand for adequacy and accuracy of observation, their methods are largely those of common sense and logic (precise definitions, consistent use of concepts, and so on).

Linguists, however, have paid considerable attention not just to concepts but also to methods. There is a general consensus among linguists about methods of reconstructing earlier stages of a language or of assigning languages to their ancestors. It therefore becomes possible to operate with an assurance approximating the "proof" of natural sciences in describing the origin of language forms, whereas the analytical methodologies of other branches of the anthropological sciences are not so formal, rigorous, or uniform.

Some argue that historical origins are not only difficult to ascertain but are uninteresting, since they say nothing about the total structure or framework within which given cultural forms function. For example, certain forms of family structure can be found in different parts of the world, even though they are not historically connected. (See, for example, Oscar Lewis 1966.) It is therefore pointless (so the argument goes) to assign any one instance of such forms to a particular ancestor, since the existence of like but unrelated forms elsewhere shows that the alleged ancestor is not necessary to explain and account for the existence of the form in question. It is therefore more useful (so the argument concludes) to look at how the form functions within the total social, economic, and cultural environment, and to explain its existence in terms of that environment. In Jamaica today, the strong resistance to teaching African history, either above or alongside European history, and to the strengthening of ties with Africa as a recognition of Jamaica's historical affinity with Africa, is an echo of this argument.

It is generally true that a custom, cultural form, or institution will tend to be meaningless outside its social context, but this assertion needs qualifying. The claim of anthropologists like Radcliffe-Brown (1952) and Malinowski (1945) that societies are natural systems all the parts of which are interdependent, each serving in a complex of necessary relations to maintain the whole, and that their history is irrelevant to an enquiry into their nature, is too extreme.

This position, known as structural functionalism, is based on an assumption of homogeneity and stasis in human societies. Modern societies, however, are characterised rather by heterogeneity, change, and conflict, and are therefore best described as "plural". Some cultural forms become recessive and archaic, and the people who practise them become marginal. This may create "dysfunctionalities", an aspect of functionalism not envisaged by Malinowski and Radcliffe-Brown. Societies and cultures have always been subject to change, but change has become a defining feature of modern societies. No theory of society and culture can ignore this dynamism. The structuralist-functionalist restriction seems most appropriate to "primitive" cultures that are already presumed to be old. Enquiry into the earlier history of these "primitive" cultures is often little more than speculation and conjecture. Modern societies (in the sense of having just emerged) – including Jamaican society – are different. In modern societies the past is very much part of the present; our understanding of contemporary society and culture in Jamaica will be deepened by an exploration of Jamaican cultural history.

All things both social and natural are both "being" and "becoming". Viewed from a vertical perspective, they are in constant evolution; viewed from a static or horizontal perspective, they are in a structural relationship with one another. These two perspectives should not be confused, though they may be fused conceptually. Jamaican society and culture is at the same time both being and becoming. My research suggests that some aspects of the structural relations between elements of "being" are really a reflection of the dynamic evolutionary process that has taken place and is still taking place. I shall discuss this dialectic at different points in this book. However, my main emphasis will be on evolutionary aspects of Jamaican society and culture. It is not only eminently valid to ask where Jamaican culture came from, what evolutionary processes brought it to its current state, and what factors were at play in these evolutionary processes; it is also humanly and politically essential that a community or society or nation be aware of its cultural heritage, for it is not just a cliché to say that "a people without a past is a people without a future". I will therefore assume that there is no further need to elaborate on the need for an historical view of the culture of African slaves and their descendants in Jamaica, even if my conclusions may lack the kind of proof associated with the exact sciences.

However, we must be sure that what we seek to do is worthwhile. It is not enough simply to match up contemporary Jamaican cultural forms with contemporary African cultural forms in order to classify Jamaican culture as African (or non-African, if no plausible matches are made; or "mixed" if matches with more than one other culture can be established). Such a procedure would have only very limited value, e.g. for establishing a cultural typology of the world on the basis of selected common features. As we have seen, even unrelated cultures share common features, and in itself such a classification would say nothing about historical affinities. Rather it would help to identify cultural absolutes or universals and generalised cultural traits. Though this might help to enlighten our understanding of the human condition, it would say little or nothing about genetic and derivational relationships.

I am therefore not claiming that there has been a "mixture" of African and European elements in Jamaica. I accept that it is not useful to view Jamaican culture as a mechanical pitchforking of elements of culture like bundles of hay from one culture to another. What I cannot accept is that in order to understand the culture of Jamaicans or any of its elements we must study it only as it works in its actual new setting, by its own mechanisms, under drives and incentives not inherited from the past or borrowed, but engendered by the new institutions. Such a restriction would fail to account for Jamaica's cultural differentiation, which has led some anthropologists to call Jamaican society "plural". This differentiation can often be conceived as a continuum of variants (I will return to this concept of continuum, which must be central to any study of Jamaican culture, in later chapters). Jamaica's cultural differentiation reflects both the different historical experiences of different groups in society as they continue along cultural paths blazed by their forebears; and their present dynamic interaction. This interaction is apparently leading to the emergence of a common value system and "national" traits that are prompting some anthropologists to reject the idea that Jamaican society is plural.

It is important to go beyond the folkloristic tabulation of "quaint" artifacts and the matching of them with counterparts in Africa. We must deal rather with evolutionary processes and seek explanatory models that can cover most data and answer most questions about the development of Africa-based Jamaican culture, and Afro-American culture in general. These questions include not only what things "survived", but why they survived; why are there more, and different, survivals in some areas of Afro-America and in some segments of each individual Afro-American society than in others; and is "survival" the most appropriate term for conceptualising Africa-based culture in the New World.

Needless to say, these evolutionary processes take place within, and are influenced by, a specific social context. Cultural traditions are seldom transmitted intact from one setting to another. They change in different ways, according to how the new social contexts vary. Black cultures of the New World, all of them plausibly derived from the same African cultural tradition, encountered different social settings in each island or continent zone. The similarities between them can be accounted for by similar social settings. Cultural traditions constantly adapt to new conditions and new needs, even when they do not "migrate" and are not subject to intense revolutionary, social, and political change (such as contact with another culture). When a people migrates, it may find in its new social setting either conditions that are conducive to the maintenance of its cultural traditions, or conditions that force it to adapt and even to change drastically. Whether these adaptations or changes should be conceptualised as "continuities" and "discontinuities" or as "creative adaptations" is something that must be demonstrated *a fortiori*. A cultural form may undergo such drastic change as a result of social pressures that it seems more a "creation" than a "continuity". But perhaps the issue is a terminological one, or one of perspective: those who opt for "continuity" take the historical perspective, while those who opt for "creativity" take the synchronic perspective. A sociological approach, structural or functional, stresses creativity, whereas an historical and cultural-anthropological approach stresses continuities and discontinuities.

The task of anthropologists must be to construct a model or a framework that can deal with culture both as "becoming" and as "being": both as an evolution from a given cultural base, however much transformed, and as a creative response to and structural component of social context.

Orthodox historians may dissent from the resort to anthropological methods in what purports to be a "history" of Jamaica. Today, history has progressed from chronology to interpretation and from data to theory, but still it has largely limited itself to politics, constitutions, economics, and society. This is not altogether different from traditional historiography. When royalty and aristocracy wrote their own history or employed chroniclers to write it for them, they tended to dwell on things that were important to them: wars, conquests, royal successions, constitutional changes, and the like. Changes at the top inevitably brought changes in the focus of historical research. Bourgeois history focussed on institutional change, mercantile expansion, colonialism, and imperialism; implicit in it was a view of the "masses" as objects of history, and never as its subjects. The few times that the "masses" did anything worthy of a historian's attention was when they reacted to the actions of their rulers (or, in some charitable writings, when they resisted the iniquities of ruling-class villains).

Caribbean history has adopted these concerns. It has viewed its subject from the angle of the ruling classes, and has traditionally focussed on the policies of the British Parliament and Government towards Jamaica, as exercised either from England or through the agency of Governors and Colonial Secretaries in Jamaica. Its concern is for documentation and "proper" sources. This fixation on documentation and written sources is viewed as a universal historiographical "methodology". Documents and sources show us how the ruling classes, being highly literate and bureaucratic, viewed themselves and the societies they ruled. For that, documents are indispensable.

In nations that are culturally homogeneous and politically, socially, and economically more or less integrated, ordinary people participate in society's institutions, so that constitutional, institutional, and economic history is relevant to their lives. Jamaican society before the end of the nineteenth century (and, to a lesser extent, after it) was so deeply divided that documents alone can give little insight into the lives of most people. Historians of the legislative system, of trade, of the educational system, and of the "Church", both before and in most cases also after the end of the nineteenth century, pass silently over the lives of the majority of the population. Similarly, the intricacies of constitutional change in the West Indies, however fascinating, tell us more about the mentality of the colonisers than of the colonised. So though we find histories of sugar, the medical services, schooling, welfare institutions, and the "Church", we find few or none about food crops, bush medicines, burial societies, pocomania, market systems. For this there are two main reasons. First, Black culture was considered backward and not worthy of historical study. Second, it could not be studied because there were no "documents" about it. Black culture therefore came to be seen as "folk" culture and was consigned to anthropology and folklore studies.

Still, new questions are being asked about Caribbean history. Rather than simply asking why England or France abolished slavery, what were the differences between British, Spanish, French, and Dutch slave systems and so on, historians are looking more and more at slave revolts and other forms of resistance. Rather than simply study the history of, say, sugar as an economic enterprise or a form of technology, historians are beginning to look at independent peasant movements.

Documentation can only be a feature of those societies – they have always been a minority – that value the written word above the spoken word. In order to develop a history of Jamaica and the Caribbean that brings the ignored majority to the foreground, we must utilise additional techniques and methods.

The thesis of this book is that Africans arrived in Jamaica from the end of the fifteenth century, but most significantly from the middle of the seventeenth century, bringing with them aspects of their homeland culture. No group of migrants, however well organised and well prepared, can transmit an entire culture to a new location; and the Africans, far from being organised and prepared, were forcibly extracted from their homelands, with which they then lost virtually all contact. Some aspects of African culture could therefore not be brought to the New World. Political and economic institutions and a full array of tools, instruments, and foods, could not be easily transported. What could be transported were acquired skills, memories, habits, predispositions, cognitive orientations, and language – all beneath the surface of consciousness, and persistent even in the worst conditions. Such resources were applied to the task of adapting to the new environments. If at first a displaced people could not bring its currency, its markets, and its systems of accumulating capital, private or corporate, to the New World, once it began to produce goods in the new environment, it could call upon its collective memory and predispositions to organise such systems in conformity with the new conditions. This would be my interpretation of the development of peasant market systems in Jamaica.

The term culture has many meanings and dimensions. It is a property of individuals[1], and it is a property of societies, since without humans interacting there can be no culture. Some aspects of culture, e.g. institutions, are located in society; others, e.g. world view, artistic sensitivity, language, and non-verbal communicative devices and strategies, are located in individuals. People who share these common properties and who participate in the same institutions and organisations belong to the same "culture". The word "same", of course, must be loosely interpreted. A culture is a continuum of variation. Different individuals possess "commonly shared" cultural features in different ways, to different degrees, and in different conglomerations; for example, dialect differences in language. So it is difficult, if not impossible, to demarcate precisely the area of a culture or the body of people who subscribe to it.

This leads me to two observations. First, it makes no sense to say that "Africans were stripped of their culture", except in the most obvious and trivial sense that they could not take all their cultural institutions and trappings with them to the New World. Historians must determine what aspects of their culture enslaved Africans took with them through the Middle Passage, and what aspects they could not take with them. To do so they need a theory of cultural transmission; information about the culture of African slaves in the early period of the colonisation of Jamaica; and reconstructions of the past based on data from contemporary Jamaican culture.

My second observation refers to the notion of "African culture". Clearly Africa is a continent with a vast number of peoples and cultures. However, Sub-Saharan Africa, or Black Africa, has certain unique traits that set it apart from the rest of the world. The notion "African culture" does not mean that all inhabitants of the Sub-Sahara region share a common set of cultural traits or institutions in which they all equally participate. It merely means that they have more in common with each other than with any other human groups. The conglomerate of Africans arriving in Jamaica would belong to an "African culture" in this sense. Many scholars have described this cultural zone, and within it some have established cultural subzones that are even more homogeneous. One such subzone is West Africa, from where the vast majority of New World Africans came. Studies have shown that West African languages, religion, social organisation, music, and art can be considered to a large degree as one system.

This does not mean that all West Africans are alike; at certain levels they are similar, at others they are not. Most West African languages are genetically related, i.e. they are offshoots of the same common ancestral stock; synchronically they are similar in their deep structure, but their surface structures are different and most of the languages are mutually unintelligible. If it is true that these languages are offshoots of the same ancestral stock, the peoples who speak them were probably once related, before migrations and invasions split them up. If contemporary languages share linguistic features derived from a common ancestor, it can be assumed that there will be other commonly derived cultural features too. Just as today we can identify subgroups of more closely related languages, so too there may be subgroups of more closely related cultures.

The notion that the deep structure of West African languages may be similar while the surface structures are dissimilar can also be applied to other aspects of West African culture. In linguistics the idea of deep structure has been formalised and it is widely accepted and used, but this is not true of other anthropological sciences. Nevertheless, anthropologists frequently refer to "African" culture and even more frequently to "West African" culture. Mintz and Price (1976: p. 1) believe that "enslaved Africans in the New World, although drawn from different parts of the continent, from numerous tribal and linguistic groups, and from different societies in any region ... shared a certain number of underlying cultural understandings and assumptions". Maquet (1972: p. 5) talks of a "common quality" in Africa. His illustrations of this "common quality" are from art and language; "similar conclusions may be drawn from areas of culture other than art or language. Social institutions (such as marriage, the family, political organisations), belief systems and world view also display common qualities throughout Sub-Saharan Africa."

We can now proceed to examine what aspects of this "culture" were brought to the New World and to Jamaica, what kinds of conditions it met there, and how it evolved under these conditions. For this, we need a theory of cultural transmission and cultural change. In the ensuing chapters, we shall look closely at three important aspects of culture: religion, music, and language. "Culture" will be understood as a complex whole, the property of people engaged in constant and continuous social interaction. The methodological assumption here is that cultural subunits (religion, language, morals, arts, and so on) can be isolated for the purpose of investigation. But it is important not to lose sight of culture as a complex whole, particularly since it is important to know precisely how and to what extent such a whole was created from the diverse African (sub)cultures taken to Jamaica.

Map of West Africa

Map of Jamaica

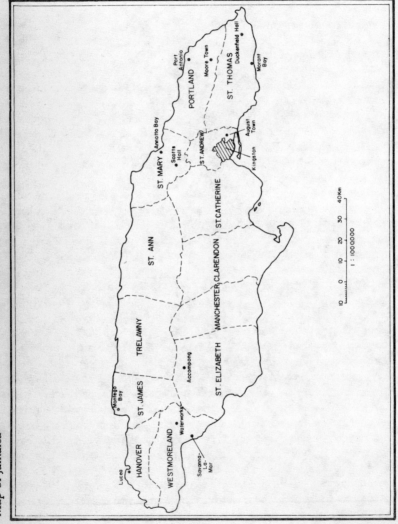

1
Cultural Contact and Cultural Change

It is generally agreed that culture is structured and patterned, that is, that cultural institutions (e.g. kinship systems) are structured and cultural behaviour is not random. This does not mean that cultural institutions and cultural behaviour are fixed and inflexible; they vary from individual to individual and from era to era, though there are limits to this variation (Herskovits and Bascom 1959: p.1). Variation in individual or group beliefs, in individual behaviour (including language), or in individual relations to cultural institutions may be the result of changes over time that affect different groups and individuals differently.

Today, cultures are changing at a dizzy rate. In earlier periods, cultures were more conservative and resistant to change, but even then they were not immutable. Cultural change is greater today because communication and contact between peoples has increased. This is not to say that communication and contact between societies is entirely new. Cultural contact has been a main factor in cultural change throughout history. It may be because of academic Eurocentrism or because large-scale cultural contact in effect began with the age of European expansion; whatever the case, almost all studies of cultural contact have been of contact between Europeans and indigenous peoples of other continents. Anthropology thus has two important themes and interests: the structure of "primitive" societies and cultures, and cultural contact.

Nineteenth century students of cultural change and cultural development looked at culture in general rather than cultures in particular. They addressed questions such as the origin and development of family systems, whether polygamy and promiscuity preceded monogamy, and the origin and development of religion. They attempted to show, explicitly, that humanity had been progressing from childhood to maturity, and that so-called primitive peoples were still at the stage of childhood. Even now some anthropologists still subscribe to this theory, and most nonspecialists in Europe and North America still tend to see the difference between "primitive" cultures and "modern" societies as one of quality. Whereas some mild ethnocentrism – a gentle insistence on the good qualities of one's own group – is probably to be found in all societies, in Euro-American societies "ethnocentrism has been rationalised and has been made the basis of programmes of action detrimental to the well-being of other peoples" (Herskovits and Bascom 1959: p. 1). In the Euro-American tradition, forms of belief or behaviour peculiar to other cultures are usually seen as inferior and abnormal. Thus the word "primitive", applied to non-Euro-American cultures by anthropologists in the sense of "traditional" and "not having undergone great change", has acquired the connotations of "savage", "barbarian, and "uncivilised".

Cultural relativism is the term used to express the notion that fixed, immutable, absolute values do not exist, but rather that "judgements are based on experience, and experience is interpreted by each individual in terms of his own enculturation" (Herskovits 1973: p. 15). For Herskovits, even "such intangibles as right and wrong, normal and abnormal, beautiful and plain, are absorbed as a person learns the ways of the group into which he is born ... Even the facts of the physical world are perceived through the enculturative screen, so that the perception of time, distance, weight, size and other 'realities' is mediated by the conventions of any given group". In this view, value systems are neither "better" nor "worse", but simply different.

The terms "normality" and "abnormality" are also meaningless when used to describe differences between cultures, and can only be applied (if at all) within one particular cultural frame of reference. For example, spirit possession is quite normal in the context of some African and Afro-American religions; it is structured and ordered, and has nothing of the hysteria, purposelessness, instability, or meaninglessness attributed to it by Euro-American psychiatrists and others. Similarly, polygamy functions quite normally within the social psychological and economic systems of African societies and creates no more or no less tensions and strains than does monogamy in Euro-American societies. Where Africans are not subjected by Europeans, their mild ethnocentrism predisposes them to prefer their own culture over the Euro-American one. The chief criterion for evaluating a cultural institution or belief is whether it fits coherently within the culture as a whole, and whether it satisfies people's material and spiritual needs. This is not to say that there is no absolute morality. But absolute morality must be derived by observing universal tenets of morality. Thus all human societies distinguish between right and wrong, operate systems of respect and deference, and believe in supernatural forces. However, a society may become "degenerate" or "decadent" when its value system is no longer adhered to by the majority and when social control and penalties no longer operate.

So contact between Europe and Africa did not mean that Africans inevitably had to change because they were inferior. Moreover, the changes that took place in African culture as a direct result of contact with Europe cannot be seen as "improvements", and in fact the reverse may be true. A cultural item that fitted coherently and organically into an African cultural system may become marginal and pathological in the New World cultural complex. Language structure and function and family organisation may be examples of this. Cultural contact and the ensuing cultural change are extremely complex processes involving many factors, including adaptability to change, resistance to change, the degree of compatibility between the cultures in contact, the degree and nature of social interaction between the peoples in contact, and the distribution of power. This last factor, power distribution, is probably what accounts for perceptions in terms of "superiority" and "inferiority" and is extremely important both for triggering cultural change and for determining the direction and degree of that change. In other words, we must develop a broad theoretical framework to study cultural contact; such a theory would have both explanatory and – one would hope – predictive power. We would then have to examine the specific nature of African-European contact to see precisely where it fits into such a framework. In developing this framework, we must discuss general factors in cultural contact that determine the directions, intensity, and nature of cultural change. Not all these factors have the same determinacy. Some are mutually countervailing, others are mutually reinforcing; it is the configuration of these mutually countervailing or reinforcing factors that ultimately determines the kind of cultural change that will take place.

We must first distinguish between two types of contact: one that is sporadic, occasional, and (in today's world) electronic; and another that is based on constant interaction between members of two cultures in the same place. Contact of the first sort is virtually universal: almost all the world's cultures are in contact with Euro-American culture and are changing as a direct result. I am not concerned here with this type of contact. However, contact of this sort is the same as contact of the second sort in one important way: economic relations between the cultures in contact largely determine the nature of the cultural change that happens. Euro-American culture has spread to various parts of the globe without a commensurate spread of cultural influences to North America and Europe from the rest of the world. In other words, economic imperialism and cultural imperialism have constantly interacted with and reinforced each other. Economic imperialism has opened the way for Euro-American culture to spread abroad and to provoke varying degrees of cultural change in the rest of the world; cultural imperialism then becomes a conscious policy on the part of the Euro-American economic system in order to preserve and extend its dominance over the rest of the world.

Economic relations constitute one aspect of the distribution of power between societies in contact; and the distribution of power is the chief factor determining the direction, nature, and intensity of cultural change. In the case of slavery, power is the control by one society over the life and death of individuals of the other. In other cases, power may manifest itself as the control of capital and the means of production by one group, while another group stays generally dispossessed. The uneven matching of power between two societies, as in the case of slavery, results in massive cultural change in the subject group, which is forced – if it is to survive – to adopt (or adapt) some of the cultural forms of the dominant society. This extreme unevenness of power was the main reason why many indigenous groups of the Americas became acculturated when brought into contact with British, French and Spanish people; and this process of acculturation is still going on today. In Canada, by contrast, the two cultures (or subcultures) in contact, Anglo-Canadian and Franco-Canadian, are less unevenly matched, even though the Anglo-Canadian group (or its Anglo-American affiliate) economically dominates the Franco-Canadian group. In this situation the cultures of both groups change in the direction of a common "Canadian" value system, but the culture of the economically subject group changes far more. Many Franco-Canadians learn good or fluent English, even to the point where French is relegated in their language behaviour to a subordinate role. As an institution, the French language of Canada is changing massively as a result of influences from English; in those speakers for whom it becomes subordinate its inner form (or structure) deteriorates. The English language undergoes no such changes, except where it is learned by Franco-Canadians, whose attempts to use it result in deviations from the Anglo-Canadian norm of English.

Another important factor in cultural contact is the nature and degree of interaction between groups. This can vary widely, as too can the sorts of cultural change produced by it. In some cases, all members of both groups in contact may have complete access to all institutions and activities; in others (e.g. slavery), such access may be extremely limited for one party or for both. Complete access may only theoretically be possible, since members of one group may not wish to participate in the institutions and activities of the other. In most cases of contact, power is unevenly distributed, so the desire of the subordinate group to participate in the institutions of the dominant group will be greater than vice versa. As a result, cultural change will be greater in the subordinate group and smaller in the dominant group. In some well-known cases, for example present contacts between indigenous peoples of South America and Hispanic peoples, the indigenous peoples remain quite marginal to the dominant Hispanic institutions and pick up only smatterings of Hispanic culture.

If individual members of each group in contact interact frequently and intensely among themselves, they will participate less in each others' institutions. High densities of in-group interaction will lead to the maintenance of a group's culture, while high densities of out-group interaction will lead to cultural change (more of course in the subordinate than in the dominant group).

The different conditions of contact experienced by different subgroups of the cultures in contact is another major aspect of interaction. Not all subgroups and not all individuals have the same experiences, which leads to what I referred to in the previous chapter as the continuum of cultural differentiation. It is difficult to make general statements about which subgroups will participate most in the institutions of and interact most with individuals of the other culture. Each instance of cultural contact must be examined to determine the precise picture. It is interesting to note that in some situations the privileged classes of both cultures in contact will interact more with one another than in others, leading to their greater cultural integration; while, in others, the pattern is more likely to be that of a dispossessed subgroup of one culture interacting (but on a far more limited scale) with the privileged subgroup of the other. This happens, for example, when domestic servants recruited from one culture are employed in the homes of the privileged classes of the other. Ultimately, each individual will have a different experience of interaction and will work out individual strategies for participating in whatever institutions are accessible.

The nature of this interaction can be posed in terms of learning conditions, i.e. the opportunities available to the members of one culture for becoming familiar with and "learning" forms of the other. Probably the most effective conditions for such learning are participation and interaction. But where these are limited, members of the culture undergoing change may acquire only a partial knowledge of the forms of the other culture and the learned forms may appear as imperfect, even pathological, versions of the "target" culture. These new forms may then become negatively valued; the resulting stigmas may then be transferred to the individuals who manifest them and thereby serve as a main justification for the social, economic, and political exploitation of these people.

Where cultures are in contact, formal opportunities for learning may be chiefly provided through schools. Schools will then be both cultural institutions to which either all or only some have access, and institutions that dispense formal instruction in virtually the entire culture. In this way the school can serve one of two functions: it can provide people from one culture with the opportunity for formal instruction in the new culture toward which they are moving, or it can preserve and impart knowledge of the culture from which these people may be moving, that is, the "dying" culture. The school is then an instrument of both cultural change and cultural persistence or revival. The school is also an effective instrument for spreading cultural imperialism: for fostering notions about the innate or achieved superiority of one culture.

Social mobility (or the lack of it) also influences the nature and degree of interaction and participation. Interaction and participation may be relatively immutable, or they may have a propensity to widen and increase. Change may result from the unconscious attempts of one group to learn the culture of another, but change may also be conscious when individuals perceive the acquisition of the culture of the dominant group as a means of social mobility. In the latter case they consciously learn cultural forms of the dominant group in order to "improve" themselves socially and economically. On the other hand, in cases where interaction and participation are fixed according to inflexible social laws, there is no socioeconomic mobility and no motivation to learn "correct" forms of the other culture. Motivation is a psychological matter; it has to do with both a perception of possibilities for upward social and economic mobility and with an individual's self-image. These things are individually located; they differ from person to person. They are another important factor in the emergence of the continuum of cultural differentiation that characterises cultural contact.

Where interaction and participation are fixed and immutable, they are mainly of the in-group sort. In such cases there is little or no motivation to learn the "correct" forms of the other culture, and the in-group orientation acts as an effective barrier to acculturation. In-group interaction may even result in positive resistance to acculturation. Groups with a highly developed sense of ethnic solidarity (often the result of exploitation and discrimination) will resist acculturation; they will preserve their ethnic identity in order to strengthen their chances of survival.

There are a number of other, lesser factors that must be mentioned to complete this theoretical framework. First of all, there is the demographic factor – the relative numerical strength of the populations bearing the cultures in contact. The demographic factor influences the density of interaction, for if one population is much larger than the other, some of its subgroups or individuals may not directly experience cultural contact.

The location of contact must also be considered. A culture displaced to a new setting must inevitably adjust to the new environment and to the locally based culture or cultures with which it comes in contact. I have already argued that a displaced people cannot take its entire culture with it to a new place. The original inhabitants of this new place will usually be in a better position to maintain their cultural traditions. Contact may also take place on neutral grounds, though that does not often happen; when it does, both cultures must in some measure adjust.

The number of cultures that come into contact will also influence the nature of cultural change. I have assumed up to now that at any one time and in any one place only two different cultures will meet. But there is always the chance that more than two cultures will meet, and when this happens, cultural change becomes more complex, since it has several points of departure and several different potential goals or models. New cultural forms in this situation will be quite complex amalgams without easily identifiable ancestral roots.

A variant of multiple contact is when one or more of the cultures can be subdivided into regional or other varieties. These are sometimes referred to as "subcultural" differences; they complicate matters enormously by making it far harder to trace antecedent forms. Great care must be taken in studies of cultural contact to identify subcultural variants. As we have seen, the term "African" and terms such as "European culture", "French culture", "Anglo-Saxon culture" are as crude as they are broad, and mask a wealth of cultural and subcultural variations.

Even now this framework is far from complete. A demographic breakdown of the populations in contact by age and sex, an analysis of psychological factors such as a people's capacity to innovate and adapt, a study (where applicable) of the politics of the colonial power, and various other factors must be kept in mind in describing cultural contact, for in some cases they may turn out to be crucially important. Factors such as these will be adduced where necessary, but I shall not consider them further at this point.

I shall now examine the results of the interplay of the factors discussed so far. Cultural change, as I understand it, is a process affecting one or both (or all) of the peoples in contact; this process is often analysed in terms of the concepts acculturation and assimilation. These concepts refer to the changes that one culture undergoes under the influence of another culture. In both cases change within the culture is in some general way (explored below) in the direction of some other culture; in the case of acculturation the change is incomplete; in the case of assimilation it is complete. These concepts refer to stages in a movement whereby a culture changes to the extent that it may become indistinguishable from, or fused with, another culture. Particular forms and institutions within one and the same culture behave differently in this process. Herskovits (1938) has proposed two concepts in terms of which change may be studied and described: syncretism and reinterpretation. Both represent in slightly different ways the process by which and the form in which the native tradition is continued (hence "continuities") or survives (hence "survivals") and forms from the other culture in contact are incorporated into the developing culture.

The other important factor in explaining cultural history and change is the ecological, social, economic and political context. A culture may respond for example to climatic changes (e.g. drought), to victory or defeat in war, or to economic developments. Some scholars have claimed that the ecological factor has operated in an exceptional way in Afro-America, and they view Afro-American culture in terms of innovations or creations, rather than as continuities or discontinuities from an African base. It is not always clear whether such scholars believe that African continuities are insignificant, or simply that the creativity hypothesis is more fruitful as a general methodology. If the latter is the case, then the issue need not delay us further, since it is part of a more general debate between those who favour a synchronic or functional approach and those who stress the diachronic or historical aspect. If their claim relates to the substance of Afro-American culture, then it is necessary to know whether they believe that Afro-American culture is exceptional. For example, more or less the same religious forms can be found in some African towns as in parts of Afro-America. They may indeed be "innovations", in the sense that all change is innovation or creation, but they can also be interpreted as changes from a common traditional base.

Price's belief (1980: p. 195) that the Maroons of Suriname "were faced with nothing less than the task of creating a whole new society and culture" is extreme, for it implicitly denies that they were able in some measure to reconstruct a pattern of society and culture that they knew in Africa. Maroons did probably "work out" new patterns of social order and cultural forms; but much depended on which groups fled to the forests first or in largest numbers, for pioneers set a pattern to which other groups had no choice but to accomodate. In the following chapters I shall argue that in Jamaica the Twi set such a pattern.

Few people would completely deny the "contributions" from West Africa to Afro-American culture. For example, Price (1980: p. 196) speaks of "general cultural orientations" and Mintz (1970) of "those aspects of the ancestral cultures [that] they could carry in their minds". My own belief, argued in this book, is that not just "pitch, intonation and timbre" but entire functioning languages were carried to Jamaica and can still be found there even now. Not just "general cultural orientations" or "religious beliefs" but entire religions were carried to Jamaica and struggled to maintain themselves in hostile conditions; not just "artistic or aesthetic orientations and preferences" but African musical instruments and a repertoire of songs and performances for religious and secular occasions. It is interesting to examine the different ways in which these cultural forms changed in different contexts, or – conversely – stayed intact. Price (1980: p. 204) justifiably derides those earlier scholars who "view Suriname Maroon societies as a little Africa in America", for ever since the fifteenth century there have been no wholly intact "African" cultures, even in Africa, either in the towns or in the villages.

One of the pillars of the "creativity" hypothesis is that there is a great variety of African cultures; and that this, together with the alleged mixing of slaves in the New World to reduce the chances of plotting and resistance by members of one ethnic group, prevented significant African cultural continuities in the New World. This study will challenge that belief, which is disproved not only by the Jamaican case but probably also by Haiti and Cuba; in all three places one African people dominated and assimilated others. Even where this did not seem to happen, the basically uniform culture shared by Africans of diverse ethnic origins and transmitted to a basically uniform set of environments in the New World led to parallel changes and developments in different parts of Afro-America. As Abrahams and Szwed (1983: p. 8) remarked, "there is simply too much contrary evidence for us to accept Mintz's argument without some real qualifications ... Whenever Afro-Americans could interact with one another, there emerged a set of expectations, attitudes, and feelings which in great part derived from past practices. These encounters would naturally draw upon the shared experiences in Africa and the New World."

Handler and Frisbie (1972: p. 36) conclude their study of music in Barbados with the view that "similarities in fundamental West African musical forms and expressions (and the sociocultural contexts in which they were found) provided a common basis for interaction among persons coming from different cultural backgrounds and a foundation upon which a shared musical tradition was established and perpetuated in New World societies." They openly oppose this opinion to that of Mintz (in "Foreword" to Whitten and Szwed, 1970: p. 8) that "the cultural heterogeneity of any slave group meant that what was shared culturally was likely to be minimal. It was not, after all, some single 'African culture' that was available for transfer nor even some generalised African cultural substratum." However, Handler and Frisbie see no contradiction between this opposition to Mintz on this particular point and their acceptance of Mintz's broader view that ultimately Afro-American cultures "depend upon creativity and innovation far more than upon the indelibility of particular cultural contents."

The current creativity vs. continuity debate has mainly addressed the culture of Black people in North America. There has been much debate of late about whether a "Black culture" exists in the United States. This question has generally been posed within the context of slavery and the effects of slavery on the culture and psychology of enslaved Africans. Elkins (1976) sums up the different positions on slavery as "damage" or "resistance". To put it crudely, the "damage" theory holds that the powerlessness, exploitation, and brutalisation of slaves resulted in their complete psychological and cultural degradation, leading in extreme cases to the creation of the personality type known as "sambo".[1] For example, the alleged destruction of the African family under slavery, mainly through the indiscriminate sale of its members and, especially in the earliest years, the shortage of women slaves, is said to account for a number of allegedly negative personality, moral, and behavioural traits among Western Hemisphere Blacks.

Supporters of the "resistance" position do not suggest that the system of slavery was permissive or benign, and maintain that slavery was rapacious and degrading, but still they prefer to emphasise the efforts of the slaves to resist, to assert themselves, and to develop their own positive culture. They believe that this culture cannot be seen merely as a "reaction" to White oppression. New historians, such as Blassingame (1972), focus on the community life of slaves, and present a picture of it as one "in which family [the slave family was not destroyed either], religion and a body of lore served as mechanisms of resistance against the debilitating effects the slave system was formerly supposed to have had." Elkins (1976: p. 278).

This "resistance" position has become very popular among Black ideologists and scholars and also among some White scholars and it is not incompatible with my position here; but it is still inadequate. First, it either ignores or fails to deal satisfactorily with the apparent contradiction between the view of slavery as a brutal, oppressive, and degrading institution and the view that slaves were able to develop their own positive cultures. Second, it presents the development of this culture in too many ways as a reaction to Whites and to slavery (though it sets out to do the very opposite). Third, it presents slave culture as a development of the period of slavery. It is not clear what culture the slaves had before they were slaves. Nor is it clear at what point slaves began to "develop" this culture and whether they existed in some kind of cultural void before embarking on this process of cultural development or creation.

Although many scholars still accept that New World Afro-American cultures have their roots in Africa and that continuities from the ancestral culture persist wherever Africa-derived populations form communities in the New World, North American writings on slavery and the culture of slaves nonetheless stress the creation of a distinctive culture rather than the continuity of African culture(s) transplanted to the New World. Both sides in the degradation vs. resistance debate share the general position that slavery was the decisive factor – either by completely destroying or infantilising the Africans; or by imposing on them White European forms of culture (which, because of the harshness of slavery, they imperfectly assimilated); or by in some way allowing them to create a distinctive culture, institutions, and organisations. In other words, the main focus is on slavery as an institution and the effects slavery had on the lives and culture of the slaves. Even authors who take the position that slaves resisted and triumphed over the dehumanising effects of slavery, and that Africa is the mother continent for New World Blacks, are still inevitably within the orbit of the "creativity" school. Thus Levine, in a work on songs and folktales (1978), argues that slave songs constitute a distinctive cultural form, but that they owe less to White influence or African origins than to the circumstances of American slave life; and he speaks of the slaves "carving out independent cultural forms". Accordingly, he presses all the evidence and data into the same mould: for example, he represents folktales as a psychic adjustment to slavery insofar as they show how "the weak must make their way in a world of hypocrisy and superior power – by tricking not only the strong but also each other". But, as Elkins (1976: p. 282) observes, many of Brer Rabbit's tricks seem gratuitous and purposeless, and he can be downright cruel to defenceless weaker people (Brer Rabbit sacrifices his own wife and children to save himself). Elkins understandably asks whether the "adjustment" represented by these tricks can be considered positive.

The "creativity" or "resistance" position is in some ways a static model of Afro-American culture and is in no way dynamic or developmental. Did Africans "create" culture at every main stage in their New World history? Of course they did, just like every group in human history. It is axiomatic that culture is not inherent in a people but emerges within a given historical environment. On the other hand, culture has its own historical flow; true, its course and rate are affected by environment, but the response and adjustment to this environment are fashioned from within the inherited resources of the culture. One main problem with the "creativity" or "resistance" thesis is that it focusses on slavery and the environment, and the culture generated thereby. It neglects the time dimension, and considers neither the culture of Africans before enslavement, nor the different stages within the period of slavery, nor the aftermath of slavery. It refuses to consider the possibility that pre-slavery cultures may have largely determined the response and adjustment of slaves to slavery. There is no doubt that animal stories featuring a spider and other animals existed in the pre-slavery culture of slaves. These tales expressed a morality that Africans brought with them into slavery. But they were also part of the picaresque narrative tradition, many of the elements of which are hard to square with the image of downtrodden slaves triumphing over their oppressors. On the other hand, other elements in the African moral tradition must surely have helped slaves deal with their oppression. One reason folktales persisted during slavery was because they and their performance were an important part of African communal interaction that helped mould a new African community from diverse African elements.

A similar analysis can be applied to slave religion. Rawick (1970: p. 151) rightly rejects the creativity view that religion was a release from the day-to-day world of work and a refuge in the promise of salvation, but reaches a methodologically similar conclusion – that "the religion of the oppressed usually gives them the sustenance necessary for developing a resistance to their own oppression". Slave religion may have been all of these things to some or all Africans, but it was – certainly in the case of Jamaica – first and foremost the continuity of an ancestral religion. True, there was an important link between religion and resistance; but religion was taken to Jamaica from Africa and was an important basis for resistance; it was not created during the course of that resistance.

Needless to say, it is often difficult to say for sure whether a particular cultural form is a "continuity" or a "creation". For example, is the fact that Suriname Maroons farm far from their villages merely an African continuity or did this practice develop in order to ensure food supplies if and when the village was razed by the European torch, as sometimes happened? Or was it a tradition from Africa selected under the pressure of new conditions, i.e. a combination of both? As it turns out, this particular custom is not confined to any one period of Jamaican history or any one part of Jamaica, though it is also characteristic of Jamaican Maroon society. Lewis (1845: p. 40) noted that his slaves kept their provision ground some distance from their homes.

In opposition to the view that Afro-American culture was suddenly created during slavery, or that "new" cultural forms are created by every successive generation or at every new social conjuncture (in which case the word "new" is rendered largely meaningless), I shall try here to account for the continuous development of the culture of African people throughout the entire period of the post-Columbian history of Jamaica and indeed of other areas of the Caribbean, with particular emphasis on linguistic evidence. I start from the assumption that cultural change is continuous and that the idea of continuity from an African base is the best way of accounting for the particular segment of Jamaican culture (and Afro-American culture) with which we are here dealing.

I am not suggesting that this historical approach is completely satisfying, since *post hoc ergo propter hoc* is not a principle of causality. Explanation in the social sciences remains a problem that the functional approach cannot resolve. The creativity hypothesis often does not even attempt to specify the conditions of causality or the mechanisms through which the particular cultural form is produced. Creativity, as a psycho-genetic attribute, cannot be verified or substantiated outside the forms that it is alleged to generate. We therefore cannot support the claim by Rawick (1970: p. 149) that "there is no more creative and innovative culture in the New World than that of black Americans". Afro-American culture is no more and no less creative that other New World cultures. The kind of creativity demonstrated by Afro-Americans is probably a legacy of Africa. Price (1980: p. 214) fails to see this when he contrasts the "relatively unchanging features of [Suriname] Maroon artistry which are based on a broadly African set of features" with "the celebration of artistic innovation and individual creativity which guarantees that Maroon arts are ever changing, inventing and playing with new forms and techniques", which is "American". African and Afro-American music, storytelling, language, dance and games can likewise be analysed in terms of an inventiveness within a tradition. Finally, the creation model is based on certain questionable assumptions about Africa and enslaved

Africans in the New World; these assumptions include the idea that African culture is heterogeneous, and that no holistic culture integrated Africans in any one New World society. True, this is not the same as saying that Africans "had no culture", as Westerners used to think, or that Africans were stripped of their culture during the Middle Passage and under slavery. According to this traditional view, Africans set about picking up what smatterings of European culture that their undeveloped physical and intellectual faculties allowed. The conclusion was that their descendants can be said to have "culture" only insofar as they master a European-derived culture. On the other hand, creation theorists claim that Africans could not be said to have had a culture, because of their forced extraction from Africa and their enslavement in the New World, and that they therefore immediately set about creating a new culture when they began developing social relations with one another (and with Europeans).

This creativity thesis is true in the sense that, as I said before, no displaced people can transfer its entire culture from one location to another. But it takes a very restricted view of culture – one restricted to those institutions that humans develop to organise and direct their social behaviour. Yet these constitute only one aspect of culture, and it is this aspect that displaced peoples are least capable of preserving. Even so, my claim in this book is that when a displaced people sets about developing new social relations in a new environment, and with them new institutions, it often first falls back on memories of, or habits or predispositions acquired from its ancestral cultures to build these new institutions. I conclude that to understand these institutional aspects of culture, as well as other less institutional aspects of culture such as music, cognitive orientations, religious beliefs (as against religious ritual and organisation), and language (as structure), it is best to begin with a description of the base, then to determine which aspects of the base did not "migrate" along with the displaced persons, and finally to examine how the base persists, is transformed, or generates "new" institutions in the new setting. This book, rather than treat Jamaican religion as a pathological reaction to extreme social-psychological deprivation, as many other studies do, begins by looking at African religious belief and practice and goes on to examine how it was transformed on Jamaican soil.

Two sorts of cultural institutions or modes of behaviour fall outside this treatment. First, there are those that cannot be related *a fortiori* to any known cultural base or heritage, or whose origins are hotly debated. In other words, given what we know about the nature of "proof" in human sciences, it will be difficult or impossible to match each cultural item with a cultural base. Note too that it will be even more difficult to show *a fortiori* in every case how the new environment and social conditions led to the creation of new cultural forms. Second, there are those that have been introduced or borrowed from the contiguous culture and that have no parallel in the receiving culture. When Africans were exposed to European languages, European music, or European religions, they did not at first assimilate them exactly as they were (although some of their descendants did so), but transferred to the "learning process" elements from their own native languages, music and religion, some groups more so than others. But where descendants of Africans came to form trade unions, Westminister-type political parties, and the like, for which they had no parallel institution in their ancestral culture, the search for continuities is by definition pointless. Even here, though, it would be interesting to know whether modes of organisation, communication, and leadership typical of Jamaican trade unions and political parties do not have their bases in an African tradition of organisation and communication. (See, for example, descriptions of political meetings in Jamaica in Alleyne 1963. Similarly Dammann (1964: p. 248), discussing the influence of traditional religion on modern African politics, shows that it played a role in the organisation of the Mau Mau uprising and that in Ghana political meetings begin with a libation to the ancestral spirits.)

The concept of base, or point of departure, goes hand in hand with the concept of target. When two cultures are in contact, acculturation and assimilation can be seen as a movement away from the base towards the target. Some individuals or groups will complete this movement further than others, for their experience of contact will be greater. This means that manifestations of the same cultural item can be ranged along a scale representing degrees of approximation to the target or, inversely, degrees of continuity from the base. This, as I shall show below, is a useful way of conceptualising the different manifestations of, say, language or religion in Jamaica and of accounting for them within the same historical-analytical framework. This scale is a theoretical construct and does not imply that every cultural manifestation (linguistic, religious) can be convincingly and *a fortiori* shown to have reached a particular point, relative or absolute, of approximation to the European norm or "target", nor does it mean that "target" was, or is, a psychological reality for Africans and their descendants (see below and Chapter 6 – Language).

Where the two cultures in contact are very different, and where learning conditions are extremely poor, with virtually no corrective pressure, the subject group will be under enormous pressure to change in the direction of the "target" culture; but there will be massive continuities from the native culture; and these will persist for a relatively long time, unless conditions arise that are favourable to their complete elimination. Social conditions largely determine the presence, degree of pervasiveness, and duration of those base features that are transferred to the newly developing culture.

There are two different aspects to this kind of cultural change and development. There is the objective structure of the particular cultural item, whose different manifestations embody different degrees of continuity from the base; and there are the ways in which individuals or groups relate to these cultural items in their different manifestations. As individuals traverse the acculturation process, they traverse different manifestations of the same cultural item, gradually retreating further from the base and arriving closer to the target; but this process is not smoothly unilinear. In Jamaica some individuals may follow a European religion and speak a European language, while they also practise new forms of religion and speak new forms of language embodying varying degrees and types of African continuities.

While this acculturation, represented by different degrees of continuity of the base and different degrees of approximation to the target, is going on, alongside it the subject culture (or aspects of it) may continue to be practised by some individuals in a virtually intact form. These people may remain cut off from the general acculturation process; or they may become caught up in it so that their behaviour oscillates along the acculturative scale. For example, some individuals may continue to use an African language or to practise an African religion while at the same time learning forms of a European language or religion. However, the main trend in situations of contact between Europeans and Africans in the New World is for the subject culture to undergo progressive loss or decay.

The loss or decay of the subject culture is rapid but gradual. It decays both in its inner form and in its outer manifestations. Language, for example, gradually loses items of vocabulary and items at other levels of structure; these losses are either net and final or else are made up for by replacements from the second language. Since loss in inner form is in reality loss of competence or loss of recall on the part of speakers, it goes hand in hand with a reduction in the number of domains in which the language is used and in the functions for which it is used. The subject language progressively loses speakers (as they become monolingual in the new language) so that eventually it is spoken only by a few specialised groups (e.g. old folk and religious leaders), or preserved only in a few specialised functions and media (e.g. religion and songs). Finally the point is reached where "speakers" recall only a few items of vocabulary or a few expressions; when these people die, the language becomes fully extinct unless a cultural revival breathes new life into it. This is what has happened to African languages and, *mutatis mutandis*, African religions in Jamaica. I shall elaborate on this in later chapters.

It remains to spell out in a little more detail the development of the contact modality of one cultural form – again language. As we have seen, this process may be viewed analytically as the gradual adoption of the dominant language by speakers of the subject language. This process is characterised by transfers (often called, inappropriately, "interferences") from the subject language to the dominant language; these transfers are so massive in the initial stages that it is more reasonable to consider the phonology and to a less extent the syntax as still related genetically to the phonology and syntax of the subject language. Other kinds of deviations from the "target" language norms may be interpreted as further up the acculturative scale (though they are not always recognisable as such). There are therefore differing degrees of deviation that can be represented on a time (or diachronic) axis as well as on a social (or synchronic) axis. Society does not move in lockstep through the progressive stages of linguistic acculturation. Different social groups experiencing different sorts of contact tend to move at different rates. But in the course of time society as a whole moves closer to complete acculturation, with any one generation of learners moving closer to a complete adoption of the new language and to an elimination of features transferred from the (former) subject language than the generation that precedes it. Social values are inevitably assigned to the different levels of speech that thus emerge. The standard norm of the "target' language is the most prestigious; the most deviant form is the least prestigious.

"Target" is, as I have already said, a theoretical construct, and there is no empirical or psychological evidence that the majority of Jamaicans view a standard norm of English as the "target" of their linguistic acculturation. There may even be evidence that part of the general resistance of Jamaicans and Afro-Americans to domination and extinction – a resistance most dramatically expressed in slave revolts – was and is a resistance to cultural assimilation. In other words, the preservation of deviations from the standard norm of British culture (or the enduring continuity of African-derived features) may be an indication of ethnic solidarity of New World Blacks in the face of 300 years of British and later North Atlantic cultural imperialism.

Today, the pattern of cultural dynamics in Jamaica is extremely complex, and the concept of "target" is less palpable than ever. Today there is even less evidence that a British standard norm, or even a Jamaican standard norm close to the British one, serves as a "target" in Jamaica. If the acculturation process is seen as a continuous movement from a West African base to a (British) target, one could even say that today a reverse movement is taking place; this movement may not be back toward the former base, but it is certainly away from the former target. Perhaps one could say that some sort of crystallisation is now taking place, with the movement freezing (so to speak) at its present point on the acculturative scale.

Needless to say, the nature of the "target" has been constantly changing over the years and centuries. In the early period of contact, "British" culture was represented in a number of regional varieties (Scottish, Irish, Welsh, Northern English, Southern English, and so on); more recently, the North American derivative of British and European culture has greatly influenced cultural developments in Jamaica. These variations within the target would need to be seriously examined in a work of synthesis of the sort proposed in the Preface, but here they will be taken into account only insofar as they help to clarify the *African* contribution to Jamaican culture.

In sum, the process of cultural contact and cultural change is extremely complex, and involves continuity, adaptation, atrophy, innovation, reinterpretations, and remodellings. Even the groups involved in contact lack clear definition. We tend to think in terms of European vs. African, Christian vs. Pagan, and so on, but these labels obscure the complexity of the issue. Moreover, the processes of interaction between cultures are constantly and continuously influenced by economic, social, and ecological factors. These processes cannot be dealt with in one study. For that we need a series of cumulative studies that build upon one another's findings. This study is only a beginning in that process and presents only one perspective.

2

The Provenance of Africans and Capsules of their Culture

The Africans whose culture, together with that of their descendants, forms the subject matter of this book came to Jamaica in three great migrations: (i) during the period 1498 to 1655; (ii) during the period 1670 to 1808; and (iii) during the period 1841 to 1865.

The first period was that of the Spanish occupation of Jamaica. Some claim that Africans were among the first "discoverers" of the "New World", since they took part in the expeditions from the ports of Castille and Portugal; others say that Africans may even have "discovered" the New World before the Europeans (Van Sertima 1976).

Iberian cities such as Seville, Cadiz, and Huelva had large Black African populations in the fifteenth and sixteenth centuries; these Blacks helped to populate Spain's young possessions in the New World.[1] In Seville, for example, which was Spain's largest city in 1594, there seemed to be as many Blacks as Whites according to many contemporary observers (Pike 1967: p. 344–5). Estimates of slaves imported into Europe range from 35,000 (Deer 1949: p. 283) to 100,000 (Luttrell 1965: p. 68) for the period 1400–1500 (this latter figure includes exports of slaves to the Canary Islands and São Tomé). Curtin (1969: pp. 18–20), after critically examining a number of other estimates, concludes that 50,000 slaves were imported into Europe during the whole of the slave trade, most of them during the fifteenth century. Therefore some of the first Black slaves arriving in the New World, and in Jamaica in particular, came from Seville and other southern cities or from the Canary Islands, and some had even been born in these places. In Spain it was relatively easy for Blacks to gain their freedom, so large numbers of freedmen migrated to the New World from Spain (Pike 1967).

According to Morales (1952: p. 268 ff.), the main dates for the arrival of Africans in Jamaica during this period were as follows. In 1509 a small number arrived with Juan de Esquivel. In 1523, 300 slaves were sent to Jamaica, but not all arrived. In or around 1530 there was an *asiento* obtained from the King of Portugal to ship 5,000 Africans to the New World; of these 700 were destined for Jamaica. In 1534, 30 slaves arrived from Portugal or Cabo Verde. Toward the end of the sixteenth century there were complaints about the lack of slaves. In 1588, 150 Africans were abandoned by a French ship on the coast of Jamaica. Towards the end of the century the slave population must have reached 1,000.

Wyndham (1935: p. 266), without naming a source, cites a census taken by the Church in 1611 to show that there were 696 Spaniards, 107 Free Negroes, 558 Slaves, 74 Indians (Nation), and 74 Foreigners. Long (1774: p. 388) says that when the Spaniards were defeated by Venables, they had with them "1,500 Negroes and Mulattos, many of whom were slaves". Curtin (1969: p. 25) estimates that 183,900 slaves were imported into Spanish America between 1521 and 1640. The vast majority of these went to the Greater Antilles (including Jamaica), but Curtin does not arrive at an estimate for each island.

In this early period, the Spanish colony of Jamaica hardly changed in size or importance. Africans were always outnumbered by Spaniards and today there is little, if anything, to show that they were present on the island in that period. Since their culture would in any case probably have been at least partly intermixed with Hispanic elements, it would be difficult to separate them from similar admixtures introduced as a result of nineteenth and twentieth century contacts between Jamaicans and Cubans. For example, there are Spanish-derived words in Jamaican vocabulary, but it is impossible to say whether they go back to the period 1498–1655.[2] *Shampata* is a Jamaican word denoting a peasant shoe with a wooden sole; it comes from Spanish *zapato*. The intrusive nasal consonant *m* in Jamaican *shampata* is a feature that recurs in many areas of the Caribbean where Africans were implanted and may be viewed as an African continuity (*see* below under Language). The intrusive nasal also occurs in English-derived Jamaican words, e.g. *nung* "now", as well as in the Maroon language (Saramaccan) of Suriname.

The most important event in the first period of Jamaican history is connected with the invasion by British forces in 1655. During the following five years of struggle, African slaves are said to have at first sided with their Spanish masters against the British; after the defeat of the Spanish resistance they took refuge in the inaccessible interior of the island and waged guerrilla warfare against the British (Morales 1952: p. 275). According to Morales, when the Spaniards finally left Jamaica in 1659–60, 300 Black slaves refused to follow them to Cuba, and instead took to the mountains. Thus the "Maroons" came into being. Some later runaways probably joined this original band, which developed over the centuries into today's Maroon societies. It is widely believed in Jamaica that the Maroons have some Spanish admixture, but there is no evidence to prove it.

Curtin (1969: p. 18), citing J.L. de Azevedo, *Epoca de Portugal Econômico* (Lisbon, 1929) and J. Melo Barreto, *História de Guiné 1418–1918* (Lisbon, 1938), says that Guiné de Cabo Verde, as the region from Senegal to Sierra

Leone was then known, was the main source in Africa of slaves for Europe, the Atlantic Islands, and the Spanish Caribbean in the fifteenth and early sixteenth centuries.[3] This places them in the Mande group of languages, which includes the subgroups Bambara, Wolof, Mandingo, Fula, and Jola (or Dyula). Morales (1952: p. 273), however, says (but without adducing evidence) that most Africans brought to Jamaica during the Spanish period were "Cromantis". The main support for this assertion is the fact that the Portuguese, who shipped almost all the slaves to Europe and the New World in that period, had set up a fortress on the Gold Coast (now Ghana) in 1482. This fortress, called El Mina, was the only European fortification on the coast of Africa until the Dutch established one a few miles away in 1612 and the British another (really a trading port) in the same area in 1631 (Laurence 1963). If slaves were taken from the vicinity of the fortress, they would indeed be Cromanti[4] (otherwise known as Asante or Ashanti), and would have belonged to the linguistic subgroup called Kwa. For the period 1526 to 1550, which is documented, Curtin (1969: p. 101) provides the following table, which shows the continuing importance of *Guiné de Cabo Verde* as a source of slaves:

Table I   Export of slaves from West Africa by country 1526–1550

	Average Annual Exports	
	No.	%
Senegambia	499	23.5
Guinea-Bissau	543	25.6
Sierra Leone	56	2.6
Cape Mount to Cameroon	272	12.8
Congo-Angola	714	33.7

Source: Philip Curtin, *The Atlantic Slave Trade* (1969)

This table suggests that in this period the vast majority of slaves came from Guiné de Cabo Verde and the region of the Congo River (where the cultures are Bantu). Curtin thinks that the majority of these Bantus were destined for São Tomé. The area of provenance is already rather wide, stretching from one end of the Sub-Saharan Atlantic Coast (Senegal) to the other (Angola).

The origin of Africans shipped to Jamaica and the New World up to about 1550 remains largely a matter for speculation. Some mysteries remain. For example, it is a mystery (if it is true) why the two geographical extremes of West Africa, Senegambia and Angola, were the main slave-exporting regions, even though it was in the middle region that the Europeans had their only settled presence.

The period from the latter half of the sixteenth century to 1640 is better documented, for this was the period of the *asientos* (or licences) issued to permit the supply of slaves to Spanish America. These licences specified the number of slaves (in terms of *piezas de India* or units of manpower) to be carried to America and the section of the African coast from which they were to be taken. But the *asientos* are not entirely reliable as evidence. There was no strict policing of the licences, so that shippers did not always stick to the geographical areas to which they were assigned. Shippers operating under *asientos* were often more interested in trading in goods other than slaves and used the *asiento* as no more than a passport to the African coast. Moreover, it is difficult to know from how far inland slaves were brought before they were assembled on the coast for shipment abroad.

Chaunu (1955–60) has published tables drawn from *asiento* records for 1555–1640 showing the provenance of slaves; Curtin (1969) has critically appraised these tables. Note that there are problems with Chaunu's geographical terminology. Thus Curtin concludes that Chaunu's "Cape Verde" and "Canaries" refer to the whole area earlier designated as Guiné de Cabo Verde, and that Chaunu's "Guinea" includes the area from the Sierra Leone River down to the Bight of Benin. Chaunu's table (vol. 6: p. 402–3) is reproduced overleaf as Table II.

Table III (p. 33) shows that at first "Cape Verde" was the dominant source of slaves (as it had been in the fifteenth and early sixteenth centuries) but was later overtaken by "Guinea" and "Angola". The importance of "Guinea" at the beginning of the seventeenth century was probably due to the coming into effective operation of the Portuguese fortress at El Mina (Gold Coast). This makes it easier to reconcile these figures with Morales' claim that most Africans in Jamaica during the period of Spanish possession were "Cromantis".

Jamaica's specific position in all this is not clear. Jamaica was neglected by the Spaniards because it had no gold, and there was little growth in the number of slaves in Jamaica during the Spanish occupation. The Spanish Crown was unwilling to grant licences for the island; as we have seen, toward the end of the sixteenth century there were complaints about the lack of slaves. Years passed without a single African arriving. At the turn of the sixteenth century, Jamaica probably had about a thousand slaves, and slave deaths were offset only by the small number of Africans licensed by the Crown to serve the Governors and Abbots. Some slaves were acquired illegally, for example by taking them off ships that had called in at Jamaica to refuel (Morales 1952: p. 275). With the arrival of the British the number of slaves was further reduced when the Spaniards took some with them to Cuba. The 300 or so that remained to fight the British (and in some cases to fight the Spaniards) left no important mark on Jamaican culture. It is likely that Africans under the Spanish regime rapidly completed the process of acculturation that had already begun in the Iberian Peninsula, and became fully assimilated to Hispanic culture.

Table II
Distribution of slave ships authorised by the Spanish government, 1551–1640, according to region of supply in Africa.

Period	Total	Canaries	Cape Verde	Guinea	São Tomé	Angola	Mixed	Un-known
1551–55	15	-	15	-	-	-	-	-
1556–60	15	-	15	-	-	-	-	-
1561–65	25	-	25	-	-	-	-	-
1566–70	9	-	9	-	-	-	-	-
1571–75	16	-	11	4	1	-	-	-
1576–80	2	-	1	-	-	-	-	1
1581–85	22	-	16	2	1	-	3	-
1586–90	59	6	7	25	3	1	15	2
1591–95	105	3	18	26	-	6	51	1
1596–1600	188	11	8	90	1	4	17	57
1601–05	97	20	2	22	-	4	1	48
1606–10	174	-	2	96	-	3	3	70
1611–15	9	-	1	2	-	2	-	4
1616–20	139	-	6	17	7	104	2	3
1621–25	125	-	8	14	5	82	16	-
1626–30	59	-	-	-	-	50	6	3
1631–35	80	-	1	2	2	64	8	3
1636–40	83	-	1	2	-	76	4	-
Total	1,222	40	146	302	20	396	126	192
%		3.3	11.9	24.7	1.6	32.4	10.3	15.7

Source: see Table I

Translated into *piezas de India* and then into bodies by Curtin, the reconstructed picture of slave origins from 1551 to 1640 is shown in Table III opposite (Curtin, 1969: pp. 106–7):

Table III Slave origins 1551–1640

Year	Total	Canaries	Cape Verde	Guinea	São Tomé	Angola	Unknown
1551–55	2,100	-	2,090	-	-	-	-
%	100.0	-	100.0	-	-	-	-
1556–60	2,100	-	2,090	-	-	-	-
%	100.0	-	100.0	-	-	-	-
1561–65	3,500	-	3,480	-	-	-	-
%	100.0	-	100.0	-	-	-	-
1566–70	1,300	-	1,250	-	-	-	-
%	100.0	-	100.0	-	-	-	-
1571–75	2,200	-	1,530	560	140	-	-
%	100.0	-	68.7	25.0	6.2	-	-
1576–80	300	-	140	-	-	-	140
%	100.0	-	50.0	-	-	-	50.0
1581–85	3,100	140	2,360	420	140	-	-
%	100.0	4.5	77.3	13.6	4.5	-	-
1586–90	8,200	1,810	1,230	4,130	420	330	280
%	100.0	22.1	15.0	50.3	5.1	4.1	3.4
1591–95	14,600	2,370	4,370	5,410	-	2,320	-
%	100.0	16.2	29.9	37.0	-	15.9	-
1596–1600	26,100	2,200	2,900	19,660	200	1,200	-
%	100.0	8.4	11.1	75.2	0.8	4.6	-
1601–05	13,500	5,600	550	6,150	-	1,190	-
%	100.0	41.5	4.1	45.6	-	8.8	-
1606–10	24,200	90	550	22,500	90	960	-
%	100.0	0.4	2.3	93.0	0.4	4.0	-
1611–15	1,300	-	250	500	-	500	-
%	100.0	-	20.0	40.0	-	40.0	-
1616–20	19,300	70	970	2,430	970	14,460	420
%	100.0	0.4	5.0	12.6	5.0	74.8	2.2
1621–25	17,400	-	2,120	2,210	760	12,270	-
%	100.0	-	12.2	12.8	4.4	70.7	-
1626–30	8,200	-	440	70	-	7,690	-
%	100.0	-	5.4	0.9	-	93.7	-
1631–35	11,100	-	140	800	340	9,420	420
%	100.0	-	1.3	7.2	3.1	84.7	3.8
1636–40	11,500	-	210	560	-	10,770	-
%	100.0	-	1.8	4.8	-	93.3	-
Total	169,900	12,280	26,670	65,400	3,060	61,110	1,400
%	100.0	7.2	15.7	38.5	1.8	36.0	0.8

Source: see Table I

1670–1805

The second period of migration is by far the most important inasmuch as it laid the foundations for contemporary Jamaican society and culture. In 1655 British forces landed in Jamaica and in 1660 the Spaniards finally surrendered and escaped to Cuba (Morales 1952: p. 375–6). In 1670 all military campaigns and international intrigues to do with Jamaica came to an end and the island was officially ceded to Britain. As a result the nature of the colonisation of Jamaica changed: sugar plantations became the basis of economic and social organisation. This in turn led to the massive importation of African slaves and the arrival of large numbers of British colonists. It was during this period that the acculturative processes that culminated in the culture of contemporary Jamaica first began.

Both before and during the establishment of British rule in Jamaica, contact took place between Britons and Africans both in Africa itself and on some islands of the Caribbean that had become colonies of Britain earlier; the contact in Jamaica after 1655 was in a sense a transposition of this earlier contact. Contact happened in the castles, forts, and lodges (or "factories") set up to trade in slaves and goods on the West Coast of Africa, and in the African townships or villages nearby, some of which had sprung up as a result of the British presence. Africans were employed in these forts and factories, and slaves were housed there, sometimes for more than six months, until a ship was available to take them to the New World (Lawrence 1963). During this period the slaves had some exposure to British culture, particularly to the English language, as a preliminary to the closer and more enduring contact in Jamaica. The Middle Passage across the Atlantic, which sometimes lasted as long as three months, provided another opportunity for cultural contact – particularly linguistic contact – between Britons (or Europeans) and Africans. It was in the coastal factories and during the Middle Passage that some institutional aspects of African culture began to give way to new kinds of relationships between Africans of different origins. For example, Africans transported on the same ship developed strong bonds that survived into the New World.

Slaves imported to Jamaica, both in this early period and throughout the later history of the slave trade, were not necessarily assembled by British traders or taken to Jamaica on board British ships. The Portuguese and the Dutch, joined later by the British, were the main importers of slaves to Jamaica, and Cartagena (Colombia) and Curaçao (the Dutch West Indies) became important centres for distributing slaves to colonies all over the New World. Jamaica too was an important centre for the re-export of slaves (Curtin 1969: pp. 25, 141, 145, 219).

Only in the area of language has there been any claim that this contact between Jamaica-bound slaves and Portuguese left any cultural residue. Some linguists believe that all Atlantic "creoles" are progenies of a

Portuguese "pidgin" or lingua franca allegedly used by traders on the coast of Africa (and indeed along the entire trade route to India and the Far East) (Cassidy 1960, Stewart 1962, Thompson 1961, *inter alios*). Insofar as the vernacular language of Jamaica can be termed a "creole", it too would have origins in this Portuguese "pidgin". But since there are no known vestiges of any Portuguese influences coming directly into the language and culture of Jamaica (except through Portuguese-speaking Sephardic Jews who migrated to Jamaica chiefly in the latter half of the seventeenth century), the claim remains unsubstantiated.

It is true, however, that the Portuguese began visiting the coast of West Africa in the middle of the fifteenth century, and that before the end of the century they and the Spaniards began populating their own countries as well as their New World colonies with slaves. When other nations began trading in West Africa, they made use of the Portuguese language or some form of it. The Portuguese castle of El Mina on the then Gold Coast served as a model for castles and forts built later by other European powers.

Before 1612, when the Dutch built a fort at Mouri about 13 miles away from El Mina after having failed to capture it from the Portuguese in 1596, Portugal and Spain were the only nations with trading stations on the African coast. In 1637 the Dutch succeeded in capturing El Mina and five years later the Portuguese had only one stronghold left in West Africa, at Cacheu just south of the Gambia River in what is now Guinea-Bissau. After 1637, the Gold Coast, which was the main trading area in the seventeenth century, remained divided between the Dutch and the British, whose forts dotted virtually the entire coastline.

Lawrence (1963: p. 245) has this to say about the British presence on the coast of Africa:

An English trading-post (called Coromantin)[5], which probably originated in 1631, is said to have been converted into a fort in 1638, but the venture did not succeed. In December 1645 news reached El Mina that the "English ship Hope had 24 guns and many people on board, 20 of whom were stationed on land in order to rebuild the ruined fort". The work must have been completed or nearly so by 1647, when the chaplain went to El Mina and invited six Dutch officers to pay a return visit.

The other important area in the early period of trading was the region around the Gambia River. Although there were probably no really big factories there before 1665, traders – especially British traders – were active along this river. Their ships could navigate great distances up it and they also traded from small forts that were set up from time to time and that changed hands frequently.

It is important to distinguish continuous contact in fixed settlements from sporadic contact. The castles, forts and lodges, and the African towns near them, were bilingual or multilingual. This was not so of other forms of contact. Where ships stayed only long enough to fill their holds with goods or slaves, people may have used Portuguese "pidgin" or some derivative of *sabir* as a vehicle for bartering. In areas of continuous contact, however, Portuguese "pidgin" would at best be no more than one factor in a multilingual situation, and would be a minor factor in language development even in areas where Portuguese were settled. The main factors everywhere in areas of continuous contact would have been European languages in their full form and African languages.

Finally, it is essential to remember that Jamaica under the British was first colonised by Europeans and African slaves from Barbados, where they had gone some 40 years earlier.[6] LePage (1960: p.17) claims that in 1675 one group of British planters and nearly 1,000 slaves moved from Suriname to Jamaica when Suriname was taken over by the Dutch. The early British Caribbean colonies grew not so much independently as by movements of population from other British colonies. Voorhoeve (1970: p. 55) describes this pattern:

> Surinam had been occupied by different successive groups of Europeans before Willoughby (of England) planted a new colony in 1651; but there is no evidence that survivors from former settlements remained in that year. The rising sugar industry created a shortage of land in Barbados. Willoughby sent 100 men to settle a new colony in Surinam. Fifty more people followed the next year. The colony was captured by the Dutch in 1667, recaptured by Barbados that same year, but handed over again to the Dutch in 1968 according to the peace treaty of 1667. Before the colony was handed over, 67 of the most important English planters emigrated to Surinam with 412 slaves. In 1680 the last group of Englishmen and slaves left, leaving only 39 Englishmen behind. The English planters were not allowed to take slaves acquired under Dutch rule out of the colony, so it was mainly old slaves who left ... The old slaves were ... taken to other British colonies like Jamaica.

According to Patterson (1967: pp. 134–53), Barbados supplied one-third of all slaves imported into Jamaica between 1655 and 1674, one quarter between 1675 and 1688, and then some 5 per cent between 1689 and 1701. This means, according to Curtin (1969: p. 58), that "about 16,000 slaves moved from the Eastern Caribbean to Jamaica between 1655 and 1701." These first slaves set a cultural "pattern" that others, arriving later, had in some degree to follow. This was especially true of language, since underlying every other problem of coping or survival was the problem of communicating. In other respects too the earliest arrivals and the first generation of creole slaves (Africans born in the New World) would have served as models. Since Jamaica was settled so much later than the Eastern Caribbean (including Suriname), there can be no doubt that creole slaves were among those transferred there under the British occupation.

Anyone who wishes to study the demography and precise ethnic origins (i.e. provenance in Africa) of early Jamaican Blacks must therefore look too at the situation in the Eastern Caribbean and particularly in Barbados. There has been much research and debate on how many Africans were brought across the Atlantic as slaves. Unfortunately there is little agreement either on global figures or on figures pertaining to particular territories. The estimates by P. Curtin (1969), a leading authority, have been seriously questioned by Inikori (1982: pp. 19–20), and his global figures have been revised upwards. Here, global figures are not as important as the proportion of Africans to Whites, and in particular the relative size of different African ethnic groups in Jamaica.

LePage (1960), Patterson (1967), and Curtin (1969) have published studies on African slave demography in Jamaica. LePage and Curtin go to great lengths to arrive at figures, and adduce a great wealth of detail; reading them, it is easy to lose sight of the wood for the trees. Here I will confine myself to examining their conclusions, especially in so far as they relate to patterns of growth rather than precise figures and to patterns of provenance at different periods of the slave trade.

For the formative period up to the end of the eighteenth century, Curtin (1969: p. 56) presents a comparative picture as shown in Figure 1 on p. 38.

In the case of both Barbados and Jamaica (and, with few exceptions, of the whole of Afro-America), the population figures are considerably lower than the estimated slave imports. Curtin, for example, estimates that some 747,500 Africans were brought to Jamaica during the slave trade and Inikori (1982) offers an even higher figure. The size of the African population in the New World during the relevant period is far lower than these figures would lead one to predict. The shortfall must be seen as a result of the harsh conditions that the slaves met in their new surroundings.

The regional and ethnic provenance of Africans is crucial to the reconstruction of the cultural history of Jamaica, but it is extremely difficult to know. Some records are incomplete and unreliable. Others use imprecise terms or refer only to large geographical areas such as "Guinea". Still others merely give the name of the port, factory, or fortress from which the slaves were shipped. But in many cases the slaves were captured far into the interior or on coasts other than the one from which they were shipped, so that it is impossible to determine their exact origins. LePage, Patterson, and Curtin have come to some tentative conclusions about patterns of regional and ethnic provenance of African groups in Jamaica and the West Indies. Curtin (1969: p. 158) concludes that of the British colonies, "Jamaica presents the best possibility of construct-

Figure 1 Slave populations in the Caribbean, 1650–1790

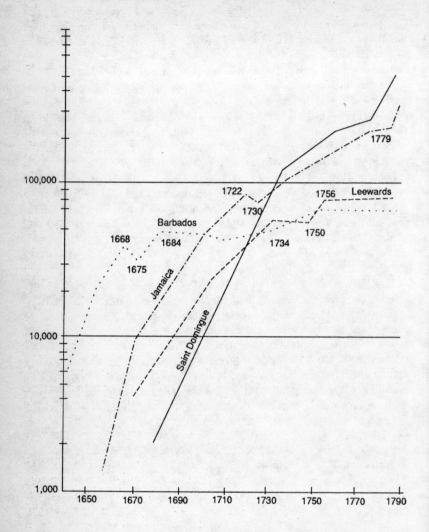

ing a relatively reliable and complete cross-tabulation of changing ethnic origins through time." Curtin's table is reproduced as Table IV on p. 40.

The estimates in Table IV are extrapolated from a number of samples of Jamaican imports by ethnic origin collected by LePage and Patterson. The most interesting estimate is the one for the Gold Coast in the period 1655 to 1701. The relatively small percentage (6.3) of slaves estimated by Curtin to have been imported from the Gold Coast contradicts the assessment of Patterson and to a lesser extent that of LePage. Patterson's conclusions are important (1967: p. 142):

> During the earlier half of the period between 1655 and 1700 the largest single group of slaves came from the Akan and Ga-Andangme peoples of the coastal strip of Ghana (Gold Coast). Many of these, coming from the Eastern Caribbean, were already seasoned and were well placed, both historically and socially, to impose their own pattern of behaviour and speech on the creole slave society which was then in its nuclear stage. Forty percent of the slaves entering the island during the last quarter of the 17th century came from Angola, the particular tribal provenance of which is uncertain since this was one of the areas from which slaves came from a considerable distance inland ... Although only 20% came from among the coastal tribes of Ghana during the later half of this period, these would doubtless have assisted in consolidating the Akan and Ga-Andangme bias which the young creole slave community would already have had.

LePage concludes (1960: p. 74) that "of the overall British slave-trade, in period one (1655–1702), Senegambia, Sierra Leone, the Windward Coast, the Gold Coast and Whydah were each contributing roughly one-quarter of the slaves". At another point (p. 75), LePage seems partly to contradict himself: "Despite the preference shown in Jamaica for Gold Coast slaves, these could have at no time constituted the major part of slave imports. It is possible that during the seventeenth century they made up the largest single group from any part of the coast."

Barbados was, as we have seen, an important source of the African population of Jamaica in its formative years (one-third of it between 1655 and 1674 and one-quarter between 1675 and 1688). Unfortunately LePage and the other scholars have not specifically researched the ethnic origins of Barbadian Africans in the formative period. All that we can say is that the records show that "up to 1663, the slave trade to Barbados was practically a Dutch monopoly" (Curtin 1969: p. 53). The Dutch played a major role in bringing the "sugar revolution" to the Caribbean, and in the seventeenth century the large numbers of slaves they shipped across the Atlantic were mostly destined for colonies of other nations. By 1624 the Dutch had expelled the Portuguese from their settlements on the Gold

Table IV
Slaves imported into Jamaica, 1655–1807: a speculative approximation by coastal region of origin

Origin	(1) 1655–1701	(2) 1702–25	(3) 1726–50	(4) 1751–75	(5) 1776–91	(6) 1792–1807	(7) Total
Senegambia	4,200	6,700	8,600	1,000	2,600	4,600	27,700
%	4.8	10.5	6.7	0.6	2.1	2.7	3.7
Sierra Leone	800	4,700	9,200	–	–	–	9,200
%	0.9	7.4	7.2				25.5
Windward Coast	11,400	5,100	11,400	28,500	–	10,300	81,400
%	12.9	9.9	8.9	16.5	–	6.0	10.9
Gold Coast	5,500	22,300	34,700	67,300	47,100	13,900	190,800
%	6.3	34.8	27.1	39.0	38.3	8.1	25.5
Bight of Benin	24,300	19,500	16,900	23,800	18,300	–	102,800
%	27.6	30.5	13.2	13.8	14.9	–	13.8
Bight of Biafra	6,800	1,000	27,900	43,300	49,500	83,500	212,000
%	7.7	1.6	21.8	25.1	40.2	48.6	28.4
Central Africa	34,800	4,800	17,700	8,800	5,500	59,500	131,100
%	39.5	7.5	13.8	5.1	4.5	34.6	17.5
Unknown and other	200	–	1,700	–	–	–	1,900
%	0.2	–	1.3	–	–	–	0.3
Total	88,000	64,000	128,000	172,500	123,100	171,900	747,500
Annual average	1,900	2,700	5,100	6,900	7,700	10,700	4,900

Sources: LePage, "Jamaican Creole," pp. 61–65, 74, 84; Patterson, The Sociology of Slavery, pp. 134–5, 137–9; Edwards, British West Indies, 2: pp. 60–80; Board of Trade Report, part III.

Coast and had captured the El Mina fortress. According to LePage (1960: p. 30), "it is probable that most of the slaves shipped by the Dutch at this time (17th century) came from the Gold Coast".[7]

Though many authors are cautious about drawing firm conclusions, much evidence suggests that the Gold Coast was the main source of Jamaica-bound Africans in the formative period (1660–1700).[8] By 1640 the Dutch had broken the Portuguese monopoly on the West African Coast and had become chief suppliers of slaves to the New World colonies of other nations (they themselves had as yet no colonies). They set up their headquarters at El Mina, on the Gold Coast. The Dutch became the principal supplier of slaves to the British Windward and Leeward colonies (and to Suriname), whence quite a few settlers migrated to Jamaica at the beginning of the British period. They also supplied Jamaica directly through the slave depots at Curaçao and St Eustatius. When the British themselves entered the trade as shippers, "all the English joint-stock companies which succeeded one another in the title to the monopoly of the slave trade to the British Caribbean and American plantation made the Gold Coast their headquarters, the main factory being at Coromantin and subsequently, after the incorporation of the Company of Royal Adventurers, at Cape Coast Castle (Cabo Corso)" (LePage 1960: p. 30).

By about 1655, "all the Negroes brought to Barbados, Jamaica and the Leeward Islands came in English ships" (Patterson 1967: p. 126, citing A. Newton, *The European Nations in the West Indies*, p. 282); and Patterson (p. 128) believes that "it can be said with some plausibility that the Gold Coast was the single largest source of the Monopoly Companies' slaves during this time (1655–1700)". Most slaves shipped from the Gold Coast came from areas near the coast and not from the hinterland, unlike in other trading areas. As we shall see later, the languages and culture (Akan culture) of this area are highly homogeneous – far more so than other slave-trading areas. This is a very important key to understanding the cultural history of Jamaica.

The other main source of slaves for Jamaica in this formative period were the interlopers, that is, ships that violated the legal monopoly of the Companies. Since interlopers left no records of their activities (which continued to be illegal until 1968), their contribution is difficult to assess. According to Curtin (1969: p. 54), the Royal African Company found that 29 per cent of all English ships landing slaves in the British West Indies in the period 1679 to 1682 were interlopers. Thus he reconciles his own estimate of total yearly imports (6,950 slaves) with that of the Royal African Company (4,010 slaves).[9] On the basis of a comparison of Company records and records of interlopers for the period 1698–1700, Curtin concludes that "the interlopers had been steadily gaining on the Company" since being legalised.

42 Roots of Jamaican Culture

The interlopers acquired slaves from wherever they could: not only the
Gold Coast but also the East Coast and Madagascar. But most agree that
Angola was their main area of supply.[10] However, slaves shipped from
Angola were acquired far into the hinterland, and were nowhere near as
homogeneous as Gold Coast slaves. This suggests that Gold Coast Africans
who came to Jamaica in this period had a stronger group identity than
Africans of other ethnic affiliations and more cultural resources, even if we
cannot be sure of their exact numbers.

Throughout the rest of the period of the slave trade, the Gold Coast
continued to be an important area of supply. Curtin estimates that the
Gold Coast contribution never fell below a quarter of the total, except at
the very end of the trade, in the period 1792 to 1807. Patterson passes over
the period 1792 to 1807 because of lack of statistical evidence; he estimates
that in the period 1730–1790 the Gold Coast contributed "a little over 40%
of slaves" (1967: pp. 136–38). LePage lumps the Gold Coast with other
regions for the period after 1725 so his figures are less useful.

The way in which Europeans stereotyped their slaves and the
preferences they developed on the basis of these stereotypes are also
important in assessing the position of Gold Coast Africans in Jamaica.
Jamaican planters seem to have preferred Gold Coast Africans, though
planters in the Eastern Caribbean thought them rebellious and disliked
them. Jamaican planters were said to have especially disliked Ibos, who
according to Edwards (1793: pp. 88–9) were "the lowest and most wretched
of all the nations of Africa", and were morose and prone to suicide. But
these preferences had little apparent effect on the distribution of slaves.
The slave trade was not generally organised efficiently enough for
planters to pick and choose. Usually they took what was available. In any
case, Jamaica was a huge market. The local demand and the re-export
demand probably often outstripped supply.

1841–1865
The third period of migration was roughly between the years 1841 and
1865, when an estimated 10,000 Africans were brought to Jamaica as
indentured agricultural workers (Schuler 1972: p. 70). In the immediate
post-emancipation period there was a general exodus of workers from
Jamaican sugar plantations, where they had previously worked as slaves.
This, coming on top of the general decline in population under slavery,
created a labour shortage that threatened the existence of the colonial
system. To get new manpower and prop up the decaying agricultural
economy, steps were taken to promote African immigration to Jamaica.

The new African migrants came from two main sources. After abolishing
their own slave trade, the British tried to stop that of their competitors
and established what were in some degree meant to be temporary
settlements for liberated Africans in Sierra Leone and St Helena. Jamaican

Maroons who had earlier been sent to Nova Scotia were also subsequently shipped to Sierra Leone. Emigration to Jamaica and other colonies in the West Indies was seen as a means of establishing permanent settlements for these liberated Africans and of propping up the old colonies. The other source of new immigration were foreign slave ships intercepted in or near the Caribbean; the slaves aboard these ships were re-routed to Jamaica and other British colonies.

The British Government officially approved African emigration to the West Indies in 1840. Most migrants arrived during the years 1848 to 1850, when Africans "constituted the only source of additional labour" (Roberts 1954: p. 238) in the West Indies; moreover, the Brazilian slave trade reached its peak in 1849, which meant that British patrols could make more interceptions. The Brazilian slave trade ended in 1852, the same year in which Chinese immigration began, and for some years after that African immigration subsided. In the late 1850s, when large numbers of slaves were taken to Cuba, immigration of liberated Africans to Jamaica picked up again. The main supply of liberated slaves virtually dried up when slavery was abolished in the US in 1864 and "by 1865 the immigration of Africans into the British West Indies was virtually at an end" (Roberts 1954: p. 239). Of the estimated 10,000 African migrants to Jamaica during this period, the vast majority came from the settlement in Sierra Leone. Roberts (1954: p. 255) estimates that every second African migrant to the West Indian colonies came from Sierra Leone, most of them before 1853. The next main source of African migrants was St Helena; the smallest number were Africans liberated in the West Indies and "processed" in Rio de Janiero and Havana.

The chief ports at which African immigrants to Jamaica disembarked were Morant Bay, where most immigrant boats stopped for landing instructions before proceeding to the other ports, Kingston, Savanna-la-mar, Lucea, Montego Bay, Annotto Bay, and Port Antonio. The demand for labour was acute in the parish of St Thomas-in-the-East (Schuler 1972: p. 6).

The main ethnic groups migrating to Jamaica from Africa during this period were Bantu and Yoruba. Bantu "from the Kongo-Kwango cultural area" (Schuler 1972: p. 7) seem to have predominated in St Thomas. The evidence for this is the persistence of linguistic forms of Kikongo origin in St Thomas and the practice of Kumina religion there (see Chapter 4 on Religion and 6 on Language). According to Schuler (1972: p. 13), Yoruba from Western Nigeria were "the other dominant group in Jamaica [and were] generally known as the Nago people". These Yoruba were concentrated in Duckenfield, St Thomas, and in Westmoreland, which acquired the second largest contingent of Africans. Remnants of the Yoruba language have been preserved in the Waterworks/Abeokuta area of Westmoreland.

The Gold Coast as a Culture Area

The Gold Coast slave-trading area extended from Cape Appolonia to the River Volta (Edwards, vol. II, Bk IV, Chs 2 and 3). This area is almost conterminous with the former British colony that became the modern Republic of Ghana. It is a relatively small area with a rather homogeneous culture, despite the fact that it was rent by political divisions at the time of the first contacts with Europeans. This cultural homogeneity is most obvious in the case of language, but it can also be detected at the level of religion, music, social organisation, and so on.

The main ethnic groups of the Gold Coast are Asante, Fante, Nziani, Agni (Ivory Coast), and Brong, all of which are subsumed under the designation Akan (see Map of West Africa on p. 9). These peoples speak very closely related languages or dialects; some of these languages, like Twi, spoken by the Asante, and Fante, are mutually intelligible. A comparative survey suggests that these Akan languages are among the most highly "developed" in West Africa, in the sense that they have undergone a relatively large number of changes from the original ancestral language. This is extremely relevant for an analysis of the dynamic development of language in Jamaica. Some characteristic features of West African languages have changed so greatly in Akan languages that they are no longer immediately recognisable as such. For example, in many African languages, nouns are arranged in classes or categories, each with a distinctive prefix that is extended to adjectives and verbs in the same sentence. This exists in Akan only in a very reduced, almost relic, form. Bantu languages, which are an extreme case, have up to 19 different noun classes, but some Akan languages have only one overtly marked noun class for which the class prefix is optional.

Tone, or pitch, plays an important role in most West African languages: it can be the only distinguishing feature between two words which have the same pronunciation in terms of sounds. This feature is also present only in reduced form in Akan. According to Stewart (1971), it is doubtful whether Twi can properly be considered a "tone language". In examining the development of West African culture in Jamaica, we should therefore view it not statically but within the framework of a dynamic evolution that was already underway in West Africa itself in the sixteenth and seventeenth centuries.

Other aspects of culture besides language were also common to the different ethnic groups designated as Akan. Christensen (1959: p. 257) says that "the various Akan peoples speak mutually intelligible dialects and exhibit a high degree of cultural homogeneity so that much of what is stated here about the Fanti will also characterize other Akan groups". This thesis is partly confirmed by Busia (1954: p. 191) writing about the religion of the other major Akan group, the Asante:

The Ashanti form part of the larger body of Akan-speaking peoples widely distributed in the Gold Coast who have in common a number of social institutions, religious beliefs and rituals; but the traditional cosmology of the Ashanti differs significantly from that of some other Akan groups.

The Asante and Fante peoples believe in the existence of a Supreme Being, called variously Onyankopon, Nyankupon, Odomankoma, and Onyame, who created all things in the universe. The lesser spirits or gods, called *abosom*, derive their powers from their creator, Onyame, and inhabit and animate trees, animals, rivers and other natural things. For example, one of the symbols of *Onyame* is Ananse Kokuroka "The Great Spider"; and the goat symbolises the Earth Goddess *Asaase Afua*, a daughter of Onyame. The widespread sacrifice of goats among the Akan is associated with the veneration of *Asaase Afua* (cf. Meyerowitz 1951: p. 76). Finally there are the omnipresent ancestral spirits (*nsamanfo*) who bring the wider world of the spirits into direct and constant contact with the world of the living and provide the link between religious beliefs and social organisation. Akan society is matrilineal: individuals belong to matrilineal clans made up of members who claim descent from a common ancestress. The spirits of her dead matrilineal descendants form the *nsamanfo* (or *asaman*).

The Supreme Deity Onyame has no public temples. In old villages each Akan compound has an altar to Onyame, the *Nyame dua* or Nyame's tree, on which offerings are placed in a basin, pot, or gourd fixed in a three prong fork (cf. Meyerowitz 1951: p. 75). According to Busia (1954: p. 192), "though many of these altars were to be seen in Ashanti villages some twenty years ago, they have now become extremely rare ... This, however, has not affected the belief in the Supreme Being." The Supreme Being has become so distant that he can only be approached through the intermediary deities (*abosom*) and ancestral spirits. It is these spirits that are in constant communion with the physical world, largely through the medium of priests.

The main prerequisite for priesthood is possession by one of the lesser deities (Christensen 1959: p. 257). These deities "come down on the head" of a person (male or female) either during ceremonies that involve drumming and singing or when the person is alone in the forest. The priest then considers that he or she has been chosen by, and become the devotee of, the possessing spirit or god. Whenever subsequently possessed by that spirit, he or she becomes a mere medium "behaving and speaking as compelled by that spirit that possesses him" (Busia 1954: p. 194).

Priests may undergo a period of apprenticeship in which they deepen their knowledge and understanding of the deity they are serving – the knowledge acquired includes "dancing, how to call his deity, and the construction and use of charms" (Christensen 1959: p. 257). The other main area of specialisation is healing, in particular knowledge of plants and herbs, and of how to use them and where to find them. In Akan culture, priests and priestesses are therefore both medical and religious practitioners.

Two other groups perform roles akin to that of priests. The Fante term *obosomfo* (literally "people of the gods") indicates according to Christensen (1959: p. 258) "those priests who serve deities of foreign provenience and who lead cults whose popularity is based on their effectiveness as an antidote for evil magic." The *adurunsinyifo* are primarily medical practitioners or herbalists who serve apprenticeships of several years during which they are instructed in the nature, use, and habitat of herbs, as well as in the art of charms and divination. In Akan cosmology illness may be caused either by physical conditions or by supernatural forces, so the practitioner must be versed both in herbal healing and in identifying and dealing with supernatural influences on human lives. They therefore specialise in charms and divination, of which the primary technique is spirit possession (Christensen 1959: p. 262).

Through their communication with the deities, priests can help people to achieve a wide variety of goals: to become pregnant, to find lost articles, to reap rich harvests, or to solve personal problems. Europeans often call this magic, and distinguish sharply between good and evil magic. Akans, however, do not seem to make such a sharp distinction. They seem to believe that "good" and "evil" are two sides of the same coin, meaning that what is good for one person may be bad for another. According to Christensen (1959: p. 265), the Fanti believed that "any priest can cause death or illness if properly approached".

"Witchcraft" is related to religious activity and very relevant to Jamaica. I mentioned it earlier when discussing the role of the *obosomfo* in combating evil magic. Rattray (1916: p. 313) writes:

> Witchcraft was essentially the employment of anti-social magic. The belief in its general prevalence was largely due to the fact that certain forms of illness resulting in death could not otherwise be accounted for ... poison in some form or other was often an important stock in trade of the professed witch.

The Twi word for "witch" is *obayifo*. The *obayifo* is, according to Rattray (1916: p. 47), the servant of *Sasabonsam*, meaning "evil spirits" or "devil"; *sasa* also refers to a person possessed by an evil spirit. *Sasabonsam* and *obayifo* are essentially at enmity with the priests (*okomfo*), but the "witchdoctors" could play a positive (though marginal) role in religion. Their Twi name (*bayi komfo*, literally "priest of witchcraft") suggests as much. Williams (1932: p. 132) writes:

No doubt the *obayifo* affected at times the role of medicine man ... Practically, in a general way, the differentiation (between 'good' and 'evil' magic) was in the specific object of the rite ... and also in the wide divergence in the ingredients employed, just as the knowledge of vegetable qualities, good and evil, was used for curative or destructive purposes, according to the profession of the herbalist.

Ellis (1890: p. 12) writes that among the Twi there is a high degree of village autonomy in the worship of deities: "On the Gold Coast there are no general objects of worship (observed by the whole of Twi-speaking tribes), few tribal, and many local." He speaks further of "a thousand different villages possessing each a god, each of whom resembles all the others in general attributes and functions but is believed to be essentially separate and individual". He contrasts this with the situation among the Ewe-speaking people of the Slave Coast (see below) where "the same gods [are] worshipped, under the same name, in every town and in every considerable village, represented by images modelled in a common plan, and possessing in every case identical attributes and functions"(p. 13). The organisation of the priesthood among the Ewe was much tighter and more institutionalised than among the Twi. Differences such as these were important for the development of religious organisation in the New World. As we shall see, the religion and gods of the Ewe had a better chance (other things being equal) of surviving in the new environment.

It is important to quote at length Opoku's description (1974: pp. 288–292) of Akan worship:

> Corporate worship is accompanied by singing, drumming, and dancing and the principal actor is the priest or priestess, assisted by attendants. The music is provided by the drummers and the singing by the worshippers (spectators). The Okomfo stands in the middle of the gathering, while the singers with the aid of the drummers pick up song after song. The Okomfo begins his preparations several hours before the congregation arrives, and included in these is abstention from sexual relations the night before, in order that he may remain ritually pure. By the time the actual worship begins, the Okomfo is in a state of possession. Most of the time during public worship is taken up by the performance of "akom", or religious dance.
>
> The "akom" usually opens with "ntwaaho", in which the priest spins round and round, while the singers call on God, the Creator, Mother Earth, or the particular deity being worshipped.
>
> The next dance, "adaban", is usually accompanied by songs of invocation and supplication. In this dance the priest dances straight backward and forward and his dancing may be accompanied by a song.
>
> In the "abofoo" dance, which usually follows the "adaban", the priest

imitates a hunter tracking down an animal. This dance is symbolic of the deity, who, like a hunter, hunts down evil. The "abofoo" may in turn be followed by "abofotia", which is similar to "abofoo".

There are numerous dances, all of which are symbolic, and at every public worship, most, if not all the dances would be performed. The Akan priest is certainly a "dancing priest", as Nketia correctly asserts, and this is clearly in evidence on occasions of public worship.

It should be mentioned that at such gatherings for public worship, it is not only the deity being worshipped who makes his appearance; other deities, who are believed to be attracted by the music, descend on the priest, who at once changes his dress and varies his steps to portray the characteristics of the visiting deity. Nketia wrote: "The dance motions are interesting to watch, but the combination of these with trembling motions, leaps and gesticulations instills awe and terror into the onlookers. For believers, there is assurance of the divine presence in all these, for while trembling and falling into ecstasy a priest is no longer himself but the embodiment of the spirit of his god working through him. The words that fall from his lips, his suggestive gestures, and any features he introduces into the drama such as impersonations of creatures, climbing of trees, etc., are carefully noted."

There are periods of rest during public worship when the priest may deliver messages from his deity through an "okyeame", interpreter. He may walk round the circle and shake hands with worshippers and onlookers. The sick may be brought to him so that he may touch them or prescribe some medicines for them.

At the end of the performance, when the deity takes his leave of the priest, the latter collapses into the arms of attendants and is carried into the sanctuary. Later on, his personality, which had been displaced by the god during the time the priest was under possession, returns and he is usually unaware of what had transpired, having been simply a medium who spoke and behaved as the deity wanted him to.

After the departure of the priest, the drummers and singers may continue while the congregation may then dance. The period of such public worship may last for a whole day or a whole night; and the purpose is to contribute to the spiritual edification and the renewal of faith of devotees, as well as dedication of converts. It is not only officials who perform at public worship, the whole congregation participates. Usually at public worship, drinks and meals are served, and this provides an opportunity for communion between the deity and his "children", and between the members of the congregation and each other.

Worship in Akan religion is both ritualistic and liturgical. In the case of ritual, it follows a set pattern, "the way it is done", and adherence to properly established procedures ensures the efficacy of the ritual performed. The liturgy is embodied in the songs, prayers, and praises sung to the deities and also in the language of the drums.

Prayers

As a result of the Akan's awareness and acceptance of the fact of his dependence on a power superior to himself, the power which determines his destiny, the Akan offers prayers through which he makes his petitions known. Prayers are usually made up of petitions and requests for material blessings – health, longevity, prosperity, children, protection from enemies and death, blessings and prosperity on the town, more money, more produce from farms, prosperity and blessings on all well-wishers, and condemnation to all who wish others ill. As the officiant prays, the onlookers express aloud their concurrence with, or approval of, the contents of the prayer, after each pause by saying "Ampa ara" (It is just the truth) or "Yonn" (Yes indeed!).

The Slave Coast

This trading area was centred on the region now known as Benin (formerly Dahomey), but also included part of what is now Togo to the west and part of what is now Western Nigeria to the east. Most slaves originating from this area belonged to a rather homogeneous grouping now known as Ewe, and known in the eighteenth century as Popo or Pawpaw. Slaves were traded mainly in Whydah and Ardra. Apart from Ewe, slaves belonging to the Nago ethnic group (a subdivision of the larger Yoruba family) from the former Oyo and Benin empires (Patterson 1967: p. 122), in what is now Western Nigeria were also shipped from these places.

As we have seen, all authors attribute great importance to this area in the early period of the slave trade. It apparently became ascendant at the turn of the eighteenth century. John Atkins (*Voyage to Guinea*, 17, p. 168) claims that in the first decades of the eighteenth century it was "the greatest trading place on the Coast of Guinea selling off as many slaves, I believe, as all the rest together." As usual, the Portuguese were there first, followed by the Dutch. The British then contested Dutch control of the Coast and the Royal African Company was able to maintain a base at Ardra. However, by the 1730s the French had acquired the greatest share of the Slave Coast trade; they populated their New World colonies, especially Ste Domingue (Haiti), with shipments from this area.

Patterson (1967: p. 142) estimates that 30 per cent of the slaves arriving in Jamaica in the last quarter of the seventeenth century came from this area and that between 1700 and 1730 the Slave Coast was "quite possibly" the largest single source of slaves, but that numbers fell rapidly between 1730 and 1790 after the Dahomeans imposed their authority on the area and the French began to monopolise the trade there, cutting off the supplies to British colonies.

This area was therefore a major source of slaves during the early period of the British colonisation of Jamaica, though less so than the Gold Coast in the first half of the period 1655 to 1700 or Angola in the second half of the same period. Moreover, its culture was relatively homogeneous; this is also important for assessing its impact on Jamaica. According to Patterson (1967: p. 132), "from the Slave Coast at least three-quarters of all the slaves came from among the Ewe speaking tribes which presently inhabit the state of Dahomey while the remaining quarter came from among the Yoruba peoples of the upper sections of southwestern Nigeria". Herskovits (1938: p. 8) writes that

> within this area, the people represent a unit, both culturally and ethnically ... There can be no question that minor differences exist today, as they did exist, between cultures of the various peoples who comprised the Dahomean state. There are differences in speech, but these are of a dialectic character; differences in religious belief, but merely in the names of deities or the emphasis placed on a particular deity, and so for all phases of culture.

The language of the Slave Coast is commonly known as Ewe. One of the main Ewe dialects is Fon (or Fongbe), spoken by the Dahomeans who subdued other peoples in the region and established a powerful kingdom in the eighteenth century. Ewe is a Kwa language, closely related to Akan; their syntactical structures are similar but their lexicons are different.

Worshipping the spirits of ancestors provides the link between social organisation and religion among Dahomeans, just as it does with the Akan people. Ancestor-spirits mediate between their living worshippers and the gods that personify the forces of the universe. Ewe-speakers, like Twi-speakers, believe in the existence of spiritual beings that inhabit the natural world and control human existence and events in the material world. Ewe-speakers propitiate and worship the in-dwelling spirits of animals and natural and physical phenomena (including pestilences such as smallpox). The Supreme Deity, Mawu, remains rather distant from the affairs of mortals; people rarely, if ever, pray or sacrifice directly to him. Lesser deities, generally called *vodu* or *edro*, are more involved with humans; they are similar to the *orisha* of the Yoruba and the *abosan* of the Akan.

Senegambia and Sierra Leone

That part of the West African coast south of the Senegal River and including the area south of the Gambia River was known to slave traders as Senegambia. The Senegal and the Gambia were the only rivers found to be navigable and trading ships were able to travel up them for great distances. All European slave powers used these rivers to penetrate West

Africa. LePage (1960: p. 74) says that a quarter of all British slaves came from Senegambia in the period 1655 to 1702, though later the proportion dropped sharply. However, Curtin estimates that Senegambia provided only 5.7 per cent of British slaves in the initial period, and he is supported by Patterson (1967: p. 116).

The main ethnic groups from Senegambia mentioned in the records are the Mandingo (or Malinke) and the related Bambara, Serer, Fula, Wolof, and Jula (also called Floop).

The Portuguese were the first Europeans to stake a claim in Senegambia; previously they had been active mainly in the Canaries, Madeira, and Cape Verde. In 1455 a Venetian known as Cadamosto sailed up the Gambia River under the auspices of Henry the Navigator. The British and French began sending ships up the Gambia towards the end of the sixteenth century. They subsequently carved up the area and created the colonies that have now become the independent republics of Senegal, Gambia, Sierra Leone, Guiné, Mali, and Guinea-Bissau.

When the Europeans arrived in Senegambia, the Mandingo were dominant and the Kingdom of Mali was flourishing. The territories occupied by the other ethnic groups were interspersed with Mandingo territory; wars alternated with periods of friendship. The Mandingo established a form of protectorate over the Gambia valley, and their language was commonly used by neighbouring groups. The Mandingo seem to have entered the Gambia valley from the east or south, or from both directions. Their capital, Manding, was in the upper Niger valley, which they entered either from the south, as Bantu, or from the northeast, in which case they had Arab links. They then spread westward along trade routes to the Atlantic.

The Mandingo were among the most heterogeneous peoples in Africa. Before the arrival of Europeans, Senegambia had been the site of intense cultural interaction, and continues to be so today. The various ethnic groups had only a limited sense of territorial loyalty.

The Mandingo (and the Bambara) were ruled by a hereditary King, or Mansa, who was political leader, religious leader, guardian of justice, commander-in-chief of the army, and keeper of traditions. He was the earthly representative of all Mandingo ancestors, and could appeal to them to bring happiness or – if he so wished – misfortune.

The Mandingo and the Bambara deify the spirits of their ancestors and believe that natural phenomena are charged with spiritual power. The deified spirits of ancestors protect the village and family that they inhabit, and animate woods, caves, hills, and rivers, which are sacred. The divinities that invest natural phenomena are represented by various symbols (called "fetishes" in most studies) that play an important role in the people's lives. Each village has a sacred tree, generally a baobab or tamarind tree, that protects it against evil spirits.

The other main element in Mandingo religious organisation is the secret societies. These are headed by a high-priest and served by an oracler who interprets the will of the society's deity, by a sacrificer and by a multitude of initiated members. The divinity is consulted on all sorts of occasions, and sacrifices (generally of a chicken) are made.

In Mandingo culture as throughout West Africa, music and dance are closely linked to the practice of religion as well as to important social events and festivals such as planting, harvest, birth, marriage, circumcision, excision, and burial. Instruments include various types of drum, string and wind instruments, and the xylophone. The griots have become famous for their epic songs and story telling, through which history and traditions are recorded and handed down.

Fula (Fulani, Foulbe, Peul, etc.)

The groups referred to as Fula are extremely complex in composition. They have wandered over the whole of Senegambia, sometimes mixing with the Mandingo and at other times remaining uneasily aloof from their neighbours. By one classification, the Fula divide into three main groups: the nomads, who are the most Semitic of the Fula and who seem to be closest to the ancestral type; the semi-sedentary groups, who generally prefer livestock rearing over agriculture, though they practise both; and the sedentary groups, who have moved furthest south and have mixed most with other peoples.

Fula political organisation was similar to, but on a smaller scale, than that of the Mandingo. Villages were headed by a gerontocracy and organised into "tribes". Both village chiefs and tribal chiefs were assisted by councils of notables. Fula society, like Mandingo society, was typically divided into nobility, castes, and slaves.

The extended family is not widespread among the Fula. Each married male has his own house, which he builds alongside his father's with the help of his father's servants or of his friends. He works apart from his father and inherits a share of cattle designated as his at the time of his birth. However, the father continues to exercise patriarchal authority over such households.

Islam already began to spread in Senegambia before the Europeans arrived there, and it continued to spread despite competition from Christianity (though the rate of progress slowed somewhat). The Fula embraced Islam more than any group, but some still practise pre-Islamic religions either in pure or in syncretic form. Most of all, they preserve a strong belief in the spirit world.

Wolof

According to Quinn (1972: p. 24), language is one of the few distinguishing features of Wolof culture. Wolof social structure was quite similar to that of the Mandingo (and Bambara), the Fula, and the Serer.

Jola (also spelled Dyula)

The Jola, who are closely related to the Serer, seem to have lived mainly around the mouth of the River Gambia before they were driven south by the Mandingo. Quinn (1972: p. 26) says that they had warred so much among themselves and suffered so much from Mandingo aggression that their society was virtually anarchic by the 1800s. Unlike the other populations of Senegambia, the Jola were resistant to influences from other ethnic groups. For example, they preserved their indigenous "animist" religion and remained virtually untouched by Islam.

The Bight of Biafra

This is the region around the Deltas of the Niger and Cross rivers, often referred to as Calabar, the name of its most important trading area (New and Old Calabar). The other main trading stations were at Bonny. The main ethnic groups in this region are the Edo-speaking Yoruba-related peoples in the famous Benin Empire in the western part; the Igbo, who live toward the east and are by far the most numerous; the Ibibio, who include the major Efik branch; and the Ijo. Most slaves exported from the Bight of Biafra were probably Igbo. By the last quarter of the eighteenth century this region had become the main source of slaves for Jamaica.

The Edo were related to the Yoruba by language and culture. Yams are their major crop and staple diet, as they are of the Yoruba. Edo households usually have two farms, a large one far from the village and a small one close to it. They prepare farm-land by cutting down the undergrowth, allowing it to dry, and then burning it. They often leave taller trunks standing after cutting off the branches and use them later as supports for growing yam vines. Yam mounds are made by hoeing up heaps of soil in rows at regular intervals. Seed-yams are split into sections suitable for planting and pressed into the sides of the mounds. Corn is generally planted in rows between the yams; and plantains, okra, and other vegetables are distributed around the tree stumps left in the field, along the boundaries, and in other spaces (Bradbury 1957: p. 23).

The Edo believe in a Supreme Deity, Osa, and in a series of lesser deities, the most important of which is Olukun, God of Fertility and Wealth, who is often worshipped more frequently than Osa. Other important deities are Ogun, "God of Iron", whom the Yoruba also worship; and Osun, "God of Medicine". The Edo also worship ancestor spirits that protect, punish and cure their descendants, and recognise spirits that inhabit rivers, trees, and so on.

Igbo

The Igbo seem to have been numerous in Jamaica and other parts of the New World, but not culturally influential. This may have been due to culturally determined personality characteristics. Whites commonly stereotyped African slaves, but there may be a kernel of truth in their opinion of the Igbo, whom they saw as introverted and given to depression or resignation; they also reported high suicide rates among them. Another interpretation of suicide is that it is a form of resistance; but suicide as a form of resistance is not incompatible with suicide as the result of depression and alienation. Dr Ena Campbell, in a letter to me, offers an alternative interpretation of this view of the Igbo. She claims that the Igbo are *extroverts* who encourage individualism and self-actualisation within well-defined boundaries. Thus in traditional Igbo society the acme of success was to be wealthy enough to buy membership in title societies. Igbo society is horizontally segmented into relatively autonomous villages, and "there seems to have been no broader organization in their history" (Shelton 1971: p. 5). Only those groups close to the Igbo/Benin border had developed the institution of the chieftaincy. They had no centralised government, and were organised in autonomous gerontocratic villages or groups of villages. This probably meant that they lacked the ethnic solidarity and interaction that would have been necessary to perpetuate and impose forms of their culture in the new environment in Jamaica. According to Dr Campbell, Igbos would become depressed on the plantations, where they could not perform and excel as individuals. In this interpretation, what looked like introversion was in fact a pathological reaction that sometimes resulted in a personal form of revolt (suicide) rather than in organised group resistance (of the sort associated with the Asante).

Yoruba

In the far west of the Bight of Biafra were the Empires of Benin and Oyo. Here too the Portuguese were the first Europeans to establish trading posts, and they remained the most influential power in the region until the second half of the seventeenth century. Bradbury (1957: p. 21) believes that the Portuguese trading posts and Catholic missions were probably abandoned in the 1660s, when the Dutch, and later the British, became the major European powers in the Yoruba region. Yoruba Africans came to the New World throughout the period of slavery and also in the later third period of migration of Africans to Jamaica.

The Yoruba have become one of West Africa's best known ethnic groups. During both the period of slavery and the colonial and post-colonial period in Nigeria, many writers have written about them.

It seems that the Yorubas' sway once extended much more widely than it now does. According to Johnson (1921: p. 15), the Yoruba had power over peoples as distant as the Asante and the Ga of the Accra region of what is now Ghana; "certainly, until comparatively recent times, the Popos and the Dahomeans paid tribute regularly to Oyo as their feudal lord."

The Yoruba believe in the existence of a Supreme God, Olurun or "Lord of Heaven", who does not intervene directly in human affairs but acts through the intermediary of lesser deities (*orisha*). They also worship and invoke the spirits of ancestors. Among the lesser deities are Ogun ("God of War" or "God of Iron"); Sango ("God of Thunder"); Esu or Elegbara ("Satan"), who can be propitiated by offerings and invoked against one's enemies; and Ifa ("God of Divination").

The Yoruba closely associate medicine with the supernatural. Several kinds of doctors are engaged in divining and combating evil powers by means of bush medicines (drunk or rubbed onto the body) and "fetishes". Medicines can be used to protect as well as to harm; people associated with harmful medicines are known as *b-erhia* or "spoiling doctors" (Branbury 1957: p. 60).

Congo

The term *Congo* refers to a river, among the biggest in the world; to the area around the river basin, especially that part south of the river; to a country (or rather two countries – the People's Republic of the Congo, with its capital at Brazzaville, and the Democratic Republic of the Congo, now called Zaire, with its capital at Kinshasa); to a slave-trading area; and to a culture area. No two of these references are conterminous, and the slave-trading area includes parts of modern Angola as well as of the two republics of the Congo. Patterson (1967: p. 124–5) defines the slave-trading area as stretching from Cameroon in the north to Rio Negro in Angola in the south, but he admits that few slaves from the Cameroon and Gabon found their way to Jamaica.

In 1484 the Portuguese reached the mouth of the River Congo, then apparently called *N'Zadi* (interpreted by the Portuguese as *Zaire*). They established relations with the Manikongo, ruler of the Kingdom of the Kongo, and by the early 1500s had begun to trade in slaves in both the Kingdom of the Kongo and the outlying regions. Toward the end of the seventeenth century the British, especially British interlopers, began to trade in the Congo area.

According to Patterson (1967: pp. 142–3), "forty per cent of the slaves entering the island (Jamaica) during the last quarter of the 17th century came from Angola" (presumably meaning the entire "Congo" area). During the eighteenth century the number of slaves from this source fell rapidly and it was not until the last 17 years of the trade that there was a "striking reappearance of slaves from South West Africa, particularly from the region of the Congo" (Patterson 1967: p. 143). As we have seen, in the third period of migration (1841–1865) most Africans migrating to Jamaica came from this region.

The peoples of the Congo all belong to one ethnic group, the Bantu, who are thought to have migrated to the lower Congo river basin from an area just south of Lake Chad. Between AD 500 and 1000 they spread out in every direction, displacing and mixing with the earlier Pigmy inhabitants of the Congo basin. Although there is a great diversity of languages and dialects in the area, they all belong to the Bantu family. Beside these Bantu mother tongues, trade languages are spoken widely in the Congo: Kiswahili in the east, Kikongo in the west, Chiluba in the south, and Lingala in the north.

Merriam (1961: p. 23) classifies the people of the Congo according to his concept of "culture clusters", and identifies as the most important clusters the Kongo (west), the Mongo and Kuba (north), the Lunda and Luba (south), and the Warega and Mangbetu-Azande. If the syllable *Ba* is prefixed to any of these names, the resulting compound denotes the people belonging to the cluster.

The Bakongo had a very sophisticated political system and are renowned for their art and industry. They mined iron ore and smelted and worked it into a fine array of tools, weapons, ornaments, and musical instruments. They also forged copper, casting it through the lost-wax process into statuettes, jewellery, and religious objects (Merriam 1961). They were brilliant weavers: they mainly used vegetable fibres stripped from the leaves of the raffia palm tree.

According to Van der Kerken (1919: pp. 42 ff), religious beliefs vary among the different Bantu groups, but "il semble cependant y avoir entre elles un fond commun". All believe in a Supreme Being: called *Nzambi* (Mpungu) in the west and north, among the Bakongo, the Basuku, and the Bayansi; *Chembe* or *Jambi* among the Bakuba; *Mungu* in Swahili; *Kalunga* or *Villie Mukulu* among the Baluba; and *Kabiza-Pungu* in the south east. This supreme omniscient creator is (as usual among West African Peoples) quite indifferent to the affairs of the human world; the Bantu people do not specifically worship him or sacrifice to him (Lamal 1965: p. 170). He is sometimes involved in moments of great sorrow or great joy, but only as an impassive and impartial witness.

Besides this supreme divinity, spiritual beings with different attributes and powers, good or bad, inhabit mountains, rivers, forests, caves, and springs, and must be propitiated by worship. Some are represented by an external object (called Kishi), such as a clay leopard. Christians have wrongly interpreted this as "idolatry" and "fetishism".

Bantu people worship ancestral spirits who, in return for protecting family members, receive prayers, and offerings such as goats. Ancestral spirits communicate with the living through dreams and can be reincarnated, particularly in their grandchildren. They often manifest themselves among the living as animals.

The Bantu believe that nature is alive with hidden forces (good or evil) and that priests with specialised knowledge and abilities can control and make use of these forces. They practise divination to uncover evil doings or to reveal the past or future, calling on ancestral spirits to pronounce the divination. For the Bantu, magic and medicine are closely related, as they are in other West African cultures. Curing is done by herbal infusions, magic, or offerings to the ancestral spirits assumed to have been offended. The diviner, the magician, and the doctor are highly appreciated and honoured in Bantu society.

Spirits of the departed, called *bamvumbi*, or *banzambi* (hence West Indian *jumbi*) constantly intervene in the world of the living. They come back to frighten the living and are endowed with unusual powers. Lamal tells of a "woman late coming from forest or lake; she returns terrified to the village declaring having seen some '*bamvumbi*' or '*banzambi*'; they were small with ash coloured skin and red hair like the *Ndundu*" (i.e. "albinos"; cf. Jamaica *dundus*).

People are considered to have a soul as well as a "shadow", conceived of as an emanation from the body (Lamal 1965: p. 183). To step on a person's shadow is an insult. A corpse on the way to burial no longer has a shadow. The soul separates and roams round the body; it may later become a *mvumbi*.

Invisible forces constitute part of reality for the Bantu. The kind of materialist philosophy that associates reality only with what can be seen, weighed, and measured is contrary to Bantu philosophy (Lamal 1965: p. 207). In the Bantu belief system, the cosmos is full of invisible forces that dwell in the material, visible world, including the "vital forces" of animals, plants, and objects (such as stones) that produce fire.

For Bantus, to know a person's name is to know that person's essence or profound nature. Bantus therefore take care (or at least did so in the past) not to reveal their names to strangers. If a boy climbs a tree, he is not addressed by his real name; to do so might provoke an injury. People have birth names, circumcision names, and nicknames by which they are known in their villages. Nicknames often tell something about a person's looks or behaviour.

Bantu children are especially fond of riddles; proverbs and folktales with a moral purpose can be frequently heard in the villages. According to Merriam (1961: p. 23), Bantu music emphasises rhythmic devices and techniques, and is played in a great diversity of styles and on a great variety of instruments, in particular drums (including "talking drums"). One of the big dance drums is called *ngoma*, which is played sitting.

In the following section I will look more closely at some cultural institutions from regions of West Africa relevant to the history of Jamaica. I do not pretend to present a rounded picture of these cultures, but merely to sketch some of their salient points. This approach is compatible with the general aim of this study, which is not to discuss Jamaican culture as a whole, but to examine selected institutions that best demonstrate the historical processes outlined in Chapter 1.

Religion

West African religion, both in its exoteric form – as understood by ordinary people – and its esoteric form – as understood by priests and philosophers – has a basic structure common to different ethnic groups.[11] This structure has changed over time, particularly in the cities (see below), but my summary here ignores these changes and my comments are assumed to be valid from 1600 through to the present, particularly in the villages.[12]

The essential elements of this basic common structure can be summarised in seven points:

(i) There is a constant interaction between religious forms and social forms; social order is guaranteed by the observance of religious ritual.

(ii) Religion links the natural world to the supernatural world, bringing living people into contact with deities through the intermediary of ancestors. Together with the living chiefs, the Supreme Being, the deities, the departed ancestors, the priests and the magicians constitute a system of authority.

(iii) The world is a vast spiritual arena. There is no rigid dichotomy between sacred and secular, between natural and supernatural.

(iv) There is a supernatural god, a unique creator, who is often androgynous or associated with a goddess who can be his twin sister. Beneath this supernatural god are a number of hierarchically organised immanent deities and spirits. These may be ancestors,[13] important historical personages, deities of the elements (thunder, lightning, wind, water, fire, iron), or spirits that invest natural phenomena (trees, rivers, hills, rocks). Some deities may possess special persons (especially priests and dancers) whom they "ride" or "mount" and through whom they express themselves. Other deities merely protect people, for which they are offered sacrifices or respect and homage in the form of food and taboos. Deities sometimes allow diviners and priests access to the supernatural world and the invisible. The lesser spirits may intervene benevolently or malevolently in the daily lives of humans, and religious practitioners may invoke their assistance for either "good" or "evil". Ancestral spirits are particularly important. According to Field (1961: p. 197), most Ga people are in practice more afraid of offending these spirits than of offending the gods. Ancestors are held to be born again in their descendants. Elderly people are respected and revered in part because they preserve the memory of the dead and are chronologically closer to the ancestors (Ellis 1887: pp. 128–9). If burial rites are improper or incomplete, they may interfere with or delay the entrance of the deceased into the spiritual world and cause the soul to linger as a restless and malevolent ghost.

(v) "Rites of passage" are celebrated at major points in the life cycle of humans and of society (birth, death, marriage, harvest, and so on). Prayers, sacrifice, the drinking of alcohol, and spirit possession play an important part in these rites, which are interwoven with music and dance.

"Mounted" devotees dance to the accompaniment of songs and music, leading some commentators to talk of "danced religions" (Raboteau 1978: p. 15, Herskovits 1967, vol 2: pp. 114–116).

(vi) Divination is practised by marginal religious practitioners who reveal people's future, often believed to be predestined. In some cases diviners also cure people by revealing the causes of their illness, and by telling them where, and how, and to whom propitiatory sacrifices should be made. Diviners can also see the invisible and are often closely associated with priests. The diviners' activities are considered legitimate and generally approved.

(vii) Magic is distinguished from religion in that whereas the priest prays to the divinity of which he is the servant, the magician commands and has a firm belief in his own powers. However, some magic is part of the legitimate manipulation of supernatural elements, and is often associated with religious ritual. Froelich (1964: p. 190) reports that "the interaction between magic and religious rite is frequent in West Africa. On the occasion of agricultural rites, the priest prays to the spirits of the Earth and at the same time scatters powders and other magical objects designed to strengthen the germinating power of the seeds or to keep away thieves and sorcerers." The magician protects against sorcerers and invisible evil beings; he cures people, makes women fertile, ensures and protects harvests, wards off destructive forces, provides antidotes, guarantees success in examinations, ensures safe travel, and so on. As a healer, he has expert knowledge of the pharmaceutical and spiritual uses of curative plants. The same person is therefore both doctor and magician (whence the term "witchdoctor").

African religions seem to have been particularly flexible and hospitable to external influences. Deities originally belonging to one religion and to one ethnic group have spread to and been accepted by other groups. Froelich (1964: p. 89) speaks of the "tolerance" of the Dahomeans in adopting new deities. African traditional religions are not fixed and immutable but in constant evolution (Parrinder 1950, 1953). Froelich (1964) gives two examples of the genesis of new cults initiated by people to whom supernatural forces revealed curative and other effects of medicaments; these cults then spread far afield. Dammann (1964: p. 238–9) points to a progressive secularisation of African religion as a result of internal processes. Magic formulae lose their constraining character and become folklore; dance becomes more of a diversion than a part of religious ritual; religious words lose their power; the worship of ancestral spirits is replaced by magical practices. These internal dynamics must be taken into account when considering the evolution of African culture in Jamaica.

Perhaps the most significant thing about African religions from the point of view of the cultural history of Jamaica is the emergence of religious syncretisms that combine Christian or Islamic elements with elements of traditional religions; analogous processes are common in Jamaica and the New World. Froelich (1964), Balandier (1953), and Parrinder (1953) have discussed these African syncretisms, some of which are more christianised, others more traditional. For example, the Zionists of South Africa practise traditional kinds of relations between the priest and the faithful, spirit possession, prophetising, and faith healing. They exalt African values, and teach individual salvation and access to the heavenly city. Many are strongly political and proclaim the redemption of the Black race by its prophets.

Froelich (1964) lists the following characteristics of syncretic religions in the Congo: there is a Saviour, who is the founder of the religion and a God Creator who makes Himself accessible to the faithful; adepts believe in faith healing, made possible by a special act of God, and they acknowledge martyrs, in particular the Saviour himself, who is a new Black Christ; they practise various food taboos, hold feasts in honour of their ancestors and recognise a hierarchically ordered clergy.

Esoteric aspects of West African religion – the philosophical meaning underlying religious practice and religious symbolism – have been neglected by British and American anthropologists. French and African scholars, however, have studied the total body of knowledge and belief expressed in African mythology and in the symbolism of African rituals. The summary that follows draws heavily on African and French sources, plus a few English-language sources such as Washington (1972). It is difficult to discuss continuities in areas that have to do with cognitive and philosophical structures, for such structures cannot be observed directly and there has been very little research on them, either under slavery or since slavery. I shall confine myself to noting similarities and parallels between Africa and Jamaica, but without going into depth.

Africans are deeply religious people but there are no dogmas or "sacred scriptures" in their religion. African religion pervades the whole of a person's life and activities, transfusing them with religious expression and meaning transmitted symbolically by paintings, sculptures, wood carvings, brass castings, rituals, dances, songs and music. There is no rigid dichotomy between the secular and the religious. Religious symbols, rites and beliefs play a unifying role in society; they are the supreme safeguard of the fundamental needs of the people and of the basic relations that constitute the social order – land, cattle, rain, health, family and clan. Individuals can no more detach themselves from their religion than they can detach themselves from their roots in the kinship group that is so all-pervading and binding in traditional African communities. Washington (1972: p. 20) describes traditional African religions (like North American Black "cults") as "seeking ... the power of the spirit of God in all times, places, and things, because without that power, man is powerless. Unless man attunes himself with the power of God, in himself or in the vessels he

chooses to permit his power or spirit to reign, man is impotent."
Superficial writers have called this spirit a "fetish", on the mistaken
grounds that it is the objects themselves (rather than the in-dwelling
spirits that they symbolise) that are worshipped. They also wrongly
claim that "ancestors are worshipped". However, it is not a case of
"worshipping people who are dead", but of paying homage to the power
and spirit that once dwelt in those now dead and that lives on after them.
According to Washington (1972: p. 27), offering food and drink to the
departed is a token of fellowship, hospitality, and respect; "the drink and
food so given are symbols of family continuity and contact". According to
Meyer-Fortes (in IAI 1965: p. 133), "ancestor worship" is the
"representation or extension of the authority component in the jural
relations of successive generations ... It is not the whole man, but only his
jural status as parent, vested with authority and responsibility, that is
transmitted into ancestorhood." Washington concludes that (p. 30) "the
heart of traditional African religions is the emotional experience of being
filled with the power of the spiritual universe."

Society and Economy

Agriculture and livestock rearing are the basis of the economy in
traditional West African societies. According to Skinner (1973: p. 209),
every Dahomean was a farmer; no matter what his occupation, he
cultivated a plot of ground. The main crops are grain and – in the tropical
coastal areas – root vegetables. Soil is prepared by clearing the land of
trees and bush and then burning them. Under the system of shifting
cultivation a piece of land is farmed until the soil is exhausted, and then a
new area is brought under production. Under the fallowing system, a
section of previously cultivated land is rested and allowed to lie fallow
for a number of years until its fertility is restored. Under both systems
crops may be rotated. Gibbs (1965: pp. 556–7) provides a detailed account of
West African farming:

> In the beginning of the dry season, the farmer clears the bush, lopping
> the branches of the smaller trees and burning them. He then makes
> heaps a yard apart and plants his yam sets. When the rain begins, he
> interplants early maize at the sides of the heaps, harvests it in June and
> plants late maize. The yams are harvested in October. In the second
> year he interplants a variety of crops: maize, peanuts, cotton, beans,
> cow-peas; and, in the third year, cassava. Each year, weeding is a major
> task in the wet season, although a cassava crop gets little attention ...
> The details naturally vary from one area to another; for instance Guinea
> corn replaces maize in the savanna, and cassava is more important in the
> south. A number of other crops grow without much attention: peppers,
> plantains, citrus fruits, kola nuts. The Yoruba farm is a tangled growth

of crops and fallow. Young men sometimes form a small group and work on each other's farm in turn. Wealthy men can call their friends together, provide drumming and a big feast, and set them all to work for a day, but there are no landless men obliged to hire themselves out for wages.

There is a division of labour according to sex that is set by custom and can even be subject to religious sanction. Among the Igbo, for example, men plant and tend those crops and trees that need the most attention, and leave the rest to women. Men's crops include yams, pineapples, plantains, and bananas, while women's include pumpkins, cassava, corn, beans, okra, and peppers. Groups usually cooperate to build houses, bush the land, or perform other farming tasks that are beyond the capacities of a lone individual or an extended family.

Markets are important gathering places with a much broader function than simply trade. They are centres of recreation and of religious and social communication. Commodities sold at them include local agricultural and craft products, meat, live animals, and – in the colonial period – European goods such as cloth, hardware, tinned foods, and kerosene. Local farmers and housewives sometimes carry their surplus crops and craft products over large distances to these markets, which are organised in periodical cycles. Within a circumscribed area, only one market is held on any one day, so that the people in the area get the chance to visit each market in turn. Vendors are segregated according to product; some products are sold by women, others by men. The main traders at the Gold Coast markets discussed by Wolfson (1958: pp. 55–56) citing a 1602 source (Peter de Marees) were women described as "very nimble about business". According to Bohannan (1964: p. 211), transactions in most African markets involve much haggling; prices vary with the status and assumed wealth of the purchaser.

Aesthetics

It is difficult to find one term to cover music, dance, carving, folktales, proverbs, and other styles and functions of language. Ottenburg (1960: p. 67) proposes grouping them under the rubric "aesthetics", but he admits that "the aesthetic life of the African is rarely set off from other aspects of everyday existence, rather it is intimately bound up with social behaviour and religious life". It is also bound up with social control. A finely wrought mask may serve to symbolise the transposition of the wearer into the spirit or deity that he or she serves. As we have seen, music and dance accompany every major communal activity (including work) and each main point in the life cycle of individuals and society.

According to Ottenburg (1960: p. 68), innovation is commonplace in this field. "Topical songs may be based on old rhythms and melodies, but, with their texts composed for specific occasions, they are essentially creative commentaries of the present social scene. Wise sayings soon become proverbs." Innovation also happens in folktales. The basic narrative of the tales is set; storytellers add their own music and songs and manipulate dramatic elements in the story to point up its moral meaning (Bohannan 1964: p. 143). They act out their tales before audiences who join in the musical chorus and contribute stylised and spontaneous spoken responses.

Nketia (1974: p. 241) notes that "the picture that emerges from a comparative study of indigenous musical traditions is not one of mutually exclusive traditions or style clusters, but one of a network of overlapping styles which share common features of structure, basic procedures, and similar contextual relations." He adds (1962: p. 11), "Divergencies merely represent areas of musical bias ... the result of specialisations or differences in emphasis on the selection and use of common musical resources, common devices and procedures." Waterman (1952: p. 212) lists five characteristics of Sub-Saharan music:

1. Metronomic base
2. Dominance of Percussion
3. Polymeter
4. Off-beat phrasing of melodic accents
5. Overlapping call-and-response.

Waterman (p. 208) talks of the "great variety of styles actually present in Africa", including some that use harmony and others that do not, but he believes that "African music" everywhere permits "certain generalizations ... concerning the musical style of the whole area."

The most outstanding feature of African music is its polyrythmic (or polymetric) structure of complex combinations of different rhythms played concurrently. Dancing directly reflects the structure of the music, for different parts of the body accompany different parts of the polyrhythmic combination; the polyrhythms of the music are reproduced by the dancer's body.

According to Nketia (in Skinner 1973: p. 384), Africa lacks none of the world's instrument types. The main instruments used in African music are the membranophones (or drums). These include hour-glass drums, kettle-drums, open and closed bottle-shaped drums, cylindrical drums, and goblet-shaped drums. Playing methods include the stick technique; the stick-plus-hand technique (in which the hand is used for muting or beating); the hand technique (in which various parts of the hand or fingers are used); and the stick-and-armpit technique.

Other instrument types include chordophones, aerophones and idiophones. Idiophones are quite common, since they are usually made of naturally sonorous materials that need no further elaboration or manufacture. They include percussion sticks, rattles and iron bells.

Aerophones (or wind instruments) include specially treated animal horns or tusks, and in particular flutes and whistles. According to Nketia (1974: p. 586), "in Akan society the sounds of horns have a linguistic and a musical use; that is to say, what is heard as music sometimes conveys a verbal message."

Chordophones (or string instruments), such as plucked and bowed fiddles of between one and four strings, are more narrowly distributed. Jobson(1623) said that the most commonly used chordophone was a plucked string instrument made of a great gourd with a neck fastened onto it. Among the Asante, Jobson reports two main string instruments: the sanko, a zither type made of a narrow box the open tip of which was covered with an alligator or antelope skin; and another belonging to the violin family, made of a calabash and covered with deerskin. In each case the strings and bows were made of cow's hair. Southern (1971b: p. 11) mentions that the thumb-piano or box-bass was in common use. He describes it as "a box one end of which is left open; two flat bridges are fastened across the top, and five pieces of curved stick, scraped very smoothly are attached to them, and their ends being raised, are struck with some force by the thumb".

Nketia (ibid.) further remarks that within the framework of the predominance of percussive instruments, clapping hands, stamping feet and clicking the thumb and forefinger provide extra-vocal sounds that may be used in any situation. One may also resort to sound-producing instruments such as packing cases, stools or chairs, or anything that comes to hand in an improvisatory situation.

Music and dance are closely interwoven in the sense that they often accompany each other and in the sense that they fulfil the same functions in African societies. In addition to enhancing the celebration of all the phases of the human and societal life cycles, music and dance have an all-important religious function in facilitating and enabling the carrying out of religious rites and communication with the spirits and deities. According to Turnbull (1976: p. 161), "music is the prime means by which the living may commune with the world beyond, divine something of its will, and secure its blessing ... In communicating with the ancestors, words are inadequate and without power. Music has all the necessary power."

Music in Africa may be classified in terms of the context and function of its execution. There is first of all ceremonial music. According to Equiano (1789), "every great event is celebrated in public dances which are accompanied with songs and music suited for the occasion." Among the most important of these events are religious observances, birth, initiation, marriage, death, the installation of kings, and going to war. Then there is music associated with work, especially communal work; songs containing social commentary; and boat songs and the like. Finally, there is music associated with festivals, which in many cases last for several days.

African singing style is highly intense and resorts to falsetto, "shouting", and guttural noises. Acccrding to Southern (1971b: p. 16), songs commonly alternate improvised lines with fixed refrains. Typically a song consists of the continuous repetition of a single melody alternating solo passages and choral refrains, or of two different choral passages. This is usually referred to as "call and response". Often the phrases of the leader overlap with the chorus; a common antiphonal form is one in which the chorus line identifies the song and remains basically unchanged throughout the performance, whereas the solo line changes through frequent improvisations leading to the singing of two melodic lines simultaneously (Merriam 1962: pp. 67–8). Praise-singing, a kind of prose-poetry, is found in many parts of Africa. It is perhaps best known in Senegambia, where performers are known as griots. Griots have various roles and functions: they may appear as flatterers seeking patrons, as historians, or as musicians at ceremonies and rituals. One of the most interesting forms of West African music is the "song of derision", which is sometimes so powerful that the intended victim will pay the singer to stay silent (Van Nam 1948: p. 53).

According to Gbebo (1954: p. 63), music in Africa is "the combination of three things that are interdependent and never separated: dancing, singing, drumming". All occasions that demand music also demand dancing. The African dances for joy, for sorrow (as at funerals), and in order to worship; dance and religion are closely linked. According to Southern (1971b: p. 12), musical instruments are played only by men, while singing and dancing is done by women too. Onlookers join in by clapping their hands or tapping their feet. There is no real audience: everyone is involved in one way or another in the performance.

Language

Language provides the soundest evidence for the theory that the peoples and cultures of West Africa are related. True, there is an almost bewildering variety of mutually unintelligible languages and dialects in West Africa. However, this does not disprove the proposition.

There are two kinds of classifications of languages that refer to different kinds of relationships. The first is the genetic kind, which groups languages into families on the basis of their common ancestral roots. This kind of classification also yields subgroups of more closely related languages and dialects that share an immediate and relatively recent ancestor. The classification may then be presented in the form of a genealogical tree whose nodes and branches represent subgroups and whose trunk represents the original ancestral language common to all languages of the family. The other kind of classification is based on structural similarities between languages of the world; it is important for establishing universal properties of human language. Languages are classified into structural types (hence the term "typological classification"). However, languages that share the same structural features do not necessarily share the same ancestor; they need not be genetically related.

Linguistics has developed a methodology that allows inferences to be made about the earlier forms of languages in order to establish whether these languages are bifurcations of one common stock. Languages like those of West Africa whose earlier forms are virtually or completely undocumented can be classified genetically by reconstructing their earlier forms through an analysis of their contemporary forms. There is of course no necessary relationship between "race" or ethnic group and language, since one group can adopt the language of another. We must therefore separate those cases where a genetic relationship at the level of language implies ethnic relatedness from others where it does not. In the one case there is genetic transmission from one human and language stock into several human and language descendants; in the other, language is diffused from one group to another.

West African languages provide examples of both. Virtually all the languages in West Africa that are relevant to the cultural history of Jamaica belong to the same genetic family (usually called Niger–Congo). In some cases this linguistic relationship implies an ethnic relationship; linguistics then becomes an important instrument for delving into the history of populations and peoples. On the other hand, constant contact among different peoples has led to the diffusion of certain languages outside their original ethnic boundaries and to their adoption by other groups.

The main groupings within the Niger-Congo family are Bantu, Kwa, Mande, and West Atlantic. The only important West African language not represented among them is Hausa, the language of Northern Nigeria, which belongs to the Hamitic-Semitic family.

The West Atlantic group is located in Senegal, Guiné, Guinea-Bissau, and Sierra Leone. It consists mainly of Wolof, Serer, Temne, and Fulani.

The Mande group is found to the east of the Atlantic group, mainly in Senegambia, Mali, and Guiné. Its principal members are Mandingo, Bambara, Mende, and Dyula; Dyula is widely used as a *lingua franca*.

The Kwa group languages are spoken in what was called the Gold Coast region in the era of slavery and colonialism; as we have seen, they were very important in Jamaica. Kwa languages include the mutually intelligible Akan dialects (Fante, Twi, and Asante) spoken in Ghana; Anyi on the Ivory Coast; Ewe (or Fon) in Benin (formerly Dahomey); Ga, the local language of Accra (the capital of Ghana); Yoruba and Igbo in Nigeria; and Bini in Benin, which was famous as an artistic centre during the period of European expansion in Africa.

The Bantu languages are the most widespread; they are found in East,

West, and Central Africa. The most important Bantu language is Swahili, which is spoken practically all over East Africa, mainly as a second language; but Swahili was not important in Jamaica. The Bantu languages of the Congo River basin area, including Angola, are Luba, Kikongo, Lingala of Zaire and the Congo Republic, and Kimbundu of Angola.

The second kind of classification called "typological" could more appropriately be called structural classification. When linguists classify a language typologically, they ignore its geographical spread, its genetic affinities, and the genetic affinities of the culture that it is used to express; they look only at its formal structural features. This method may yield a very broad classification in terms of general patterns of word formation. Languages are then classified as inflectional, isolating, or agglutinative. In inflectional languages, words are typically composed of a root plus an inflectional ending. In languages like German, Spanish, French, Russian, and to a lesser extent English, these endings express categories such as number, person, tense, and aspect (for verbs); number, case, and gender (for nouns and pronouns); comparison (for adjectives); and so on. In isolating languages like Twi, Mandingo, Chinese, and Jamaican, words are not typically inflected, so that word order – the position of words relative to one another – is the main way of expressing grammatical relationships.

West African languages such as Twi, Yoruba, and Bambara are related both genetically and typologically; the typological relationship is largely due to the genetic relationship. These languages share structural features inherited from a common source; on the basis of the shared features, we assign them to the same typological class. Some examples follow:

(1) These languages have verb phrases made up of an invariable verb and one or more particles. These particles, which usually precede but sometimes follow the verb, either singly or in combination, express aspect and tense. According to Delafosse (1952), a verb without any particle usually expresses perfective aspect (equivalent more or less to English "I have __ed"). A typical verb paradigm, taken from Twi, is as follows (Christaller 1875):

o ba	"he comes"
o bai	"he came"
o re ba	"he is coming"
o be ba	"he will come"
o a ba	"he has come"

(2) Nouns in these languages occur in classes that may originally have been based on some shared semantic property (e.g. animateness, liquidness, and so on). This is known as the noun class system. Each class has an identifying prefix which, by a system of concord, may be copied before

adjectives and verbs. The noun class system does not exist with the same degree of completeness in all Niger–Congo languages. The most complete systems (such as in the Bantu languages, including Swahili) may have up to 15 noun classes, while others, as a result of historical evolution, retain only one class together with the vestiges of a system of concord. The system has evolved furthest in the Mande and Kwa languages (Greenberg 1966: p. 10; Alexandre 1967: p. 86–8; Welmers 1973: p. 156). Anyi, for example, has a number of nouns that begin with *a-* that have derivative (or deriving) verbs without *a-*; e.g. *arye* "food" and *ri* "to eat". According to Welmers (1946:p. 58), where nouns appear to enter into a system of classes in Fante, the prefix is almost always *a-*. Christaller (1875: p. 21–22) mentions that *a-* is the most frequently occurring noun class prefix in Twi and Ewe.

(3) Tone is a characteristic feature of the structure of Niger–Congo languages, though it is more elaborate in some than in others. In tone languages, relative pitch (the frequency at which the vocal chords are vibrated) may suffice to distinguish one word from another, e.g. *fè* "plainly", *fé* "deeply"; *óbà* "child", *òbá* "he comes" (the examples are from Twi). According to Westermann (1970: p. 43), tone seems to have largely broken down in the Mande languages. Stewart (1971) shows that tone is relatively unimportant in the Akan dialects, which distinguish only two pitch levels (high and non-high), and that distinctive tone shows signs of disappearing altogether.

The Arrival of Africans in Jamaica

These then are the elements, in one sense disparate, in another sense common and uniform, that came together in Jamaica and began a process of evolution that culminated in the present cultural configuration of the people of African descent in Jamaica. Before we go on to examine this process of evolution, we must look briefly at various aspects of the transport of Africans to Jamaica, and of their early settlement on the island, that have important implications for Jamaican cultural development.

One issue is the forced extraction of Africans from their homelands. Africans could not prepare themselves psychologically and materially for their departure to the New World, and once aboard the slave ships they had virtually no contact with their home cultures. Since European cultures were overwhelmingly dominant in slave societies, one would expect acculturation to be rapid and one-way, in other words, that Africans would strive to acquire European culture.[1] Africans were unable to bring with them all the elements necessary to preserve their original cultural traditions and institutions. Moreover, because they were enslaved they were not permitted to continue to operate some institutions of a political, legal, and economic sort. Finally, their lack of direct ties to Africa meant that they had no access to models or to a higher authority that might have helped and encouraged them to preserve other aspects of their cultures such as religion in a "pure" form.

On the other hand, forced extraction must have nurtured feelings of resistance both to enslavement and acculturation. The concept of marronage, embodying both political, physical, and cultural resistance, is essential for an understanding of cultural history in Jamaica (and in the rest of Afro-America). A symbiotic interaction developed between culture and resistance. The will to resist required the preservation of some functional distinctiveness in culture, upon which the success of the resistance depended; and the success of the resistance in turn contributed to the preservation of an African-type base culture. The Maroon communities of Jamaica and other parts of the New World are the most striking example of this symbiosis, but from the very start resistance took other forms as well, including suicide on capture, during the Middle Passage, or on Jamaican soil; poisonings; and the development of certain personality traits (the *ginal*), modes of behaviour, and forms of expression designed to confuse the master class. Poisoning was an art widely practised by slaves and widely feared by the master class; it depended on the preservation of knowledge about herbs, roots, and barks that was part of the culture and "folklore" of Africa. Language, songs, folktales, and the *sambo* and *ginal* personality types were imbued with ambiguities: they had one meaning for the master class and another for the slaves. Spirituals such as "Steal away to Jesus" are the best-known example of this,[2] but they are not the only one; other examples can still be found throughout Afro-America (cf. Reisman 1970). Finally, suicide was motivated by Africans' belief that at death their spirits would be returned to the ancestral homeland, where they would dwell in harmony with the revered ancestors (cf. Gardner 1873: p. 99). This interaction between culture and resistance was perhaps most evident in religion, which is the subject of the next chapter.

The nature of slavery as a system of production had its own implications for the development of culture in Jamaica. Slavery was a labour-intensive system of production that required large numbers of field hands; owners took no part in production, and the system depended on coercion. The supply of slaves was reasonably steady and they were under military control. There was therefore no economic need to train them, educate them, motivate them, or interact with them on any large scale;[3] nor did the master class feel any psychological or moral need to do so, since for them the slaves were without dignity. Slaves were therefore virtually free to develop their own forms of culture, which were greatly enriched by elements transmitted from Africa. The persistence of these African forms of cultures contributed greatly to the collapse of the slave system.

In the hierarchy of occupational differentiation that developed on the plantations, field slaves, who were the majority, were furthest removed from contact and interaction with the master class. It is among field slaves that continuities from Africa were strongest. Field slaves rarely interacted with people outside their own class; this group exclusiveness tended to negate the effects of the diversity of their African origins.

The structure of Jamaican society after emancipation only served to reinforce the pattern outlined in the preceding paragraphs. Subsistence farmers in isolated areas continued to interact mainly with their own sort, just as their slave parents and grandparents had done, and it is among them that African continuities are strongest.

Western writers have attached more importance than necessary to the diverse origins of Africans destined for Jamaica. As we have seen, throughout the history of Africa peoples have been displaced, conquered, and brought into contact with one another, leading to massive assimilation and acculturation. This happened even when there was no common enemy serving as a catalyst to help bring Africans together. Enslavement enabled Africans to see beyond their differences. Cultural unity and uniformity was not just an ideological construct promoted by the militants: it was a product of objective conditions, as I tried to show in my discussion of African culture and in my analysis of the interaction between culture and resistance. Slaves began to grasp this unity almost as soon as they were captured, and could sufficiently communicate their sense of it – whether through language, kinesics, drums,[4] or music – to organise revolts aboard the slave ship. Even if it is true (and not just a typical case of European stereotyping) that most revolts were hatched and led by Asante Africans, there was apparently no ethnic restriction on who might participate in such revolts. Dallas (1803 vol.1: p. 33) observes that "Negroes of other tribes joined the Maroons, but the Coromantee (Ashanti) language superseded the others and became in time the general one in use."

Travelling to Jamaica on the same ship became a very important bond for Africans, who treated their shipmates as kinsfolk. Patterson (1967: p. 150) shows that for the early slaves:

shipmate seems synonymous in their view with brother or sister ... [and] is the dearest word and bond of affectionate sympathy amongst Africans ... They look upon each other's children mutually as their own. It was customary for children to call their parents' shipmates "uncle" or "aunt". So strong were the bonds between shipmates that sexual intercourse between them, in the view of one observer, was considered incestuous.

The seeds of an African community cutting across superficial boundaries between people of different ethnic origins were therefore sown as early as the crossing from Africa to the New World.

The question of community is a crucial one. The essential characteristics of a community are stability, continuity, and constant interaction, without which the slaves would have found it extremely difficult to pursue their cultural traditions. All communities are of course to a certain extent unstable and discontinuous: the terms are relative. In Jamaica, it would be hard to argue that Maroon societies were anything but stable continuous communities. However, some scholars doubt whether the Africans who remained slaves constituted a real community, and tend to see them as no more than a motley group of individuals or as tiny ethnic groups that clung together and viewed others as strangers. Mintz (1976) has even argued that Africans in the New World were at first more a "crowd" than a community.

There is no doubt that a slave could be sold at any time, without regard for family ties. On the other hand, family units and community clearly did exist, and instability was by no means the rule. As we have seen, bonds were even forged aboard the slave ships, so that "shipmate" became almost a term of kinship. Gardner (1873: p. 179), commenting on the sale of slaves to pay off debts, writes:

At first sight, it might appear that a change of masters could make little difference to people in a servile state, but the slave formed friendships like other people (sic) and they had their allotted plantations and houses. Their love to parents and shipmates was great; and moreover if there was no wedded bond, there were relationships held by many of them as sacred.

Gardner also refers (p. 182) to the "social life" of slaves. Newly purchased slaves were generally quartered on older Africans, who were "glad to revive old memories by converse with these strangers ... The strangers would almost always look upon their hosts as parents and address them as such". This "social life" as described by Gardner was nothing less than community life. When couples came together the event was "sanctified by some little ceremony". Afterwards many lived faithfully together. There were special ceremonies to mark divorce. A *cotta* (the pad made usually of leaves or fibres from banana or plantain trees and carried on the head to support loads) was said to have been cut in two, each party retaining a half as a sign of separation (Wright 1937: p. 231). There is no way of authenticating this report.

Children were loved, old people were respected, and there were festivals (such as the festival of the new yam) and festivities. The first generation of creole slaves had shed most of the "tribal" allegiances they inherited from their parents. According to Long (1774: p. 414), "a general correspondence is carried on, all over the island, amongst the Creole Blacks".

Divisions did exist among the slaves; but it is doubtful that these were so deep as to fragment slave society into non-interacting separate and autonomous compartments. Early writers could identify different ethnic groups and different languages, but it is not clear to what extent these differences entailed ethnic rivalry or separation.[5] Schuler (1979b: pp. 67–68) suggests that before the appearance of Myalism in the 1760s "ethnic divisions existed ... The different nations tended to isolate themselves from each other, none more so than the Akan." Unfortunately this claim is asserted rather than argued or documented. It is of course not unlikely that people of one ethnic group would stick together (for ethnic cohesion is a widespread – some would say universal – facet of human behaviour and societal organisation). Moreover, there are reports of exclusively Akan slave rebellions and of festivals exclusively celebrated by one ethnic group. Schuler (1970) seems to believe that some eighteenth century revolts were ethnically exclusive, but her comment is not entirely unambiguous: "they seemed intent on limiting participation to a single ethnic group – at any rate to Africans alone" (i.e. not to creoles).

Beckles (n.d.) takes a different view. He speaks (p. 9) of:

emotional unity, and a sentimental bond [that] held the plantation black communities together. The form of unity cut across cultural lines but rarely withstood the full force of political praxis. One observer noted in 1666: "They are passionate lovers one of another; and though they are born in different countries and sometimes, when at home, enemies one to another, yet when occasion required they mutually support and assist one another, as if they were all brethren."

He also claims (but again without providing the evidence) that "the rebels must have had developed a significant level of political consciousness in order to transcend their cultural divisive tendencies, to launch a series of collective political actions against their oppressors". Price (commenting on Schuler 1970, pp. 143–4) says that "the majority of cases of strong ethnic organization that we know about among slaves occur in the 19th rather than say the 17th century", but later agrees with Schuler that the process (which he calls creolisation) that created "slave communities vertebrated by new Afro-American (rather than separate African ethnic) principles of organization" happened more rapidly in Suriname than in Jamaica.

Evidence from Maroon societies may shed light on the early relationships between African ethnic groups. According to Bilby (1981), contemporary Maroons still recognise four major ancestral spirits, each of which is identified with a major "tribe" or "nation" from which Maroons think they are descended.

> The only social context in which this notion of tribes comes into play is the traditional (religious) ceremony of Koromanti dance ... Several other tribes are cited by present-day Maroons as having contributed to early Maroon society ... All these individual tribes are subsumed under the one most powerful tribe, the Koromanti tribe.

We shall see later that there is evidence among Maroons and among Jamaicans in general of an inter-African syncretism and assimilation taking place within a broader framework of Ashanti (or Koromanti) dominance. Groups seem to have expressed their ethnicity in some areas but to have suppressed it in others, in favour of ethnic integration. This integration grew as creole slaves came to outnumber Africa-born slaves. In England too, where different ethnic groups now experience the same subjugation, hostility, and discrimination, a similar process can be observed among West Indians from the different islands of the Caribbean. On the one hand, a distinct ethnic identity is maintained and asserted. On the other hand, ethnicity is suppressed, particularly by West Indians born in England, in favour of Jamaican (as opposed to, say, Trinidadian) language, music and religion.

There probably was rivalry between creole slaves (i.e. those born in Jamaica) and Africa-born slaves; the latter were called "Guinea birds" or "salt water naygurs" by the former (Long 1776: p. 410). The creolisation of slaves is an important event in the development of African culture, for it represents the first big step toward the Jamaicanisation of this culture. As we have seen, the first generation of children born in contact situations everywhere become more rapidly acculturated than their parents. There is much evidence (e.g. Long 1776: p. 429) that in Jamaica, for example, creoles spoke better English than Africa-born slaves.

So there are elements of both stability and instability, continuity and discontinuity, in Jamaican slave society on the plantations; there is evidence of a community of slaves interacting from the very start, and other evidence of ethnic divisions and divisions between creole and Africa-born slaves. There were other forms of differentiation too: by occupation (between domestics, drivers, artisans, and field slaves); by civil status (between the enslaved and the free); and by "racial" admixture(between negroes, mulattos, quadroons, and so on). However, the discontinuities were rarely absolute. For example, even where kinship systems could not be maintained because of the absence of vital kin, basic elements of the system, such as respect for elders, could be maintained. Moreover, notions of kinship that could no longer be applied to consanguinal relations were transferred to other relations. Despite their removal from Africa and from their families, slaves continued to worship ancestral spirits in various parts of the New World, including in Jamaica (see below).

The formation of stable integrated communities by slaves was not incompatible with dominance and leadership by one ethnic group. Scholars have always recognised (cf. Herskovits 1941, Bastide 1971) that different African cultural traits preponderate in different parts of the New World. Thus Dahomey Fon predominate in Haiti, Yoruba in Cuba, Bantu in several parts of Latin America, and Twi-Asante in Jamaica and Barbados. Bastide (1971: pp. 8,11) argues that predominance is not just a question of numbers, which in any case cannot be accurately established from the records. I suggested earlier that a group may have come to predominate not because it was generally in the majority but because of its importance in the early formative period of slave society. Some ethnic groups were more coherent and unified than others, and could therefore maintain their traditional institutions more easily than their disorganised neighbours, who may have adopted their institutions. As we have seen, this frequently happened in Africa. Gardner (see below) reports religious behaviour and institutions in Jamaica that are related both in underlying principle and in detail to Akan religion; the question is whether this religion was observed by slaves regardless of ethnic origin.

Another interesting question is at what point in history was the Akan vocabulary that predominates among Africa-derived words in the Jamaican language adopted by other ethnic groups. The historical record provides no conclusive answer to this question, but there is no reason to doubt that there was some generalised acceptance of the norms established by the dominant group in the early period in Jamaica. Thus the naming of objects by Akan words was probably adopted by other groups in the early period. Gardner (1873: p. 184) more than implies as much when he writes that "the influence of the Coromantyns seems to have modified, if not entirely obliterated, whatever was introduced by other tribes" (he is referring to religion). However, the dominant group also incorporated elements from the culture of other ethnic groups. Thus the Akan-derived religion of the Suriname Bush Negroes recognises Dahomean and Bantu Gods (cf. Bastide 1971).

Finally, it is possible that while one norm was accepted in the area of, say, language, many different norms were simultaneously pursued in other areas of culture. Thus there is some evidence that Congolese Africans continued to maintain their own religious institutions while other Jamaicans were moving from an Akan base toward a number of different types of religious structure. This probably explains the persistence of Kumina in the eastern part of Jamaica.

4

African Religion in Jamaica

Africans coming to Jamaica brought with them a certain set of religious beliefs; they brought with them too a memory, individual and collective, of certain structures of religious behaviour and practice. It is quite probable (though there is no direct evidence to show so) that priests, magicians, doctors, and diviners were among those brought to the New World and that they continued to fulfil the same functions, or similar functions modified by the new conditions, in slave society. The most important difference between Africa and the plantations was that on the plantations there was little or no large-scale political organisation among slaves, so that religious practitioners had no political and little social support and were dependent on what recognition they could gain through personal initiative and self-assertion. This absence of political organisation seems a more likely explanation than ethnic diversity for the lack of an overall religious organisation encompassing the majority of Africans, either in Jamaica as a whole, in one region of the island, or even on one plantation. In Africa there was a tradition of interaction among different religions and of acceptance of the religions of other groups. In Jamaica the absence of political organisation led eventually to the fragmentation of African religion into innumerable local groups, each dominated by a priest whose individual powers largely determined how far the group's influence could spread. This in turn made it difficult to support more than a local hierarchy of priests and produced a lack of uniformity in theological concept and religious practice. A general frame of reference was handed down from Africa; within it developed a variety of beliefs and modes of worship. It should not be forgotten that Akan religion, which was apparently dominant in Jamaica, was village specific, in other words there was a high degree of village autonomy in the form of worship, unlike Ewe religion, which was organised above village level.

Finally it is possible, though unlikely, that a few of the Africans who came to Jamaica had originally belonged to that select group of philosophers, theologians, and intellectuals who enunciated on issues concerning the nature of God and the Universe and who functioned as repositories of religious lore. Whatever the case, such people were recreated in the New World and in Jamaica, where they expounded their own views on similar questions. Even so, the only evidence we have of intellectual activity of this sort dates from after the abolition of slavery.

This was either because slaves had no time or leisure to elaborate coherent systems of ideas about the nature of God and the Universe, or because observers of the period were unable or unwilling to describe such systems. This aspect of religion is vitally important, especially for a study of the African intellectual contribution to the New World, but I lack the space – and probably the competence – to discuss it here. I shall therefore stick to discussing the everyday beliefs, fears, practices, and attitudes of ordinary people.

These aspects of religion can exist without a political infrastructure and with only a modicum of social organisation. As we have seen, they were basically uniform all over West Africa. There is no doubt that they were transferred wholesale to Jamaican soil. The earliest significant description that we have of the religion of Africans in Jamaica is by Edwards (1793, vol. 2: p. 85); it was repeated by Gardner (1873: p. 184). Gardner's version (which is written in more modern language and provides additional information) is quoted here in its entirety:

> Little can be said with confidence as to the religious beliefs of these people. The influence of the Coromantyns seems to have modified, if not entirely obliterated, whatever was introduced by other tribes. They recognised, in a being called Accompong, the creator and preserver of mankind: to him, praise, but never sacrifice, was offered. Assaici was another being: to him they offered first-fruits, and the festival of the new year was kept in his honour. Ipboa was god of the sea. The devil was represented by Obboney, a malicious being. It is said that human sacrifices were sometimes offered to appease him; no Jamaica records, however, allude to such an event. The tutelary deities included the departed heads of families, and the worship of such was almost the one observed to any great extent by Africans or their descendants in Jamaica.
>
> It is and ever has been very difficult to extract from an old negro what his religious belief really was, but it seems probable that there was some idea that departed parents had influence with the supposed rulers of the world beyond the grave, and that prayers were offered to them in some such spirit as that of the Roman Catholic who appeals to the saints in his calendar. At certain times and often at the festival of the new yam, a family of two or three successive generations would gather around the grave of a departed ancestor; a sacrifice of a cock or a goat was offered, and the blood poured upon the grave. Each head of a household then offered another fowl in the same manner, and when this had been done the animals were cooked and eaten. Occasionally these acts of worship assumed a form of intense melancholy. Death had been busy in the family; one and another, perhaps the young and strong, had passed away, and just as the savage tribes in Africa sacrifice hundreds of slaves at the death of a chief, that they may serve him in the world

to which he has gone, so in Jamaican families the idea prevailed that the dead ancestor might wish some of his descendants to be with him in the next world, and the death of relatives was frequently attributed to his influence. In these cases earnest supplications were offered that those taken might suffice, and such as remained on earth be spared. More solemn and affecting were those occasions when a mother bereaved of some of her children went at the midnight hour to the grave of their dead father, taking the living children by hand; and then, while gently reproving him for what he was supposed to have done, earnestly entreated him not to take from her those who yet remained.

Among the Africans there was a wide-spread fear of charms and incantations, and the creole negroes, though not superior to the same kind of superstition, sought to preserve their property by hanging cats' teeth, feathers, and other obeah signs about.

The funeral ceremonies bore some resemblance to Irish wakes. A feast was provided, at which there was singing, drumming and dancing. When at length it was time to carry the coffin to the grave, it was borne more frequently on the heads than on the shoulders of the bearers. After a little progress had been made a sudden stop was almost sure to take place: the corpse, it was said, was obstinate, and would not go on; something was surely the matter. Presently the cause would be explained. Perhaps, just by, a man lived who had been at variance with the dead: he must be visited and soundly scolded, and then the departed spirit would rest. Quietude seemed to come much quicker if the accused person was liberal in his offers of rum.[1]

Occasionally the corpse was displeased with the mode of conveyance and this had to be changed. When at length the grave was reached and the coffin was lowered, cooked food, in which no salt had been put, was placed upon it; and in covering up the grave the attendants often turned their backs to it and threw the earth in from between their legs. This was an infallible way of preventing the spirit of the departed from returning with them to their homes. Sometimes the spirit was caught with many ceremonies in a box provided for that purpose, and then the box was carefully buried. The surviving widow of the departed was expected to go more careless in dress than usual for some few weeks; but when tired of the single state she cooked a fowl, and carried it, with the broth, to the grave, accompanied by friends who either sympathised with her or perhaps merely wished to spend a pleasant evening. A song was sung expressive of confidence in the happiness of the departed, fresh earth was piled upon the grave, some of the viands were cast upon it, and the rest eaten. More singing, and also dancing followed. No propitiatory offerings could, however, keep the departed from occasionally breaking bounds. Hence every negro trembled at the mention of duppies; these are the ghosts of northern climes. Even now, when a corpse is prepared for the grave, dressed, as is not unusual, in a full suit of clothes, the pockets are often cut away, lest the duppy should fill them with stones and annoy the living on his return. For nine days the room in which death took place was undisturbed, and a light left burning at night; nor were little conveniences to which the departed was accustomed, as water to bathe the feet, etc., omitted.

Edwards' account of Africans in Jamaica leaves no doubt that in his opinion "Koromantyns" were the dominant group both numerically and by dint of their character. Edwards also suggests (vol. 1: p. 538, vol. 2: pp. 105–6, 109) that "all nations of Africa" recognised the power of Obi and Obeahmen. However, it is impossible to say whether this religion of the "Koromantyns" was present all over the island or restricted to one particular region or plantation. There is evidence that although the Akan influence was strong in Jamaica, not all other forms of African religion were obliterated. As we shall see later, a religion of apparently Bantu origin persisted in Jamaica and evolved into what is today commonly known as Kumina; there are also clear Yoruba-type vestiges in some contemporary religious practices in Jamaica.

If Gardner's source (or his use of it) is accurate, it suggests that Akan religion in Jamaica had already begun to change. In Africa, Asaase was the female counterpart of the supreme deity, whereas Gardner refers to Asaase as "he". But it is possible that since there is no distinction in the Jamaican pronoun system between "he", "she", and "it" (all of which are rendered as *i(m)*), Asaase was pronominalised as *i(m)*, which was rendered by Gardner or his source as "he". Akan pronouns also do not express gender.

Akan religion took two paths in Jamaica: a conservative path among the Maroons, who even today preserve religious relics; and in the wider society, an evolutionary path influenced by contact with Christianity and loss of contact with Africa after the abolition of the slave trade. But in both cases there was a great deal of syncretistic mixing of different variants of West African culture. This is scarcely compatible with those views of slave life that attach such great weight to ethnic diversity and to the alleged policy of separating slaves linguistically and ethnically. In Africa, as we have seen, it was not uncommon for one group to adopt the gods of another, especially when the gods in question were endowed with attributes and powers that had a particular appeal for the adopting group. In Jamaica too it seems that the particular appeal of Akan magic (obeah) may have led to the adoption of Akan religion outside the strict Akan group. This does not mean to say that only Akan could practise obeah. Members of other ethnic groups were very highly reputed practitioners of it, just as in Trinidad East Indian obeahmen and other obeahmen from outside Trinidad, Guyanese or Grenadians for example, are highly rated.

Even the Akan adopted deities from other groups. This sort of syncretism can be found throughout Afro-America, such as the division of Haitian *loa* (gods) into nations, or "ranks", according to origin. According to Raboteau (1978: p. 26), these divisions perhaps corresponded to national divergences among the slaves of Saint-Domingue. The Rada rank includes gods of Dahomean origin; the Petro rank consists of some gods of African nations such as Ibo, Bambara and Hausa, or after African areas such as Congo, Wangol (Angola) and Siniga (Senegal). According to Bascom (1965: p. 132), "there was both fusion and protection of group identity among different African religious groups in Cuba."

Though the Suriname Maroons are predominantly Akan and generally worship Nyame as their Supreme Deity (Bastide 1971: p. 59), they have also incorporated deities from other sources, e.g. Legba from the Yoruba, Loango and Zambi from the Bantu, and *vodoun* (a generic name for certain types of deities) from Dahomey. The mixing went even further in slave plantations on the Guiana coast: there Dahomean and Bantu names have penetrated the Akan pantheon.

What I have referred to as Akan religion was a belief system rather than a system of active ritual and worship. Ritual and worship were seriously inhibited in slave society, since slaves did not control the scheduling of their daily activities. Religion therefore came to mean a belief system that remained unchanged rather than a routine of ritual observance. It has been suggested that the emphasis in slave religions on the belief in spirit forces that can be manipulated by persons, "good" and "evil", who possess certain qualities and attributes, was due to the "insecurity which the slave regime created in slaves". As we have seen, where African indigenous religions have been replaced by outside religions (Christianity or Islam), this is the belief that almost everywhere lasts longest.

Accounts later than Edwards' refer only to the "superstitions", "obeah" practices and funeral rites of slaves, though Dallas (1803: pp. 92–3) mentions that the Maroons continued to believe that Accompong was God of Heaven, creator of all things, and deity of infinite goodness; however, they neither worshipped nor offered sacrifices to him. It is striking that there is no suggestion either that new beliefs and rites had been created or that different types of Africans observed different beliefs and rites. Although there is some evidence that creole slaves may have believed less in obeah than Africa-born slaves and that obeahmen were more likely to be Africa-born than creole, there is nothing to suggest that before the early decades of the nineteenth century there were any important differences in religious beliefs among slaves. This is not to deny that some individual slaves had become Christian; it is likely that most came from the domestic group, for domestics were more vulnerable to proselytising members of the master class.

Active worship of gods, as opposed to a belief in them and in their powers, began to diminish and soon ceased to be effective. However Patterson (1967: pp. 205–6) shows that a water spirit widely worshipped in Africa, was also worshipped well into the nineteenth century in Jamaica. A *rubba missis* (according to the spelling of Banbury 1895: p. 24), i.e. "Lady of the River", was believed to inhabit each fountainhead of every inexhaustible stream of water in Jamaica. Banbury (ibid.) claimed that such streams were worshipped and that sacrifices were offered to them. Beckwith (1928) reports that at the end of the nineteenth century "dances were performed for the *rubba mama* and sacrifices of a white goat, a black cock, and silver money are made to the water being called *mamadjo* who cures diseases especially that West Indian form called yaws". Patterson (1967) writes that the reporter to a Jamaica Parliamentary Committee in 1832 said that he "had not heard of any act of superstitious reverence to trees for the last four years: they [the slaves] used to worship the cotton tree but I have not heard of that for some time". Two other accounts from the 1810s and 1820s are worth quoting, one by Stewart and one by Lewis.

> The African negroes of the West Indies, whatever superstitious notions they may bring with them from their native country, agree in believing in the existence of an omnipotent being who will reward or punish us in a future life for our good or evil actions in this ... Their superstitious reverence for certain animals, common in their own country, they retain in some degree ... By intercourse with each other, and with Europeans, the absurdity of many of their native superstitions is gradually laid aside – at least in practice. One opinion they all agree in, and that is the expectation that, after death, they shall first return to their native country, and enjoy again the society of kindred and friends... As to the creole slaves, they have no particular superstition which they have not adopted from their African forefathers and that they have not now in a great measure cast off (Stewart 1823: pp. 280–1, 274 ff).

Stewart also mentions pouring libations at funerals and sacrificing fowls on the graves of the newly dead – a tribute that mourners afterwards occasionally repeat; and stopping coffins on the way to burial at the doors of debtors of the dead person until the debt is paid.

Lewis (1845: p. 290) suggests that some form of "ancestor worship" was maintained:

> Neptune came this morning to request that the name of his son, Oscar, might be changed for that of Julius, which (it seems) had been that of his own father. The child, he said, had always been weakly, and he

was persuaded that its ill health proceeded from his deceased grandfather's being displeased because it had not been called after him ... they conceive that the ghosts of their ancestors cannot fail to be offended at their abandoning an appelation, either hereditary in the family, or given by themselves.

Lewis (1845: p. 88) also reports that "negroes [were] always ... buried in their own gardens". It may be an exaggeration to interpret this as "worship" (which is not necessarily the right term even for the treatment of departed ancestors in Africa itself), but it does indicate that the integrity of the kin group was valued and that ancestors still played a central role in it.

Two important circumstances influenced the development of religion in Jamaica. First, African theologies were continuously revitalised up to the abolition of the slave trade by the arrival of new slaves from Africa. These new arrivals maintained the integrity of African religious beliefs and strengthened traditional rituals and observances. As we have seen, there are numerous reports that obeahmen tended to be Africa-born slaves. This suggests that creole slaves recognised that Africa-born slaves had greater knowledge and were more effective practitioners of the religion to which both categories adhered. Second, very early laws were passed banning the assembly of large numbers of slaves on Sundays and holidays. An Act passed in 1696 (and confirmed in 1699)[2] ran as follows:

And for the prevention of the meeting of slaves in great numbers on Sundays and holidays, whereby they have taken the liberty to contrive and bring to pass many of their bloody and inhuman transactions: Be it enacted by the aforesaid authority, that no master, or mistress, or overseer, shall suffer any drumming or meeting of any slaves, not belonging to their own plantations, to rendezvous, feast, revel, beat drum, or cause any disturbance.

This prohibition must have put an early end to the open (but not to the secret) celebration of religion by slaves, though after the arrival of Christian missionaries in Jamaica slaves were able to celebrate their religion under the guise of Christianity. This encouraged the separation of the priest from a total structure of religious observance and led to the predominance of the obeahman operating alone. Writers of the period certainly focussed on this latter personality, and the literature abounds with descriptions of the obeahman and his activities. Later, obeah also came under legal prohibition because it became known to the British that obeah was closely allied to slave rebellions. An act of 1781 prescribed as follows:

And in order to prevent the many mischiefs that may hereafter arise from the wicked art of Negroes going under the appelation of Obeahmen and women, pretending communication with the devil and other evil spirits, whereby the weak and superstitious are deluded into a belief of their having full power to exempt them whilst under protection from any evils that might otherwise happen: Be it therefore enacted by the authority aforesaid, that from and after the first day of January, aforesaid, any Negro or other slave who shall pretend to any supernatural power, and be detected in making use of any blood, feathers, parrot beaks, dog's teeth, alligator's teeth, grave dirt, rum, eggshells, or any other materials relative to the practice of obeah or witchcraft ...[3]

From the very inception of the slave society therefore, religion and rebellion became associated in the symbiotic relationship. It is generally agreed, and the evidence is quite compelling, that slaves from the Gold Coast area, the Akan people known in Jamaica in the early period as Coromantees (with several other variant spellings), were the chief instigators of rebellion. The rebellion of 1760 was, according to Gardner (1873: p. 132), led by Coromantees and was "aided by the mysterious terrors of Obeah". Gardner adds (p. 133) that "the negroes were greatly stimulated by their confidence in the powers of the Obeahman", among whom was Tacky, the Supreme Commander. Cf. also in Haiti where the revolt led by Boukman in 1791, was inaugurated by a religious ceremony and where religion also played a significant role in earlier slave revolts. According to Mintz in the "Introduction" to Metraux (1960: p. 10) "voudou surely played a critical role in the creation of a viable armed resistance by the slaves against the master classes".

We shall see later that this association between revolt and religion remained important throughout Jamaican history. Thus Coromantees provided both political and religious leadership in slave society. The fact that their folk hero Anansi was also adopted by slaves throughout the Caribbean suggests that there was a whole series of factors favouring the retention of Akan religious forms.

The obsession with obeah in White studies of Jamaican society is symptomatic of the inability and unwillingness of Europeans to understand the culture of Africans. However, the conditions under which slaves lived, in particular the ban on religious assemblies by slaves and the need to mobilise spiritual forces for resistance and survival, probably combined to make obeah more important than other elements in the slaves' religion. The original Asante word for sorcerer (*obayifo*) was preserved in the term obeah, whereas the name of his counterpart the priest (*okomfo*), preserved among Maroons in the term *Kumfu-man* ("ritual specialist"), gave way quite early in the language of most Jamaicans to the term Myalman, based on *myal* (of obscure origin) meaning "spirit" (Myalman therefore literally means "spiritman"). There was, and still is, much confusion about the terms Myalism and obeah. Patterson (1967), Williams (1932), and DeLisser (1913) imply that the distinction between the two is fundamental to an understanding of the development of religion in Jamaica. Myalman and Obeahman are terms that emerged in Jamaica to describe religious and quasi-religious roles important not only for the Coromantees but for virtually every other ethnic group with members in Jamaica. These roles are those of priest, and those that go under the names of "medicine-man", "witchdoctor", or "sorcerer". As we saw earlier, though the priest and the medicine-man are different from the witch-doctor, and even hostile to him, still the three roles overlap. They overlapped in Jamaica too, in the sense that some people were in greater communication with and better able to manipulate the spirits and deities – qualities that are necessary for the playing of all three roles. Some writers indiscriminately lumped together Blacks who organised followers into so-called "cults" as either Myalmen or Obeahmen. But since such people were operating as individuals and in secrecy, it was more difficult, and less necessary, for them to keep their functions and activities separate. As we have seen, in Africa good and evil are not always clearly antithetical. This was even more true of Jamaica, where magic designed to harm members of the White ruling class and slaves loyal to them occupied that nebulous area between good and evil. Certainly the British viewed such magic as obeah (or "black magic", in the rather ironic terminology of Europeans). But for Africans, resorting to the power of spirits in order to resist slavery was a positive expression of religion. Those writers who reported that myal was hostile to obeah and undid obeah's evil work show clearly how Myalmen harnessed spiritual forces to resist slavery. Williams (1932: p. 146), discussing the different roles of Obeahmen and Myalmen, says that it was the Myalman who

administered the terrible fetish oath mixing gunpowder with the rum and added grave dirt and human blood to the concoction that was to seal upon the conspirators' lips the awful nature of the plot for liberty, steel their hearts to the dangerous undertaking. It was he who devised the mystic powder that was to make their bodies invulnerable and enable them to meet the white man's bullets.

Akan religion in its conservative version is still practised by Maroons even today. However, it is receding before Christianity, with which it coexists in a system of "compartmentalisation". Generally speaking there are no cross influences between the two religions. However, Schafer (1974: p. 227) reports the case of the wife of a Maroon colonel known as a strict Christian who never participated in traditional rituals but before whose house "stands a tall pole with three forked branches to support a platform. Placed on top are a porcelain basin and several drinking glasses ... reminiscent of Captain Rattray's description of Ashanti ceremonial altars, also in front of the house, utilized for offerings to Nyame."

According to Dallas (1903: p. 93), "the Maroons continued to believe, like their forefathers, that Accompong was the God of Heaven, the creator of all things, and a deity of infinitive goodness, but they neither offered sacrifices to him, nor had any mode of worship." Today Maroons still recognise Yankipong (or Nyame) as the supreme deity. They still invoke the divinity known to the Akan as Asaase in the greeting *Yankipong adu Asaase*. Below the supreme deity are the spirits of the ancestors ("duppies", cf. Twi *adope* "spirit"). These spirits are arranged in a hierarchy: the older ancestors are the most powerful, but they are rarely invoked because of their remoteness in time; more recent ancestors are closely linked to the living and exert great influence on their daily lives. The "Koromanti dance" (or "play") is the contemporary form of Maroon religious ritual. Bilby (1981) has written an excellent study and Schafer (1974: pp. 223–43) has provided a copious record of the links between Maroon religious rituals and Akan traditions.

Among the slaves Akan religion changed more radically than among the Maroons, probably as a result of the special conditions of slavery, contact with similar forms of West and Central African religions, and later, contact with Christianity.

Myalism has come to be used to refer to the dominant form of Africa-derived religion that developed among the slaves in Jamaica. It emerged as the first religious organisation of Africans in Jamaica; its characteristics are those of the typical West African "secret cult societies".

Schuler (1979b) analyses the origins and development of Myalism. However, she wrongly links Myalism to "Central African" religious movements, apparently because her only source for African religions was one rather brief article on Central Africa. E. Kamau Brathwaite, commenting on Schuler (1979a: pp. 150–155), rejects the hypothesis that Myalism originated in Central Africa and places Myalism in a wider perspective of Afro-Jamaican religious and ritual behaviour. I agree with Brathwaite, and would suggest that the significance of Myalism – as attested by Long (1774: II; pp. 416–17) – is that it was an organisation, a society, or a "movement", and as such added a new dimension to the already existing belief system.

There are records of initiation ceremonies in Jamaica (Gardner 1873: p. 162; Lewis 1845: p. 295, for the year 1817) that induce death or at least unconsciousness in novitiates and then restore them to life or consciousness by an infusion or anointment of herbs. Williams (1932: p. 141) cites A. Cardinall's description (*In Ashanti and Beyond*, London 1927, p. 238) of an initiation ceremony in a Bimoda (Gold Coast) "secret society" in which the novitiate is induced into a state of death for five days and then anointed with medicine and restored to life. No detailed account has survived of the Myal pantheon and the total structure of Myal religious beliefs. But Williams (1932: p. 145) and Bastide (1971: p. 102) affirm that the dance "myal" was performed in honour either of the minor deities accompanying Accompong, or else of the ancestors. This conforms to the general practice of West African religious worship by which the Supreme Deity was not the object of particular worship or celebration.

We next have some rather copious evidence of the beliefs held by Myalism in the metaphysical nature of man. Man possessed first of all a spirit which left him on the death of his body. It is this spirit which was believed to return to the ancestral land to dwell with the other ancestral spirits; this belief led to the absence of fear of death displayed by many slaves.[4] This spirit hovered for some days around the spot of death or burial before it embarked on its journey. Hence the elaborate burial rituals which were performed to appease or please the spirit and facilitate its journey. Later, it seems that when Africa and the ancestral homeland began to fade in the immediate consciousness of Africans and the spirits were no longer able to journey back to Africa, precaution was taken to placate the spirits of relatives and friends and to neutralise those of enemies. These spirits were known as *duppies* and the term survives in Jamaica, meaning spirits that roam after death (the idea of the journey back to Africa is apparently lost). Long (1774, vol. II, p. 416) records the term *bugaboo*, referring to a spirit of "more hostile and tremendous aspect", i.e. that of a departed enemy.

Another spirit, called the shadow, belonged to living people. The Obeahman would catch this shadow and nail it to or bury it beneath the silk-cotton tree. The owner would then deteriorate rapidly and eventually die if the shadow was not restored. The Myalman's function was to pull the shadow from its imprisonment and ceremoniously restore it to the person in whom it once dwelled (Williams 1932: p. 153).[5] Myalmen were also present at funerals to catch shadows and make sure that they were properly buried with their corporeal abode lest they bring harm to the family of the dead person.

Bastide (1971: p. 100) reports a similar belief among today's creole community of Suriname. He speaks of two souls: the *akra* (cf. Twi *kra* "soul", to which the Noun Class marker is prefixed in the Surinamese form; see Chapter 6 – Language), which is born and dies with the individual, and defends him or her against the forces of evil; and the *yorka*, which leaves the body at the moment of death and goes wandering abroad. According to Patterson (1967: p. 189), among the Ga people (of Ghana) *susuma* means both "essential aspect of the human personality" and "shadow"; moreover, an ill-defined *kla* concept is "closely related to *susuma*": when the *kla* departs, the victim dies. This is the same as *akra* mentioned above. Initial *a* is the Noun Class prefix and the consonant *r* alternates with *l* in Akan dialects, see Chapter 6 – Language. See also de Beet and Sterman (pp. 249–54) for a three soul concept among the Matawai of Suriname: *akaa* "an individual's life force"; *somba* "shadow"; *yooka* which hovers around the corpse after death before journeying to the kingdom of the spirits. A bad medicine-man may capture a victim's *kla* or *susuma* (the words are often used synonymously) and thus cause his death. Raboteau (1978: p. 32), dealing with reincarnation and the return to Africa after death, says that there are several components to the traditional African idea of the soul. An individual's personality-soul appears before God after death to account for its deeds. When a person sleeps, this soul may wander; thus dreams are the experiences of the wandering soul. There is also the shadow, which is immortal but dies with the body. Each individual has a spirit that serves as moral guide and is in fact the spirit of God within the human body.

This is one of the aspects of slave societies about which we lack detailed knowledge, resulting from the absence from them of that class of people who in Africa articulated and transmitted views about human ontology. Thus terms and concepts such as *duppy, shadow, spirit,* and *soul,* are not properly distinguished either by scholars or by ordinary Jamaicans. For example, Beckwith (1924), whose account is followed by Bastide (1971: p. 104), in describing funerary rites at the turn of the century, said that:

a cross was planted on the grave to prevent the dead man's soul from coming out and tormenting the living. Nevertheless, the dead man's spirit remained in the house for nine days, and on the last of these, every object was moved around, so that the spirit might fail to recognise its surroundings, and so depart. The funeral celebrations concluded with the sacrifice of a cock, dances, and songs (in one of them it was claimed that the soul would return to Africa) and games.

Africans adapting their native religions to the new context in Jamaica and working out a common set of beliefs and practices had a rich fund of similar experiences on which to draw, for as we have seen religious syncretism was commonplace in African society too. Local African religions were not averse to accepting influences from other religions or to accepting other gods and divinities into their pantheon, especially when these foreign gods seemed as powerful as the local ones and had attributes that appealed to people meeting them for the first time.

Christian missionaries did not start working seriously in Jamaica until toward the end of the eighteenth century, but African slaves began experiencing the power of the European god as soon as they arrived on the island. For example, it was generally agreed – including by the slaves –

that the destruction of Port Royal by the earthquake of 1694 was a judgement of God brought down on the city because of its wickedness. The first law passed after the earthquake was one proclaiming a fast on its anniversaries; the preamble announced that "it has pleased God justly to punish the inhabitants of this island for the manifold sins and wickedness committed against his Divine Majesty" (Gardner 1873: p. 193), citing *Laws of Jamaica*, vol. 1). The European habit of attributing Jamaica's frequent hurricanes and earthquakes to the vengeful work of the Christian god must have deeply impressed the African slaves, who then, as was to be expected, incorporated that god into their pantheon, especially since he possessed qualities that matched those of African deities. Moreover, the Christian god was often pitted against the spiritual powers of Obeahmen and Myalmen, and in some cases seemed to win out, for example when Myalmen and Obeahmen were put to death, despite their claims to invulnerability, for plotting or carrying out revolts. However, God, like Nyame and other supreme beings of African religions, was not worshipped as such. As we shall see later, Blacks tended to venerate and invoke the spiritual powers of other Christian figures such as the Saints, the Old Testament Apostles, the Holy Ghost, and – to a lesser extent – Jesus Christ. At first only the name of the Christian god was adopted, as part of the general switch to an English-based vocabulary. It was not until later that the attributes and characteristics of the Christian god were gradually transferred to the god recognised by African Jamaicans.

Myalism, which is the most commonly used name for the religion that developed in Jamaica during the period of slavery, began slowly to change under the influence of Christianity. On the one hand Myalism was a belief system without an orthodox dogma but with a general common core of beliefs inherited from Africa plus variant forms to which individuals or groups adhered. On the other hand it was an organisation: one that prospered and cohered in inverse proportion to the vigilance with which the ruling class policed laws forbidding slaves to assemble freely. As we have seen, religion in Africa had no dogma and was not subject to tight central control but was rather organised in "sects", societies, or villages, each with its particular variants of religious beliefs and practices. It is hard to say whether these characteristics were transmitted from Africa to Jamaica or whether it was the conditions of slavery (including the legal and logistic impediments to assembly) that fragmented religious organisation (though I suspect, in line with my general thesis in this book, that continuity was a main factor). Whatever the case, religion under slavery was fragmented into numerous local organisations, the life of each of which was often conterminous with that of the priest leader. Even so, religion was often the main unifying force in slave revolts.

Three major forms of slave religion can be identified – Myalism, Convince, and Kumina. Myalism was the broadest reference and serves as a cover term for all religious observances that developed from African religions; Convince and Kumina are two major branches of that religious tradition. Myalism must be viewed along a diachronic continuum of change beginning in Africa; and along a continuum of synchronic variation within the population at any one particular time. When Christian elements began to infiltrate Myalism, the two branches of Convince and Kumina crystallised into autonomous traditions. Forms of Myalism most strongly influenced by Christianity ended up as Revivalism (and Zionism) and as Pukumina ("Pocomania").

Slaves began to be formally instructed in Christianity toward the end of the eighteenth century by Moravians. The reason they were first in the field was apparently that four sugar estates in St Elizabeth were owned by the Fosters and the Barhams, notable Moravian families (Gardner 1873: p. 199). Four Moravian missionaries arrived in Jamaica in 1754. Later in 1783 a group of "about 400 White families and between 4,000 and 5,000 of their Negro slaves" fleeing the new Republican government in the United States arrived in Jamaica. Among them were George Lisle (also spelt Leile) and Moses Baker, two former slaves who turned to preaching Christianity in Jamaica. The spectacle of Blacks openly preaching and conducting Christian religious services was novel, and the two men attracted large followings. Gardner suggests that Lisle was rather unorthodox, holding "some peculiar views such as the washing of feet and anointing the sick" (p. 344). Curtin (1968: pp. 32–4) mentions another Native Baptist leader, George Lewis, who was born in Africa and taken to Virginia as a slave. George Lewis was among those who left the United States for Jamaica. According to Curtin, he was "a true heretic who purposely rejected the whiteman's version of Christianity in favour of his own, more African, variety"; he preached in the parishes of Manchester and St Elizabeth. The Native Baptist groups stressed the spirit at the cost of the written word. Followers of leaders like Baker or Lewis could only be baptised after they had been possessed by the spirit, which descended on the follower in a dream. To experience this dream, adepts first fasted according to a set canon and then spent some time alone in the bush. The ceremony of baptism also acquired new importance and took the form of complete immersion. Christ became a secondary figure to John the Baptist.

Myalmen immediately responded to the new cults, and became strongly associated with Lisle and Baker. According to Gardner (1873: p. 344), "some other Black men, separating from Lisle, established churches in other places. In some instances they were altogether unqualified; in others they mingled many superstitious observances with what they had learned from the scriptures". Others who remained with the churches that Lisle's and Baker's successors founded "had assumed the office of teachers and leaders"; when the original missionaries withdrew, these "superstitious and grossly immoral men were left to pursue their course with less restraint" (Gardner 1973: p. 357).

Gardner adds that:

> as a result native Baptist churches became associations of men and
> women who, in too many cases, mingled the belief and even the practice
> of Myalism with religious observances, and who perverted and
> corrupted what they retained of these ... Their leaders, or daddies, as a
> class, were overbearing, tyrannical, and lascivious, and united the
> authority of the slave driver with the darkest forms of spiritual
> despotism (p. 356).

Hogg (1964: p. 110) agrees that "the Native Baptists considered
themselves Christian, but their religion resembled Myalism as much as
sectarianism ... They stressed personal interaction with spirits more than
sin and salvation ... Some cult leaders required spirit possession (for
membership)".

Some Myalmen with leadership qualities apparently saw the cults as
an opportunity to legitimise their religious practices and develop religious
organisations. The authorities tried several times to ban "unlicensed"
priests and all non-conformist religious activity, but liberals in England
stopped them from doing so. The "ticket and leader" system adopted by
the Methodists and the Baptists, which divided the churches into classes
each with its own appointed leader, made it much easier for autonomous
churches to emerge under the control of Myalmen. Methodist leaders were
selected from among freedmen or Whites, but "in the case of the Baptists
they were generally slaves and therefore illiterate" (Gardner 1873: p.
360). Class leaders were supposed to become personally acquainted with
each class member, to visit class members as often as possible, and to report
from time to time on their conduct to the minister. According to Gardner
(1873: p. 360), in the course of time these leaders began to hold services
among the people, and after a while there were "class-houses" in almost
every negro village. Gardner says it is "unquestionable" that some of these
class leaders and their organisations were active in the rebellion of 1831
that sounded slavery's death knell in Jamaica. Waddel (1863: p. 192)
shows how class members restructured and redirected these classes. He
reports on a Baptist leader "who helped us (Missionaries) cordially in
warning the people against the Myal error ... His own class had joined the
Myal company and taken possession of his prayer-house for their
heathenish practices."

The activities of the various cults and denominations were strongly
influenced by their leaders' views on slavery. "Official" Baptists
attracted slaves by their support for equal rights and emancipation. But
though the planters accused them of incitement to rebellion and persecuted
them, there is no evidence that they advocated anything but a

constitutional path to emancipation. Local Baptist members of the official Baptist missionary organisation distanced themselves politically from the White missionaries, and one of them, Samuel Sharpe, a class-leader in Rev. Thomas Burchell's organisation, organised a strike among the slaves; other Baptist class-leaders and slave drivers, who were often one and the same person, played an important role in launching the strike (Bleby 1953: p. 109 ff). However, Native Baptists took control of the movement before the strike could get underway and organised an armed rebellion in coastal St James. According to Curtin (1968: p. 86), in the interior of the parish "was the shadowy figure of Daddy Ruler Tharp, still another leader of the rebels, from his title either a Native Baptist or a Myalman". As we have seen, by this time (1831) the distinction between Native Baptist Christianity and Myalism was often blurred.

This contact with Christianity was experienced in different ways by individual slaves and groups of slaves, resulting in a continuum of variation in popular religion that can conveniently (though not necessarily best) be expressed in terms of the volume of Christian elements in the African base cosmology. This continuum of religious variation directly parallels the continuum of linguistic variation that I described earlier. In both cases the population has "moved" in the course of history along the line of the continuum, "losing" forms close to the base culture derived from Africa; this process is continuing even now. For example, the names and to a lesser extent the attributes and functions of deities in the African pantheon have disappeared, and fewer natural objects are recognised as having indwelling spirits whose power can be exploited. Religions identified by names such as Revival Zion, Pocomania (called here Pukumina), Convince, and Kumina are merely zones abstracted from this continuum and are themselves subject to variation. An individual is located not at a point but at a zone of greater or lesser range on both the religious and the linguistic continuum. In the same way that a speaker can switch between speech levels, so an individual can switch between different modes of religious behaviour. Although these appear to be two separate systems, they are in fact simply different stages on the continuum of variation. Just as the development of so-called creole forms of language may be viewed as a solution to the problem of how to achieve a modicum of communication with White planters while at the same time forging instruments that can be used for resistance, so the introduction of Christian forms into African cosmology can be viewed as a solution to the problem of how to legitimise religious practices in the eyes of the ruling class while forging instruments of group cohesion and identity, also for use in resistance and revolts.

Kumina

Today, Kumina may be placed at one end, the African end, of the religious continuum. Even in that position, it is prone to dissolution as the inner core of its practitioners increasingly fail to observe its total set of beliefs and tenets. It has been given the appearance of a new lease of life by Jamaica's National Dance Theatre Company, which stages a work called Kumina, and by other groups some of which include Kumina adepts who perform Kumina music and dance.

Kumina is located in St Thomas, and it may not be accidental that both Convince and an important Maroon group are also located in the same eastern part of Jamaica. The historical record is thin, but it seems quite likely that Kumina emerged in St Thomas because of the presence there of large numbers of Bantu people from the Congo–Angola area. Different African religions fused but Congolese forms predominated, just as religions fused within the orbit of one dominating influence in other areas of the Americas (Bastide 1971). At this point on the religious continuum, Christianity has had only a very limited impact (some Christian figures have been introduced into the pantheon of deities, and services are rounded off with the singing of Christian hymns; David, Ezekiel, Moses, Cain, and Shadrach are among the earthbound deities of the Kumina religion).

Apart from these Christian earthbound deities, the Kumina religion also has skybound deities, of whom the highest is Oto, King Zombi, a name derived from the Kikongo language. Other Kumina deities also bear African names such as Shango and Obei. Shango is the name of the Yoruba God of Thunder and exists in the belief system of many parts of Afro-America. This is further evidence of *intra*-African syncretism. Ancestral spirits are called *zombi*, and are the "spirits of men and women, who, in their lifetimes, were dancing zombies (persons who experienced possession by a god and who danced while possessed), drummers, and obeah men" (Simpson 1978: p. 98).

Among Kumina followers, *zombi* is the word for "spirit" and is derived from Kikongo *dzambi* "god", which occurs in many parts of Afro-America (cf. Haitian *zambi*, Trinidadian *jumbi*, and Brazilian *zumbi*). But cf. p. 57, where we mention the Kikongo term *mvumbi* meaning "spirit", apparently used synonymously with *nzambi*. Kikongo is also the language of many of the songs used to invoke spirits; some Kumina religious leaders (drummers, for example) can still produce some utterances in Kikongo: see Chapter 6 – Language.

The pivotal element in Kumina religion is the worship or invocation of ancestral spirits that take possession of the living. In Kumina, when someone dies, "the personal spirit (soul) goes directly to Oto King Zambi, never to return to earth, if, in life, the person had never been possessed by a spirit (*zombi*). If a person had been possessed by a *zombi*, his soul takes on a new quality, and, at the death of the person, the soul joins all ancestral *zombi* spirits and can return to duties of various kinds on earth, including attending cult ceremonies and possessing living individuals" (Simpson 1978: p. 336). These spirits continue to be called by the names of their former embodiments (Ajax, Augustus, Mabel, etc.). Information provided by Bastide (1971: p. 108) shows that the same thing happens in Brazil, where the Macumba religion of the former Cambinda nation recognises both a supreme deity called Ganga Zumba (paralleling Kumina's King Zombi) and ancestral spirits called *zumbi*, who have names like Old John, Old Joaquin, and Aunt Marie. The word *Cambinda* provides a very plausible etymology for *Kumina*. Phonologically, there is support for a development *mb > m* and *nd > n* in African words brought to the New World (See Chapter 6 – Language). I am indebted to Beverly Hall for this observation.

Kumina is organised into nations or sects served by special deities. These nations have African names: the most frequently reported in Simpson (1978: p. 98) are Mondongo, Moyenge, Machunde, Kongo, Ibo, and Yoruba. Again we find parallels with Brazil's Macumba and with certain Vodoun sects in Haiti which are also organised into nations or mysteries; some have names similar to those of the Kumina nations (in Haiti, there are Mondingue, Mayombe, and Moussondi).

Convince
Convince is the oldest surviving form of Myalism. Gardner (1873: p. 357) reported that Convince was present during the period just before emancipation, just after the arrival of the Baptist missionaries Lisle and Baker. Myal leaders who tried to legitimise Myalism by introducing Christian elements into it and by coopting the name Baptist seem to have regarded an experience called convince as evidence of conversion. According to Gardner,

> evidence for conversion and qualification for baptism was sought not so much in repentance and faith as in dreams; but if the applicant had experienced a convince, that is, had swooned away, and while in that state had a vision, or passed through a stage of great excitement, attended by physical contortions, then all was well.

This appears to point to an evolution of the African initiation ceremony.

Moore's comprehensive study of Convince located its centre in the two easternmost parishes of Portland and St Thomas; it thins out and disappears in the neighbouring parishes of St Mary, St Andrew, and St Catherine. Convince also goes under the name Convince Flenkee (or Fankee); its members are called Bongo. Moore, on the basis of "statements by informants", concludes that Convince originated among Maroons in the

Blue Mountains of eastern Jamaica, some of whom began moving from Maroon settlements after emancipation to live among other Jamaicans. This theory is impossible to reconcile with Gardner's comment that Convince was known among titular Native Baptists (practitioners of Christianised Myalism) even before emancipation, that is, before Maroons lived among other Jamaicans. On the other hand, the Maroon religion, derived from Akan religion, was basically similar to Myalism. The presence of Maroons in St Thomas and Portland after emancipation may have reinforced Convince there.

Convince represents a stage of development at which Christian names have entered into the Myalist pantheon but attributes of the deities and attitudes toward them are based on African transmissions and continuities. God, the Supreme Being, and Christ merit little attention, being "too remote and otherworldly to be of practical value and too benevolent to be worried about" (Moore 1960: p. 4). Convince Bongo men, like Africans, look rather to the lesser deities and spirits who are more accessible and more involved in the affairs of the human world. Among these lesser spirits are departed ancestors or, more generally, people who were once members of a Convince religious group. Convince recognises a hierarchy of spirits based partly on degrees of removal from the contemporary generation, with the "strongest Bongo ghosts coming from Africa, others deriving from ancient Jamaican slaves and Maroons" (Moore 1960: p. 6). Next come the spirits of recently departed Obeahmen (assumed to have had more contact with the spirits while alive); and lowest in rank are the spirits of ordinary Convince members.

These spirits are individualistic; their own idiosyncracies are recognised in Convince ceremonies. They possess or "mount" their devotees, who in turn honour and satisfy them with ceremonies and goat sacrifices. There are similar terms and concepts in Shango, Voudoun, and other religions. According to Hogg (1960: p. 4),

> [Convince] rests on the assumption that men and spirits exist within a single unified social structure, interact with one another and influence each other's behaviour ... Bongo men believe that spiritual power is morally neutral – or that it can be put to both constructive and malevolent purposes. It makes little sense, they reason, to propitiate spirits who are neither potentially dangerous nor immediately useful. God and Christ therefore merit little attention. Bongo men focus their attention on lesser, more accessible spirits who take an immediate interest in material human affairs and have greater influence upon phenomenal events.

Convince ceremonies, like Kumina ceremonies, contain marginal Christian elements in the form of readings from the Bible and the singing of Christian hymns (but the hymns are "traced", i.e. someone reads each line aloud before it is sung by the congregation as a whole). Singing is accompanied by the clapping of hands. Christian hymns alternate with special Bongo songs sung in the call-and-response format; Bongo dances, including the "wheel" (whirling round rapidly for minutes on end without stopping) are performed to these songs. "Wheeling" is also to be found in Pukumina and Kumina, and has even appeared in some styles of "ballroom" dancing. "Wheel and turn" is also the theme of a famous mento.

Convince does not apparently use a completely esoteric language but Moore claims that Bongomen possessed by spirits use "a strange dialect of English" which his interpreters told him was "the African dialect of English" containing a number of African words. One such word recorded by Moore is *malav*, which is without doubt Kikongo in origin (cf. Kikongo *malavu*; see also Chapter 6 – *Language*, where the loss of the final Kikongo vowel is discussed).

Convince is clearly related to Kumina and Myalism. This link is illustrated by the lyric – consisting of one line sung repeatedly – of an important Bongo song. The lyric, "John see the kuruma home on a limbay", was recorded by Moore at a Convince ceremony. According to Moore, *kuruma* was sometimes replaced by its synonym *kumina* in the lyric, which refers to spirits that inhabit the limbs of trees (especially silk cotton trees). Such spirits are part of the belief system of many West African religions, as well as of Myalism and Kumina. This suggests that the terms *kumina* and *myal* mean "spirit", an interpretation supported by the fact that *myal* is apparently synonymous with "angel".

Gardner did not say whether Convince was general over the island or whether it was restricted to a particular geographical area or a special group. Since his general theme was the structure and behaviour of Native Baptist churches, it is likely that Convince was present throughout most of Jamaica. I assume that Convince was introduced into the Baptist churches by Myalists in the period just before emancipation. After emancipation quite a few Congo Africans arrived in St Thomas during the African immigration of the period 1841–1865. These people re-Africanised Myalism by introducing Kongo religious elements and Kikongo language into it. As a result they gave it an undoubtedly Kikongo name that has come down to us as Kumina. They also prevented the further movement of Myalism away from its African origins, and adopted the term Convince to refer to it.

Myal is still used in Kumina to refer to "spirit", but it is also used in a compound myal-spirit. In Kumina this myal-spirit descends on people and mounts them around the neck (Lewis 1845: p. 60). Kumina also attaches the same importance as Myalism to the silk cotton tree. Spirits are believed to reside in the branches of this tree or in the chambers formed by its huge roots, which protrude from the earth. The tree is also associated with initiation into the priesthood. According to Lewis' (1845: p. 63) account of one such initiation, the apprentice spends 21 days in the hollow of a silk cotton tree, where the spirits bring her the enlightenment and knowledge necessary for carrying out her priestly functions.

Pukumina and Revival

At important points in the continuum of religious differentiation created by the meeting of Myalism and Christianity can be found the two major religious movements known as Pocomania and Revival (this study prefers the spelling form Pukumina).[6] These movements are largely urban; freedom of assembly since emancipation plus the model of the Native Baptist churches led to their crystallisation in stable structures with a central authority and a well-defined priesthood. In West Africa the worshippers were organised into esoteric cult groups that were sometimes called "secret societies". In Jamaica these cult groups could not flourish openly or for long periods because of the ban on slave assembly. Myalism introduced the beginnings of religious organisation among slaves. The Myalman was typically the leader of a loosely constituted group of people, whereas the Obeahman operated on his own. Myal organisation became a hotbed of slave rebellion.

The loose nineteenth century-type Myal organisation survives in the form of Convince. Elsewhere Myalism became tighter and more structured, especially when it took over Baptist churches, for it not only converted these churches to Myalism but incorporated Christian elements into its own organisation.

The movement against slavery in the United Kingdom assisted this process by successfully campaigning against the proposed new Slave Code of 1826, which sought inter alia to prevent slaves from teaching or preaching under any denomination and to prevent "designing men professing to be teachers of religion from practising on the ignorance and superstition of the negroes".

Slaves closely monitored the constant conflict between the government of the colony, the non-conformist missionaries, and the British government in order to press their own interests. They appeared to embrace the Christian teachings of Methodists and Baptists, who proclaimed equality and inveighed against the sins of the colonists. The colony's rulers realised that slave participation in religious organisations plus support for their liberation by missionaries could gravely threaten colonial authority. From the very start the colonial establishment tried to crush the missionaries, or at least to frustrate their efforts. George Lisle, the freedman who in 1783 came to Jamaica from Virginia in the USA and became the first Black man to preach publicly in Jamaica under the banner of (Baptist) Christianity, was severely persecuted. Soon after he began to lay the foundations for Native Baptist churches in Jamaica he was arrested, clapped in irons, and tried on a charge of inciting slaves to rebellion (Gardner 1873: p. 343). He was arrested at least one more time, and suffered greatly at the hands of the authorities. The authorities finally decided to compete with the missionaries, and resolved "to carefully investigate the means of diffusing the light of genuine Christianity, divested of the dark and dangerous fanaticism of the Methodists which, grafted on the African superstitions,[7] and working on the uninstructed minds of the negroes, has produced the most pernicious consequences to individuals, and is pregnant with imminent danger to the community"[8] (*Journals of Assembly* vol. XII, p. 833, cited by Gardner 1873: p. 332). The Church of England then began to proselytise among and baptise slaves.

Slaves in all British colonies were more attracted to the Methodists and Baptists, the non-conformist sectarians, than to the orthodox Protestant Church. The reason is generally thought to be that sectarian missionaries championed equality and in some cases advocated emancipation. Some writers believe that the non-conformists' emphasis on the Old Testament and their "emotional" approach had a stronger appeal to Africans than the orthodox religion. Moreover, the sectarians were themselves being persecuted, and this must have created some kind of fellow feeling between them and the slaves. The Baptists, alone among churches, were willing to grant positions of leadership to slaves, and Myalmen seized the chance to set up their own "churches" where they could practise their forms of worship and celebrate their beliefs under the guise of Christianity.

This did not go unnoticed by the authorities, which set out to prevent the free assembly of slaves and the exercise of any kind of public priestly function by slaves. The Act of 1802 sought to "prevent preaching by persons not duly qualified by law" in meetings of Blacks, and prescribed special penalties for slaves who engaged in such unlawful activity. The British government rejected this Act and others that sought to restrict religious freedom, and it seems that there was continual conflict between missionaries and local authorities over the provisions of laws on religious activity. The report of a Commission of Enquiry appointed by the Assembly of Jamaica in 1828 is enlightening on this point (Gardner 1873: p. 355):

Your committee, appointed to inquire into the establishment and proceedings of the sectarians in this island, report that they have taken the examinations of sundry persons, which examinations are annexed, and find that the principal object of the missionaries in this island is to extort money from their congregations by every possible pretext, to obtain which recourse has been had to the most indecent expedients. That, in order to further this object, and to gain an ascendancy over the negro mind, they inculcate the doctrines of equality and the rights of men. They preach and teach sedition even from the pulpit, and, by misrepresentation and falsehood, endeavour to case odium upon all the public authorities of the island, not even excepting the representative of majesty itself. That the consequences have been abject poverty, loss of comfort, and discontent among the slaves frequenting their chapels, and deterioration of property to their masters. Your committee therefore feel themselves bound to report that the interference of the missionaries between the master and the slave is dangerous, and incompatible with the political state of society in this island, and recommend to the house to adopt the most positive and exemplary enactments to restrain them.

Sectarian missionaries were active in the rebellion of 1831, which was led by Myalmen and native Baptist class-leaders (insofar as the two categories were distinguishable). Samuel Sharpe, a Baptist Deacon of Montego Bay, became a sort of adviser, spiritual and political, to the rebels.

The 1831 rebellion showed up the local authorities' corruption and contempt for due process of law, compelling the British government to enforce the Toleration Act. By the time Apprenticeship was introduced, the "outward persecution of missionaries ceased, and the English Emancipation Act set any remaining doubt as to the rights and privileges of Non- Conformists forever at rest".

Freed slaves also took advantage of emancipation and the enforcement of the Toleration Act to openly proclaim and practise Myalism. According to Gardner (1873: pp. 459–60), in 1842:

several negroes residing on an estate near Montego Bay gave themselves out to be Myalmen; and in St James, Westmoreland and Trelawny thousands of deluded people became their followers. They were accustomed to meet together at nightfall, generally beneath the shadow of a cotton tree. Fowls were sacrificed and wild songs sung in the chorus of which the multitude joined. Dancing then began, becoming more and more weirdlike in character, until one and another fell exhausted to the ground, when their incoherent utterances were listened to as divine revelations. Half-demented creatures sat among the branches, or in the hollow trunks of trees, singing while others with their heads bound in a fantastic fashion ran about with arms outstretched and declared that they were flying ... Some 6 years later a Myalman Dr Taylor gave much trouble in Manchester and Clarendon drawing great crowds after him. He was sent to the penitentiary, where he was accidentally killed. In 1852 the delusion again appeared: some now gave themselves out to be prophets, and saw visions, but the firmness of the missionaries soon put an end to these practices.

Waddel (1863: p. 189), a contemporary observer, describes a ceremony he visited (with the intention of subverting it):

> We found them in full force and enjoyment, forming a ring, around which were a multitude of onlookers. Inside the circle, some females performed a mystic dance, sailing round and round, and wheeling in the centre with outspread arms, and wild looks and gestures. Others hummed or whistled a low monotonous tune, to which the performers kept time, as did the people around too, by hands and feet and the swaying of their bodies. A man, who seemed to direct the performance, stood at one side, with folded arms, quietly watching their evolutions.

Here we have the nineteenth century antecedent of twentieth century Pukumina and Revival; Gardner's Dr Taylor is the precursor of Alexander Bedward, prophet of August Town and a legend in the history of Jamaica.[9]

Curtin (1968:p. 170) mentions other "outbreaks" of Myalism in the southeast in 1846, in the countryside in 1848, 1852, and 1860, and in Kingston in 1857. Buchner (1854: pp. 139–40) describes the expressive "exotic" aspects of the Myalist religion:

> As soon as the darkness of evening set in, they assembled in crowds in open pastures, most frequently under large cotton trees, which they worshipped, and counted holy; after sacrificing some fowls, the leader began an extempore song, in a wild strain, which was answered in chorus; the dance followed, grew wilder and wilder, until they were in a state of excitement bordering on madness.
>
> Some would perform incredible evolutions while in this state, until, nearly exhausted, they fell senseless to the ground, when every word they uttered was received as a divine revelation. At other times, Obeah was to be discovered, or a "shadow" was to be caught; a little coffin being prepared in which it was to be enclosed and buried.

Banbury, a missionary, describes the 1842 "outbreak" (again from the point of view of the establishment):

> They went by the name of Myal people; they were also called angel men. They declared that the world was coming to an end; Christ was coming and God had sent them to pull all Obeahs and catch all the shadows that were spell-bound at the cotton trees. In preparation for these events, they affected to be very strict in their conduct. They would neither drink nor smoke. Persons who were known to be notorious for their bad lives were excluded from their society (Banbury 1985: p. 85).

The Myal "revival" therefore preceded by some 20 years the "Great

Revival" of 1860 in the United States and its subsequent spread to Jamaica. This is yet another case of the distortion of Jamaican history by Eurocentric scholarship. The Myalist revival of the 1840s was no less important for Jamaican religious history than the imported revival of the 1860s. Myalism went from strength to strength; it largely controlled the "great" religious revival of 1861 and laid the foundations for Jamaica's religion as it is today. According to Gardner (1873: p. 465):

> in 1861, there had been a very remarkable religious movement, known as the revival. It commenced among the Moravians and gradually extended to all parts of the island. In many central districts of the island the hearts of thoughtful and good men were gladdened by what they witnessed in the changed lives and characters of people for whom they long seemed to have laboured in vain; but in too many districts there was much mild extravagance and almost blasphemous fanaticism. This was especially the case where the native Baptists had any considerable influence. Among these, the manifestations occasioned by the influence of Myalmen, were very common. To the present time, what are called revival meetings are common among these people.

Curtin (1968: pp. 170–1) dramatically demonstrates the capture of the revivalist movement by Myalism:

> In the early days, the new convert was usually struck prostrate on the church floor; but as the movement progressed other manifestations were introduced, and these bothered the missionaries. There were oral confessions, trances and dreams, "prophesying", spirit-seizure, wild dancing, flagellation, and mysterious sexual doings that were only hinted at in the missionary reports. One missionary accepted the explanation of a follower that two different spirits were taking possession of the converts – the Spirit of Christ and another, diabolical spirit trying to undo the Divine Work. But there was no getting around it: the Great Revival had turned African. It became more and more a mixture of myalism and Christianity, ending as a permanent addition to the Afro-Christian cults. The revivalists were disowned by those who initiated the movement. The immense congregations of 1861 dwindled away, leaving the missionary churches at the lowest ebb since their decline began ... The mixture of the African and the European religions even invaded the orthodox churches, where an occasional member would be seized by the spirit during a service – a development that was sometimes disconcerting to the minister in charge.

Chevannes (1971: p. 33) lists four characteristics that link Myalism directly to Revivalism: (1) The heads of Myal people were wrapped in cloth and tied with cord and their waists were wrapped tightly in cloth; (2) Myal people considered themselves to be holy. They neither drank nor smoked and they excluded all those who were known to lead bad lives; (3) A sense of divine mission permeated their campaign to catch shadows and dig up obeah. They claimed that God had sent them to destroy all wickedness, and went about calling on people to pray; (4) They worshipped by dancing round and round inside a circle of swaying onlookers. These onlookers hummed or whistled "monotonously" while their leader stood conspicuously by, watching the ceremony. They danced until they fell to the ground in the Spirit, uttering words that were taken to be divine revelation. Note the similar behaviour of the Akan priest reported in Chapter 2, p. 48.

Myalism as a name later fell into disuse, and "revival" came to designate the religious practices of ordinary Jamaicans. Religious worship became more and more structured and organised, and individual leaders or "Daddies" won recognition far outside their own particular groups. As I have already suggested, although Pukumina, Revival, and Baptist are nominally separate, in reality they are points on a continuum of differentiation. Pukumina is the closest descendant of Myalism; Revival or Revival Zion and various forms of Baptist show greater degrees of Christian influence. These labels are of course analytic and descriptive conveniences. Followers of Pukumina, for example, generally prefer the designations Baptist or Zion to Pukumina (or Pocomania); and since these movements have no centralised authority dispensing dogma and establishing orthodoxy, religious leaders are free to choose their own individual forms of worship and their own belief systems within the general framework of Myalism. Simpson (1956: p. 342), referring to the West Kingston area, cites "one lower class informant [who] maintained that wherever one finds jumping, that is labouring in the spirit to bring on possession, one finds Pocomania". Moore (1960), referring to the Morant Bay area, says that Pukumina people set up altars on the earth for a ceremony intended to "cut and clear" away evil spirits; and that Revival Zion people use neither rum nor marijuana, while Pukumina people, especially the leaders, normally use both. Simpson (ibid.) thinks that the main differences between Pukumina and Revival Zion in West Kingston are that Pukumina puts less emphasis on preaching and Bible explanation and more on singing and spiritual dancing; that it makes greater use of witchcraft (*sic*); and that it uses more extreme techniques of healing. This suggests Pukumina is closer to Myalism on the evolutionary scale than is Revival (Zion). Beckwith (1924: p. 181) says that though many Pukumina songs are phrased in biblical terms, others contain specific references to the invocation of ancestral spirits. In the song cited by Beckwith, the great nineteenth century Myal leader and prophet Taylor is asked to "come bear me over Jordan". Brathwaite (1978: p. 52) reports that a Kumina priestess recognises a "significant difference between the African religion of Kumina and the Afro-Christian Zion", but Brathwaite detects shared elements: "kinesis/possession especially, i.e. the rhythmic nature of the worship and the taking over of a worshipper's body, mind, character, by a god/spirit".

There is a very general framework common to a number of religious groups that either call themselves or are called Pukumina, Revival(Zion), or Baptist. Part of this framework is inherited from Myalism and part has been introduced from Christianity; these elements are combined in the particular synthesis that emerged after 1860, when religious organisation became legally free (though persecution by the political and religious establishment continued). In this period people began to forget the names of African deities or believed that they belonged to Maroon deities. The deities whose names Simpson put before his informants were all of Yoruba origin. One informant told him that Revival Zionists would never use the names of African gods in a ceremony because their services must be clean and pure, that is Christian, but that some may use the names of African gods in private ceremonies. Moore (1965: p. 65), however, says that "four different groups of informers testified that African Gods come to the Revival booth during the services and stand around but do not dance ... It is interesting to note that at least three informants were possessed by both Christian Revival spirits and African Gods." Pukumina and Revival are therefore in one sense miniature versions of the larger religious continuum; African "gods" or spirits are more active and recognised in some forms of these movements, and less so in other forms. The analogy with the way in which language evolved in Jamaica is striking.

Revival Zion and Pukumina do not recognise the functional Christian pantheon, but assemble a number of figures from the Old and to a lesser extent from the New Testament, rank them in a loose hierarchy, and endow each one with a set of attributes and functions. When these Christian spirits come down on devotees (possess them), they are best identified by their idiosyncratic dance (as we saw in the case of Akan deities; see p. 45). The spiritual force of "spirits", "angels", "messengers" and ancestors is constantly invoked, as in Myalism. Simpson (1956: p. 344) says that Michael and Gabriel are "the most popular spirits" among Pukumina and Revival followers; followed by Jesus Christ, Mary, the Holy Ghost, Satan, and "beings from the DeLaurence publications".

These spirits – like African spirits – take an active part in human affairs. They punish or reward the living, and may descend on their devotees and possess them. All spirits with the exception of God and Jesus may possess their followers and be invoked by them, either to help them or to harm their enemies.

Perhaps the most abiding element of Myalism is spirit possession. Spirit possession is a feature of religious movements not far from the orthodox

Christian end of the continuum of religious differentiation. True, the An-
glican, Methodist, Moravian, Presbyterian, and Seventh Day Adventist
churches in Jamaica reject the idea of spirit possession, but even so
"members" of these churches often quietly and unobtrusively become
possessed during religious services (as we have seen, individuals in
Jamaica often switch between seemingly incompatible cultural systems).
Other self-professed "Christian" churches, e.g. Pentecostal Holiness,
Shilo Apostolic Faith, Bible Church of God, do practise spirit possession.
However, these churches only allow Christian powers to possess members
(unlike Pukumina and Zion, which allow the spirits of departed ancestors
to possess members (cf. Seaga 1956).

Rastafarianism

The most recent religious development in Jamaica is Rastafarianism; but it
cannot be placed in any straightforward way on the evolutionary scale
presented here. Rastafarianism is extremely Africa oriented, but Africa
has become here more a conscious ideological focus than an historical point
of departure for a system of religious belief and behaviour.

The role of Africa in the ideological consciousness of Jamaicans is not
easy to map out historically. In fact, this has been one of the important
areas of dispute in theories of Afro-American culture. In the earliest
period of slavery, Africa remained quite strong in the consciousness of
slaves, as the abode of the ancestral spirits. Slaves were able to accept
death with equanimity because of the belief that their spirits would
return to join the ancestors in Africa. Later this belief eroded (except that
Rastafarians believe in the desirability and inevitability of their
repatriation to Africa), but there is evidence of the maintenance of the
idea of Africa as the mother country, even though an important part of the
colonial syndrome in Jamaica has been the rejection of Africa. There are
therefore two opposing and apparently contradictory streams in the
Jamaican attitude towards Africa: on the one hand, the eroding of the
consciousness of Africa as the mother country (for example the term
"African Jamaican" is hardly ever used, whereas "Chinese Jamaican",
"Indian Jamaican", "Syrian Jamaican", etc. are common terms); and on the
other hand, a preservation of this consciousness which reaches its highest
point in Rastafarianism.

Whereas Africa remains very high among Rastafarians at the level of
ideological consciousness, there isn't very much of African continuity in the
system of religious belief and religious behaviour. For example, "spirit
possession", which, as has been noted above, remains the most abiding link
with Africa in the Jamaican religious behaviour, is totally absent in
Rastafarianism. Rastafarianism is probably an excellent example of a
cultural form being generated virtually *ab initio* out of the social
circumstances.

However, it is interesting to observe that there remain two types of African continuities in Rastafarianism. The first type is a reintroduction rather than a linear continuity, of a cultural form of African origin for which there is no historical record in Jamaica, but which suddenly appears in Rastafarian culture and religion as an expression of the intellectual and spiritual links with Africa. One such cultural form is the practice of "dreadlocks", explained by Owens (1976: p. 154) as "the fullest expression of nature" or as "an ideological heritage from the ancient days when all Ethiopians wore locks as a special sign of priesthood". Locks, similar to dreadlocks, are also to be found in Kenya among the Mau Mau and in West Africa.

Another cultural form of this type is to be found in the plastic arts. Rastafarian artists follow many of the traditions found in East Africa. According to Bryan (1984: p. 11–12), these traditions include:

1. The device of applying hieratic proportion to figures within a composition. For example, Christ is depicted as the largest figure. Another device calls for equal prominence being given to all components in the composition, both in the foreground and in the background. This is formalised in a system of vertical perspective in which objects in the background appear in the upper portion of the picture plane.
2. The human figure is depicted as a composite showing a frontal torso with profile head, feet and one breast. One full front eye is shown in the profile head.

The second type is the product of the historical process of continuity and change. Within this second type, the following may be included:

1. The use of a herb based on (pseudo-)empirical knowledge of its natural therapeutic value as well as on its mystical magical power. The use of marijuana in this way has not been documented in Africa and is, in Jamaica, an obvious import from India. However, the attribution of multifarious therapeutic efficacy to the herb may be an African continuity, as well as its religious ritualistic use and the belief in its mystical magical powers.
2. Food taboos, which are very strong among Rastafarians and which are based on the view of the oneness of man and nature. The avoidance of salt (a major feature of "ital" foods) recurs among the Maroons of Jamaica and among Kumina practitioners who use no salt in the preparation of food meant as an offering to the spirits. The place of nature in the world view of Jamaicans in general and Rastafarians in particular is discussed in Chapter 7.
3. The concept of the Earth as Mother. In many areas of Sub-Saharan Africa, the Earth is the Mother God, the closest and dearest of the deities.

Rastafarianism, according to Owens (1976: pp. 145–147) "views the Earth as a loving mother and even as God himself". Respect for the earth, as the primary manifestation of nature, is also a fundamental feature of the world view.

4. According to Nettleford (in the Introduction to Owens 1976: p. xv), there [is] hardly any place for the concept of original sin in the Rastafarian belief-system. Related to this is the rejection of "another world" where salvation is to take place (Owens, p. 141). This "now"-orientation may be an African religious and world-view continuity and underlies the strong desire to remove the inequalities and injustices of the status quo which is commonly found in Afro-Jamaican religious movements.

5. The use of drums as a major music source. In many Rastafarian festivals, drums are the only instruments used to produce music.

6. Finally, there is the belief in the magical power of the word. This is dealt with more fully in Chapter 7.

5

Music and Dance

The earliest references to slave "manners and customs" in Jamaica mention music and dancing. Gardner, writing about the period between the British conquest in 1655 and the Great Earthquake of 1692, says:

> Two or three days were given at Xmas and also at Easter, which the slaves called pickanniny Xmas. What holidays they had were usually spent in dancing. These dances were almost invariably of a licentious character. The music was produced by small hollow gourds across which were laid strips of horse hair and some of the dancers had a kind of rattle fastened to their wrists and legs. The favourite instrument was a drum, made of skin stretched tightly over a hollow piece of timber ... the dances though not graceful were energetic, at times they assumed a fancy dress character. No appendage was too preposterous, but the most correct style of thing was to affix the tail of a cow to that part of the human frame where in tailed animals that appendage invariably grows.

Gardner's account of African music in the following period (1692 to 1782) shows no fundamental changes (p. 183). Gardner undoubtedly based his observations on Edwards (1807, vol. 2, pp. 102–3), who wrote:

> In general they prefer a loud and long-continued noise to the finest harmony and frequently consume a whole night in beating on a board with a stick. This is in fact one of the chief musical instruments; besides which they have the Banja or Merriwang, the Dundo, and the Goombay; all of African origin ... Their songs are commonly impromptu; and there are among them individuals who resemble the improvisatori, or extempore bards of Italy ... Their tunes in general are characteristic of their national manners, those of the Eboes being soft and languishing; of the Koromantyns heroic and martial ... At their merry meetings and midnight festivals they are not without ballads of another kind adapted to such occasions; and here they give full scope to a talent for ridicule and derision ... At other times, more especially at the burial of such among them as were respected in life, or venerable through age, they exhibit a sort of Pyrrhic or warlike dance, in which their bodies are strongly agitated by running, leaping and jumping with many violent

and frantic gestures and contortions.

Gardner adds: "The (satirical) song usually consisted of a solo part or recitative, in which the key was varied; this was followed by a chorus." Another comment by Gardner illuminates the history of Jonkunu, a major dance and music folk festival of Jamaica:

> The rough Merry-Andrew festivities (alluded to in the earlier account) were now improved upon. About 1720 there was a noted personage on the Guinea Coast, called John Connu. In what way he got associated with such festivities is not clear; but about Xmas-time crowds of men dressed up in a fantastic manner, with cows' horns on their heads, horrid masks and boars' tusks on their faces, and followed by numbers of excited women, danced through the streets and lanes, yelling at every door – "John Connu, John Connu!" About 50 years after the introduction of this custom a number of new devices were introduced and gradually the more elaborate spectacles called "Sets" came into vogue.[1]

Clearly music was transmitted more or less intact across the Middle Passage. Its African contexts and functions recur in Jamaica, but in a less elaborate, less ceremonial, and less conventionalised form. There was music at religious services and at ceremonies connected with events such as births and deaths, but events such as the initiation of priests, the installation of kings, and going to war either did not happen in Jamaica or happened infrequently and were not accompanied by the same ceremonies as in Africa. There may have been initiation rites, chiefly associated with religious orders such as Myal. There were also war preparations by slaves preparing revolts and by Maroons preparing for battle against the colonial regime. All of these ceremonial activities were accompanied by music and dance. There were also far fewer social gatherings and festivals in Jamaica than in Africa. Music and social life are closely associated, so social changes inevitably lead to changes in music or the performance of music. Even changes in language affect music. Yet African slaves in Jamaica continued to sing work songs and social commentary songs, and to make music for festivals such as Jonkunu, and even today impromptu "plays" are still staged by Maroons.

There are clear parallels between continuity in music and continuity in religion, language, and social organisation. The trouble in analysing these parallels is that anthropology and the study of music are separate disciplines that few scholars try to straddle. Here I shall look at music from an anthropological point of view; some musicologists may question my conclusions.

Music and dance acted as a uniquely unifying force among Africans in Jamaica. On Sundays and holidays, when work was generally suspended, slaves were free to engage in their own activities, primary among which were music and dance. Given the common structure and sociology of West African music, it is likely that slaves of different ethnic origins danced and sang together, especially when the music was of a purely recreational character.

According to Waterman (1952: p. 217):

in areas (Brazil, Haiti, Cuba) where the official Religions permitted the syncretism of deities with the Saints of the Church, African religious music has persisted almost unchanged, and African influence upon secular music has been strong. In protestant areas where such syncretism has not been possible [sic], the influence of African musical patterns on both religious and secular music has hinged upon a more extensive process of reinterpretation but is nonetheless considerable, in that fundamental characteristics of West African music have been retained.

Some forms of musical expression (such as the Maroon abeng, the call-and-response pattern of singing, and work songs) have continued virtually intact. Call-and-response refers to a certain organisational procedure for both vocal and instrumental music. A soloist or a small group of leaders takes a lead and the whole body of the group or the chorus responds by singing or playing the same melody or a different melody of corresponding or varying length. This procedure occurs with drums and other instruments as well as with voice and can be heard in all types of Afro-American music, including jazz, reggae, and calypso. A variant of this procedure is the call-and-refrain form, in which the choral or group response is a standard unchanging refrain after each variable solo "call".

But music, like religion and (as we shall see later) language, has developed along several paths according to the position of certain groups (including Maroons and African religious groups) in the acculturative process and depending on the social setting in which the music is performed. The notion of surface structure and deep structure, with which we are already familiar, is also pertinent to the history of Jamaican music. In the acculturative process, European musical forms, including melodies, lyrics, and instruments, constitute the surface structure of Jamaican music, while the rhythmic framework of the African source constitutes its deep structure.

Waterman (1952: p. 209) thinks that:

the presence of the same basic concept of scale and the use of harmony in both Europe and Africa have made easy and inevitable the many varieties of Euro-African musical syncretism to be observed in the New World ... the European music which came to the African's attention must have appeared mainly as a source of new musical ideas to be worked out in terms of African concepts and techniques ... Thus folk tunes and hymns stemming from the British Isles were often seized upon by African slaves and their descendants and after suitable remodelling, adopted as American Negro tunes."

African music, like African religions and languages, incorporated European traits and with each new generation became more and more "European" along at least one of its evolutionary paths.

The sections into which I divide my discussion of the development of music and dance among Africans in Jamaica are in a certain sense arbitrary, for music, song, dance, religion, and social organisation were closely integrated in West African culture, and also among slaves in the New World. At least one African people, the Dan of Ivory Coast, has only one word (*fa*) for song, dance, and instrumental music (Delerma 1970: p. 79).

The divisions to which I resort follow conventional ways of analysing musical activity. Music, including the subdivision instruments, is separated from song, including voice. The other main division is dance. Dance is closely related to music and song, but insofar as some styles of walking are related to "dance", the relationship is not universal and automatic.[2]

Instruments

The most important instrument is the drum, which has always been used by Africans in Jamaica. The colonial authorities sometimes banned drums and drumming, but they could never effectively silence them.

Drums came in different shapes and sizes, and were made of various materials. There is some confusion about the identification of a series of drums whose names begin with *gumb-*. There are variant spellings of these drum names, of which three distinct types can be identified:

1. *gumbi* (or *gumby*) "a barrel shaped drum about 6 foot in length carried by one man and beaten by another with a stick".
2. *gumba* (or *gumbah*) "hollow block of wood covered with goat or sheep skin and beaten with a stick (in each hand)".
3. *gumbe* (or *gumbay*) "small drum formed of trunk of a hollow tree and beaten with fingers".[3]

Other drum names occur in the historical literature, but their meanings are obscure. Beckwith (1929) mentions the *bon* or the *panya*, a drum played with sticks; Edwards mentions the *dundo*, "a kind of tabor". In Trinidad the term *bum*, evidently onomatopeic, is the name of the large bass drum in a steel band.

Several drum types and drumming techniques are used today in Jamaica, but far fewer than in Africa. Special drums for use on special occasions (festivals, initiations, the instalment of kings, and the like) were not always necessary in Jamaica, where there were far fewer celebrations. Moreover, it is unlikely that any one African community used the full variety of drums known to West Africa, or that each sort of drum found its way to Jamaica. Hour-glass drums for example, are not mentioned in the historical sources. It is likely that the range of drum types and drumming techniques narrowed in the course of time, but so far there has been too little field research to conclude that Jamaica is poor in drums. Roberts, for example (1972: p. 22), observed a *tambo* drummer in Wakefield, Trelawny, who muted his drum with his heel; this drummer's son used a pair of catta sticks to beat out a second rhythm on the side of the *tambo*. Roberts adds that "a twentieth century author [apparently Helen Roberts writing in the 1920s; see bibliography] has seen square drums in Jamaica". Lewin (1973: p. 9) mentions a variety of sorts:

> side drums, revival drums, base drums, fundeh, repeater, kbandu, playing caste, bruckins, tambo, bongo drum and congo drums. Some of them are single headed, others stopped at both ends; some are played with sticks, others with hands; the players may straddle and beat with their hands, the heads of the drums are heeled on alternate beats so that the pitch is varied alternately.

Other percussion instruments from Africa are still used in Jamaica (as well as in other parts of Afro-America). One instrument in the form of a flat board beaten with sticks is called *cotter* (Beckford), *kitty-katty* (Lewis 1845), and *clapper* (among the Kumina people). *Clapper* is mentioned by Beckwith (1929: pp. 147–48), meaning stones knocked together during wakes for the summoning of spirits. The modern *shaka* (or *shak-shak*) was also brought to Jamaica and Afro-America by Africans. In the earliest period, this instrument (generally called *shaki-shaki*) was made of any receptacle (such as a box or gourd) filled with pebbles, seeds, and the like. It was either shaken by a handle or tied to the wrists or legs and shaken by dancing. Today the *shaka* tends to be manufactured according to a uniform pattern; in Jamaica it is always held by the handle. Musical instruments are no longer worn on the body in Jamaica. Other percussion instruments from Africa include: *jenkoving* "two jars with ordinary-size mouths over which the palms were brought down to make sucking sound" (Cassidy 1967: p. 245; Wright 1937: p. 237; Leslie 1740: p. 310); and the *rookaw* "two jagged hardwood sticks beaten (or rubbed) together" (Wright 1937: p. 237; Cassidy 1967: p. 385; Leslie 1740: p. 310).

Percussion instruments are still the most tangible musical links to Africa. The drum still dominates Jamaican music; even those forms of music that in choice of instruments and melodic structures are least obviously African still retain a structural equivalent to the drum sound in the form of a heavy bass rhythm that emanates from, say, a bass guitar. The central role of percussion in Jamaican music is also evident in the Jamaican habit of turning up the bass when recording music or listening to records. In a comment on Jamaican reggae music in a Jamaica Tourist Board film on the subject, a Jamaican recording engineer said: "For reggae recordings in Jamaica we push the bass 80 per cent. Over there (in the US), they say that is madness, that we are peaking. But in Jamaica we must have it at least 80 per cent."

Percussion still assumes various forms throughout Jamaica and the Caribbean (and probably throughout Afro-America too). Anything that makes an acceptable noise is banged, from bottles and spoons (or knives) – by now standard instruments in African and New World Black music – to tables, desk tops, walls, and tin cans. However, the polyrhythmic character of African music becomes progressively weaker the further one gets from "traditional" drumming associated with Africa-derived religious movements, like Kumina and Convince, or with conservative groups such as the Maroons, and the closer one gets to modern music groups that use the box bass (rhumba box) or the bass guitar. This progression culminates in the monorhythm of reggae music, which repeats one single heavy beat. But this phenomenon deserves a more competent musicological analysis, since the dance movements that accompany reggae are often polyrhythmic, suggesting that dancers are responding to a parallel feature of the music.

Percussion and a sense of drum rhythm remain Jamaica's strongest link with the African musical past. Percussive rhythms are constantly produced on all occasions and from several sources, including improvised sources like the bottle and spoon that have almost become formally recognised musical instruments. Much music is performed only on percussion instruments (accompanied by singing). This is true of institutionalised music performed by Maroons and by religious groups such as Kumina and Convince; of celebrations such as Etu and Gumbe; and of impromptu gatherings at which merry-makers grab whatever percussive devices are at hand. In such cases music consists of pure rhythm and is usually accompanied by dance. Roberts' comment (1972: p. 11) is interesting in this connection:

Meaningful sounds are the basis of African music, as they are of any music, but there seems to be value not only in the sounds themselves but also in their arrangement in orderly sequences or patterns of rhythms ... Rhythm is basic to enjoyment. Pieces with almost no tune in a Western sense are enjoyed if there is sufficient rhythmic interest.

String and wind instruments were both brought to Jamaica from Africa

and made in Jamaica by Africans working from memory. However, these African instruments seem to have given way at an early stage to parallel European instruments. There is evidence that Africans first encountered European string and wind instruments during the Middle Passage. Epstein (1973: p. 66) reports an account of a 1693 voyage from Africa to the West Indies: "We often at sea in the evening would let the slaves come up unto the sun to air themselves, and make them jump and dance for an hour or two to our bag-pipes, harp, and fiddle." Edwards (1973, II: p. 116) shows that African instruments (but not necessarily string and wind instruments) were also present on board the slave ships: "In the intervals between their meals they are encouraged to divert themselves with music and dancing; for which purpose such rude and uncouth instruments as are used in Africa are collected before their departure."

The following string instruments are mentioned in the early literature; (Clerk 1914: p. 21) claims that many were made of wood or gourds):

1. An instrument whose name is spelled *bonjour*,[4] *banjar*,[5] or *banjil*[6] in publications about Jamaica; *banza* in publications about the French islands and Haiti; and *bandore* or *banjer* in the USA. The word and instrument have evolved into the modern *banjo* . The original instrument is everywhere described as a "coarse, rough kind of guitar made of a gourd with a neck fastened on to it, having from 4 to 6 strings". Long and Gardner refer to what seems to be the same instrument as the *merry-wang*.
2. The *bender* or *benta* is described by Beckford (1790, II: p. 387) and Beckwith (1924) as a "bow made from a stick and held together by a slip of dried grass, the upper part is gently compressed between the lips, and to which the breath gives a soft and pleasing vibration, and the other end is graduated by a slender stick ..." *Benta* has also been recorded and similarly described in Suriname.
3. According to Clerk, the *tumba* is a Maroon instrument made of a large hollowed-out piece of trumpet tree across which three strings are stretched and on each side of which pieces of metal, (in place of shell) are strung.

The flute is the most frequently mentioned wind instrument. The Coromantee flute was "made from the porous branches of the trumpet tree, about a yard in length, and of nearly the thickness of the upper part of the bassoon" (Beckford 1970, II: p. 387). Lady Nugent (1966: p. 75) says that it was played with the nose. Sloane (I: p. ii) speaks of trumpets "played by Africans on their festivals" before "they were prohibited by the Customs of the Islands". Beckford and others noted the use of an animal jawbone. There is also mention of the *abeng* (also called *kiake* according to Beckwith), which today remains a living symbol of Maroon resistance.

Song

The two main factors producing change in the song structure of Africans in Jamaica were the absence of the full set of social and ceremonial occasions observed in Africa by the singing of songs, and the effect of linguistic change (see Chapter 6). African melodies sung in African languages are largely shaped by the words with which they are associated, for Africans attach more importance to lyrics than to other features of their songs (say, for example, melody). Words in the vast majority of West African languages brought to Jamaica have their own melodic pattern: each syllable has a definite pitch that must be observed and reproduced as an integral part of the word; failure to observe and reproduce the pitch of a syllable would result in a change of meaning or the creation of a non-word. African melodies must largely follow the melodic pattern of the words in the song, so that they rise and fall together with the pitch of the syllables.

In the course of language development in Jamaica, words lost distinctive pitch (or melody) patterns and the structure of song melodies thereby changed.[7] As we shall see in the following chapter, the change in the role of pitch was not absolute, nor was pitch replaced by a prosodic feature equal to English. Rather, pitch lost its distinctiveness (it no longer distinguished the meanings of large numbers of words) but high pitch generally marked those syllables that in English have main stress. (The same happened both elsewhere in the Caribbean and in modern Twi.) Syllables maintained their even timing with relatively even stress (cf. the uneven timing of English syllables with relatively uneven stress); this even stress gave melodic and rhythmic flexibility to the song line. For example, words at the end of song lines could be stressed on their final syllable (this remains a marked feature of the metric structure of contemporary West Indian calypso).

However, African lyrics continued to be sung, for the most part in connection with Maroon and Kumina religious and other ceremonies (Brathwaite 1971: p. 224; Roberts 1926: p. 348ff). There was an evolutionary split in the African song, depending on the context in which it was performed. Where African religions continued to be practised, African lyrics were used; in acculturative contexts, lyrics were composed in the language variously known as Jamaican creole or patois.

The language in which lyrics were composed, and the impact of that choice on the structure of melody, is a main criterion for classifying Jamaican music. African genres became quite rare because of the general restriction on the use of African languages (see next chapter); but songs in the Jamaican language continued to cover the full range of genres. Another useful classificatory criterion is the social context in which the song was sung. In many cases the two classifications (genre and social context) overlap.

We may distinguish between religious, ceremonial, festival, and recreational social contexts (Lewin 1974). The African tradition remained stronger in some contexts than in others. The history of the development of the structure of songs (and of the language of the lyrics) is analogous to the history of development of African religion in Jamaica. In Kumina,

> much of the music is antiphonal and sung in unison, and many of the melodies are modal. When harmony is used, the texture is rather loose and contrapuntal, with many voices spanning up to three octaves. Kumina music resembles in many aspects that of the Bakusu in the Congo, and it is interesting to note that there are Congolese words in some of the Kumina songs collected in Jamaica (Lewin 1974: p. 127).

In Convince, Christian hymns sung in a very slow, dirge-like tempo called "long-meter" alternate with Bongo songs that have distinctive rhythms and hand-clapping accompaniment and that are sung in the call-and-response format (Hogg 1960: p. 11). Roberts (1926: p. 355) records ten songs, many of them said by Maroons to be in the "Koromanti language", and concludes from a musical analysis of several of them that "there is nothing like this in European music and nothing at all like it in other Jamaican songs. It is undoubtedly African not only from the points mentioned above (tonality, minor scale) but even more so from the repetition of phrases, and the lack of development."

At the Pukumina and Revival Zion stage in the evolution of religion, hymns and choruses of Christian origin predominate; but much of the music is "improvisatory, both melodically and harmonically. Short phrases are often repeated for many minutes [cf. Roberts' comment on Kumina songs above] ... with variation both in pitch and in rhythm" (Lewin 1974: pp. 126–27). Lewin also reports "minor mode" songs as well as a rhythmic background provided by "clapping, stamping and other percussion sounds made by the worshippers".

Beckwith (1929: pp. 161–2) describes how Christian hymns are transformed during performance. Her description shows that the concept of continuity applies not only to cultural institutions over a span of time (i.e. diachronically) but also to particular instances of cultural behaviour at the moment of execution (i.e. synchronically). "Code switch" or "code movement", terms used in the analysis of speech performance, can therefore also be applied to the analysis of musical performance. Beckwith describes a St Elizabeth revival meeting as follows:

> The exercises differed in no way from those of an ordinary prayer meeting in a free congregation; that is, there were singing and prayer and some words of exhortation. But the manner of singing was noticeable. A Moody and Sankey tune was begun, accompanied by the beat of a drum,

after a bit it fell into a dizzying repetition of set phrases over and over again while the audience and the workers rocked their bodies in tune to its rhythm.

Other genres do not generally use African lyrics, but some features derived from Africa do persist in them. The genres themselves – worksongs, comic songs, songs of derision (called *jamal*, cf. Roberts 1925: p. 150), and play songs – are based on African models, though play songs in particular have come under strong European influence. But even these genres that are no longer fully African exhibit important African features. For example, the rhythm underlying the English melody in play songs is mainly African, as is the ever-present call-and-response feature. Lewin describes worksongs:

There are worksongs for digging, sugar boiling, picking cotton, pimento, and corn, planting corn, peas and yam, timber cutting, rice beating, house-cleaning, house-hauling, women's work, fishing and loading bananas on boats ... The chants took on the rhythm of the work which they accompanied, so they are as varied as the tasks which slaves had to do. Styles also developed accordingly. In digging songs, for instance, one man would be required to lead or call the tune, while the work gang sang in chorus. The leader, apart from being a confident powerful singer, would improvise lyrics and mime them in order to keep the work gang happy. Some digging songs are simple, two-phrased melodies sung antiphonally – solo followed by chorus in harmony. Others have more extended melodies usually in the major or minor modes ... The antiphonal style of singing in many of the songs harks back to Africa, but most of the melodies and harmonies are Western European in style. Only in the rice beating songs is there very strong East Indian influence.
(Lewin 1974: pp. 128–9)

Recreational music seems to have evolved chiefly in the context of Sunday and holiday festivities. When Sunday was recognised as a holy day, Saturday became the day of festivity; it was then that many changes began to take place. Originally African drums and other instruments provided the music for the "plays", as the music and dancing were called (and are still called, particularly by Maroons). There are no reports that the sexes were separated in Jamaica during these festivities, but Ligon (cited by Handler 1972: p. 30) says that in Barbados, "on Sundays, to dancing they go, the men by themselves, and the women by themselves, no mixed dancing." Other sources cited by Handler suggest that 50 years later this sexual division had disappeared. Stewart (1823) specifically describes plays as "an assemblage of both sexes".

The earliest sources on Jamaica mention a ring or circle formed by participants, with the musicians in the middle. People entered the ring to dance, and were replaced by others as soon as they became tired. Men and women danced together. According to (Long 1774: vol. 2, p. 424) and Stewart (1823: pp. 282–3), dancers advanced adroitly toward one another, keeping their heads, torsos, and limbs erect as they performed a "wriggle" (in the words of Long) or as they "writhe and turn the body on its own axis". Stewart (1823: p. 270), repeated by Gardner (1873: p. 383), suggests that songs were sung by females in the call-and-response format, and that the dancing was "indecent" or "licentious".

Stewart (1823: p. 56) describes a different acculturative path, taken chiefly by domestic slaves:

In a few years it is probable that the rude music here described will be altogether exploded among the creole negroes, who show a decided preference for European music. Its instruments, its tunes, its dances, are now pretty generally adopted by the young creoles, who indeed sedulously copy their masters and mistresses in everything. A sort of subscription balls are set on foot, and parties of both sexes assemble and dance country dances to the music of a violin, tamborine, etc... But this improvement of taste is confined to those who are, or have been, domestic about the houses of the Whites.

The circle has remained the main feature of Jamaican traditional dance, in Kumina, Maroon, and Goombay dancing. Dancers move anti-clockwise around a group of drummers. Women, both dancers and onlookers (but particularly dancers), do the singing. According to Waterman (1952: p. 215), the counter-clockwise circle dance, in which dancers make up part of the singing chorus, is common both in West Africa and in the New World. The circle periodically "explodes" when a dancer or dancers break out of line and spin a few times before rejoining it, or when two dancers face one another to perform the kind of hip movement described by Long.[8] Along this evolutionary path, singing is accompanied only by percussion instruments, particularly drums.

The main changes along the other evolutionary path are that percussion is no longer dominant and that other instruments begin to be added to carry the melodic line, which becomes an additional component in the musical structure. There is no one point at which African instruments were replaced. Different performers and performances occupy different stages along the evolutionary scale; in this century a main determinant of their place on this scale is whether they are located in the towns or in the villages.

Rural performers may still use banjos and bamboo flutes, with rhumba boxes and shak-shaks to provide the rhythm. In another context the bamboo flute is replaced by the bamboo saxophone, until finally city performers adopt the commercial European saxophone and replace the banjo with the guitar. At this stage, the circle gives way to the general "ballroom", in which not one but many pairs of men and women dance together. They have no physical contact; they face each other for most of the time, but sometimes they retreat or spin before regrouping. The song or dance most closely associated with this evolutionary stage is the *mento* (the dance itself is sometimes called *shay shay*) (cf. Beckwith 1929: p. 214). DeLisser (1919: p. 107) describes the mento as consisting of slow movements of the body, and "the point of perfection is reached when, as in Haiti, the dancer never allows the upper part of the body to move as she writhes or shuffles over the ground". According to Lewin (1974: p. 129):

> The indigenous dance music ... is Mento, a song/dance style characterised by the accentuation on or in the last of four beats in a bar. The songs are often used to ridicule and censure people within the group, so they often contain veiled or symbolic references which are fully understood by the members of the group creating or using the particular song.

Jekyll (1907: p. 216) shows how European music provides the surface structure in the form of a basic melody while the deep structure derives from the Afro-Jamaican tradition:

> Turning now to the dancing tunes, the chief difference to be noted is that they show a more marked departure from what may be called the Jamaican-type melody. Sailors bring popular songs to the seaports, and from there they spread to the country. For some time the original words are kept, but before long they get changed ... merely due to the fact that the words, referring as they do to English topics, have no interest here. So we generally find that the tunes are refitted with a complete set of new words describing some incident which has happened lately in the district or some detail of daily life. When these reflect, as they often do, upon the character of individuals the names have been changed and all evidence pointing to the locality destroyed... The music consists of three flutes, two tambourines, and a big drum ... a cassada-grater, rubbed with the handle of a spoon ... the jawbone of a horse, the teeth of which rattle when it is shaken ... stirrup irons hanging on a string [doing] duty as a triangle.

Today popular dance music seems to derive less from the mento than from the religious song. This may at first sight seem strange, but on deeper reflection it can be explained in terms of the traditional integration of music, dance, and religion in Jamaica. For Africans and their New World descendants, there was no rigid dichotomy between the sacred and the secular.

Twentieth-century Jamaican popular music (e.g. ska, rocksteady, and reggae) has a number of features that are common to all evolutionary paths. These include call-and-response (cf. Natty Dread, where Bob Marley sings the lead and the Wailers the response); vocal effects (grunts, cries and yells); body movements that are synchronised with singing; polyrhythm; and the absence of physical contact between dancing partners.

There are two variants of the ska rhythm corresponding to two dance forms. One variant can be seen as basic, and is derived from the music of Revivalism. In the dance form associated with it, the torso moves up and down and the hands alternate in a similar movement; this dance form is derived from a Revivalist dance movement called "trumping" and "labouring", a "shuffling two step dance done to a 2/2 rhythm, bending forward and up in rhythmic sequence, while sucking the breath into the body and releasing it with a grunting sound" (Moore 1965: p. 64). The second ska variant manifests an up-tempo jazz influence; the dance form associated with it, called "footsy" or "legs", consists of a rapid virtuoso movement, including vibrations, of the legs and feet (this dance form occurs in Africa and the United States among performers like James Brown).

The *ska* is thought to have emerged around the time of Jamaican independence in 1962. Its musical structure can be explained by the fact that its early practitioners were in close touch with Revival churches in West Kingston. Its lyrics, which tended to be light, were generally about love and love-making. Toward the middle of the 1960s, when the expectations raised by independence remained unfulfilled, Jamaicans expressed their frustration in the more introverted rocksteady, whose lyrics revealed a new social consciousness. Toward the end of the 1960s this trend was reflected even more clearly in reggae, which – because of a strong Rastafarian influence – represented a return to the traditional fusion of the secular and the religious and to the symbiotic interaction of religion (including music and dance) and politics.

Music and dance (like religion) brought together slaves of different ethnic origins. They were major instruments both of cohesion and of revolt – even today the *abeng* remains the most dramatic symbol of Maroon independence (and gave its name to the newspaper that in the early 1970s claimed to be the organ of revolutionary change in Jamaica). According to Sloane (1707: p. lii), the colonial regime banned the use of drums by slaves at the very start of plantation society in Jamaica, in the late seventeenth century. This prohibition was not very effective. According to Royes, (1978: p. 7),

music and dance form an instrument for spreading their [Afro-Jamaican] ideologies, attracting converts and releasing within the people a feeling of power over everyday suffering and poverty and oppression, as well as a physical closeness or even oneness with the great gods and spirits of their religion.

This is as true of Myalism as it is of Revivalism, and is true also of Rastafarianism.

6

Language

Among the most widespread fallacies about slave societies in the New World is the belief that slaves were unable to communicate with each other because of the wide diversity and mutual non-intelligibility of African languages and dialects and because they (slaves) were systematically separated so that members of the same ethnic/linguistic group would not find themselves on the same plantation. The fact is that African languages were routinely used on slave plantations and have survived in Jamaica up to today. Even if it is true that the military establishment aimed at systematically separating slaves of the same ethnic origin, there is no evidence that this policy was consistently and effectively carried out. Rather there is evidence that in some cases slaves of a particular ethnic-linguistic group were deliberately sought by planters because of certain stereotype characteristics that these slaves were supposed to have. There is also evidence that new slaves were sometimes quartered with people of a similar ethnic origin who would help them to acclimatise and learn the ways of a slave plantation.

So any discussion of the history and evolution of African languages in Jamaica must start out from the recognition that African languages were spoken quite normally on the island. However, the linguistic history of Jamaica shows clearly the significance of social context, and of the period of African migration, for the evolution of African languages. African languages, like African religions and African music, evolved along different paths according to the social context they were used in. As we have seen, the immigration of Africans (mainly Bantu) in the third period of migration (1841–1865) and their settlement in St Thomas were main factors in the persistence of the Kumina religion in that parish. The persistence of the Kikongo language among Kumina worshippers in St Thomas can be similarly explained.

Jamaica was therefore multilingual at the very start of its colonisation by Europeans. If it is true that at first most slaves were Akan in Jamaica (or on the Gold Coast, in Barbados, or in Suriname), then the number of languages would be relatively few and most would be closely related; only later would the multiplicity of languages grow and become more complex.

The evolution of African languages in this multilingual setting may be elucidated by a look at the phenomenon of multilingualism in general. Language contact is but one instance of cultural contact. A general framework for the study of cultural contact was developed in Chapter 1 (pp. 13–17); it is also applicable to language contact. It remains to look at some specific factors in language contact, including the factor of social context.

In multilingual situations the political dominance of the speakers of one of the languages involved is an important determinant of the nature and direction of language change. In Jamaica, English was the dominant language, that is the language of the military force that kept society together. Note that my use of the term language dominance refers not to the relative number of domains or functions in which a particular language is used (which is how sociolinguists generally understand the term) but to the role that its speakers play in society. But the two sorts of dominance are often interlinked: military (or economic, or demographic) power often leads to dominance as conventionally understood by sociolinguists. The dominance of English in Jamaica led inevitably to major changes in African languages, while English itself (as spoken by native speakers) changed little. As we have seen in Chapter 1, this is to be expected when the power bases of cultures or languages in contact are grossly mismatched.

When two languages are mismatched, second language learning is unidirectional: speakers of the subordinate languages learn the dominant language but not vice versa. Speakers of the subordinate languages not only learn the dominant language but surrender their own languages more or less swiftly and more or less completely, depending on the degree of unevenness in the matching of the cultures in contact. The lower languages undergo drastic change as a result of either borrowings from the dominant language or to losses in inner form as a result of growing disuse. The dominant language, however, changes little or not at all when spoken by native speakers, though it changes drastically when acquired as a second language by speakers of the lower languages. It is important to consider whether change in lower languages resulting from borrowings from the dominant language and from losses in inner form is completely distinguishable from the drastic changes that the dominant language undergoes when acquired by speakers of lower languages. Some interpret Jamaican "creole" or "patois" as a product of the continuity of African language structure with loss of inner form and borrowings from English; others as the product of drastic changes introduced into English during its acquisition by Africans. The question is: are these two interpretations mutually irreconcilable? We shall see later that the language of Jamaicans is best understood dynamically, as a "becoming". In its popular contemporary form and in older forms the "continuity" aspect is uppermost; in its modern urbanised "educated" form it is best understood as the product of centuries of approximation to English. This is why it is important to understand the process of language change rather than simply try to classify contemporary forms as genetically or structurally (typologically) related to one or another of the contributory languages. The process may then reveal multiple or changing relationships, as first suggested by Taylor (1960), though his view of the process is different from that being presented here.

Dominance is a concept that can be applied not only to relationships between European and African languages but also to relationships among African languages used within the community of Africans. Bilingualism and multilingualism were already common in pre-colonial Africa, and there must have been many polyglots among the enslaved Africans in Jamaica. It is quite likely that Twi-Asante was learned as a second (or third) language by Africans in Jamaica, for as we have seen, the Twi-Asante people were dominant in Jamaica at the start of plantation society, when differences between African ethnic groups were still sharp. There is linguistic evidence to support the idea of Twi-Asante dominance. The Maroon language of Jamaica is based almost exclusively on Twi-Asante. Slaves from ethnic groups other than Twi-Asante who joined the Maroons evidently learned the Twi language and surrendered their own. The vast majority of words of African origin in the Jamaican language come from Twi-Asante. This suggests that Twi-Asante, or at least its lexicon, was accepted by Africans of other linguistic groups in Jamaica. Dallas (1703: pp. 31–33) mentions a group that joined Kojo's maroon band,

distinct in figure, character, language and country. Some of the old people remember that their parents spoke in their own families, a language entirely different from that spoken by the rest of the negroes with whom they had incorporated. They recollected many of the words for things in common use, and declared that in their early years they spoke their mother-tongue. The Coromantee language, however, superseded the others, and became in time the general one in use.

Given the dominance of Twi-Asante (Coromantee) over other African languages, the factors that characterised contact between English and African languages probably also characterised this intra-African contact. That is to say, acculturation and language learning were probably unidirectional (toward Twi-Asante); "lower" African languages progressively and rapidly decayed until they disappeared completely. Twi-Asante, on the other hand, changed little as a result of contact with these other African languages, which by the end of the eighteenth century were on the point of extinction (just as Twi-Asante is today on the point of extinction in its contact with Jamaican and English). The process that Dallas describes is typical of the general process of language death: reduction in one domain after another until the language is spoken only "in their own families" by parents, and subsequent generations recall only "words for things in common use".

The only specifically identifiable traces that these "minor" African languages have left behind are a number of vocabulary items in both the Twi-Asante language of the Maroons and in the Jamaican language as a whole. Twi-Asante in Jamaica now contains, for example, words from Temne and Limba, which are languages of Sierra Leone. The following examples are taken from Dalby (1971: pp. 41–46):

opung	"you dead" cf. Temne *òpong* " he is finished, dead"
katègbè	"?" (apparently uttered to pacify a man in trance) cf. Temne *ketègbè* "calm(ly)"
katègbè yanu	"?" (shouted angrily in response to the above) cf. Temne *ketègbè keyi-èno* "there's no peace here"
akote	"dog" cf. Limba *kuteng* "dog" (the Jamaican form is created by denasalisation)

Social Contexts

The different contexts within which African languages were used in Jamaica gave rise to the different evolutionary paths that these languages took. There are six main social and other contexts relevant to the evolution of these languages. They are discussed in the following pages.

1. Expressive Genres such as Songs and Folktales

Songs and folktales differ from the major channel of communication, which is speech. Songs in particular preserve older forms of language, and old songs are sometimes preserved even when they are no longer generally understood. Songs in African languages make religious ceremonies and folk festivals seem more mystical and esoteric.

Sloane (1688) recorded a number of African songs (including "Angola", "Papa", and "Koromanti") during his visit to Jamaica at the beginning of the British colonial period. Roberts (1926), on a visit to Accompong some 200 years later, discovered "that songs still existed and could be sung by some of the Maroons which they designated as Koromanti songs". I myself heard songs during visits to Scotts Hall in the 1960s that were not in English or Spanish or any other language known to me; these too were called "Koromanti songs" by the Maroons. Roberts (ibid) adds that:

> in addition to their being sung chiefly with words and syllables that are not now understood by the people, they are in other respects markedly different from all others obtained at Accompong or in the vicinity or in other parts of the island...

These songs are part of a whole tradition that has been preserved among the Maroons. But this tradition is now weakening as Maroons become more and more indistinguishable from ordinary peasants. It is consistent with the general pattern of the development of "lower" languages in contact situations that these "Koromanti songs" have by now become unintelligible.

Proverbs are another conservative linguistic form. However, since their purpose is didactic, they must be intelligible to be effective. Proverbs in African languages were therefore presumably no longer used after a certain point, but were translated into (or creatively recomposed) in the developing Jamaican language. The language of Jamaican proverbs changed along with the Jamaican language as a whole (see below). But because proverbs are conservative, they changed more slowly than the language of everyday speech, so they contain a number of archaic or obsolete words and structures that serve as windows into the linguistic past. These archaic or obsolete forms represent continuities of West African language structure that are either lost from or have become weaker in contemporary Jamaican (see below).

Some of these continuities are listed below; others will be discussed in more detail later. (All the examples are from Franck 1921.)

1. Denasalisation: *cunning* becomes *koni,* which in proverbs is the normal word for "clever". Today *koni* is used only in the names of animal characters like Koni Rabbit. As an adjective meaning "clever", it is used and understood only by older country people.
2. Vowel final syllables are much more widespread in proverbs than in everyday language, e.g. *farra* "far", *changie* "change", *goadie* "gourd", *ratta* "rat", and *yerrie* "hear".
3. Hypercorrection leads to the reverse process, in which final vowels are lost, e.g. *slipple* "slippery" and *famble* "family" (cf. Krio *sipul, fambul*).
4. Initial *ny-* varies with *y-* : *nyoung* "young".
5. Consonant *v* is rare: *neba* "never", *hab* "have", *lib* "live", and *ebery* "every".

2. Marronage

This is one of the contexts in which gradual language loss or decay can best be observed. The Maroons set up independent communities separate from the colonial establishment, so they had much less linguistic and cultural contact with Europeans than did slaves. Twi-Asante challenged English for linguistic dominance in the same way as the Maroons challenged the British on the battlefield. Twi-Asante's political and military role as an alternative to English helped preserve it right through until the present, albeit with a reduced structure and fewer functions.

Twi-Asante probably flourished among Maroons during the period of slavery, but after slavery, its military and political role declined as Maroons came into closer contact with other Jamaicans; this accelerated its decay. During slavery, particularly when the Maroons were in a state of war with the British, Twi-Asante was not only tactically indispensable but was a symbol of the African identity of the Maroons, and an anchor of their pride and confidence. Later it lost its active role and became a mere symbol of independence. Today it is no longer a viable means of communication, but Maroons still use it to mark the boundary between them and others.

As we have seen, language loss or decay occurs in two dimensions: loss of inner form (structural), and loss of domains (functional). Twi-Asante was used in a far fuller form and in many more domains in early Maroon societies than it is today. Dallas (1803: pp. 33, 52–53), for example, records that "Coromantee" was the general language of Maroons in the eighteenth century. Bryan Edwards, the eighteenth century historian, was no doubt referring to Twi-Asante when he mentioned "a barbarous dissonance of the African dialects with a mixture of Spanish and Broken English" spoken by Maroons (see Dalby 1971: pp. 36–37). Today Twi-Asante is almost never used in a referential function, and evidence suggests that it has reached the terminal stage of functional decay typical of contact situations. Maroons no longer know the meaning of many of the words and expressions they remember.

It is not altogether clear when Twi-Asante finally lost its referential function. Beckwith (1929: pp. 191–3) says that Maroons whom she observed "command a secret tongue (the so-called Koromanti), and they know old songs in this speech". Beckwith was told the English translation of one of these songs:

ke re wan ke, eh eh eh eh bar me oh
kin ke ne wang kwa ke eh eh eh eh bar me oh
Ho tuck o de me du hin

We are in war who fight for our country.
War! bring the explosive, let us kill the enemy,
Good evening![1]

Beckwith added that "in Moore Town they still send signals to each other by drumbeats" and that "in Accompong the horn man calls out the name of the dead through a conch (the Abeng), and everyone listens to the signal". These three means of communication (the Twi-Asante language, talking drums, and the Abeng) are all dependent on tones (or pitches); once pitch was lost as an information unit of language, it would no longer have been possible to use talking drums or the Abeng to recreate pitch patterns.

This means that the three means of communication listed by Beckwith would live together and die together. Dunham (1946: p. 54) reports that:

> the Colonel [of the Accompong Maroons] told me that the message [of the Abeng] is transmitted not by a signal or code but by the actual pronunciation of the words and by tones which are easily distinguishable to a trained ear. Old Galibo who died last year was the last really expert hornblower.

Cundall (1915: p. 336) doubts that the Accompong Maroons were able to use more than a few words of Twi-Asante, but he may have been deliberately misled by his informants, who were perhaps wary of revealing their secrets to strangers. He himself reports that a visitor from the United States Bureau of Ethnology claimed that he "had discovered the Maroons talking their native language" on a visit to Accompong a year or two before Cundall. Dunham (1971: p. 157) mentions Accompong Maroons talking "partly in Koromantee" and "carrying on a friendly conversation with an ancestral spirit in their native African tongue". Dalby (1971: pp. 37-38) summarises his own research on this question as follows:

> Thompson (1937: p. 477) noted that "besides their ordinary speech, they (Maroons of Moore Town) have a dialect of their own which they will not disclose to the neagres [sic] (i.e. non-Maroon Jamaicans), or any person not of their race. They claim that even if they should try to disclose it secretly their comrades will hear at the very moment they are speaking; also their ancestors, though dead, will be displeased and may subject them to severe penalty". For Accompong, Williams (1934: pp. 385–386) reports the use of only a few words of the language in 1937 supplied by Colonel Rowe, with no one else in the town seeming to be in a better position; but, for Moore Town, he states that "Koromanti was in a somewhat better position ... the older people, of about 50 years of age, on the occasion of gatherings, once the rum has begun to flow, vie with one another, repeating whatever Koromanti they may remember. But strange as it may seem, this is for the most part done in poll-parrot fashion, without any concept of what they are saying. At Charles Town, Williams found that Koromanti is still a living language among them, being taught by the elders to the children; and similarly at Scott's Hall, he found that "Koromanti is spoken, and while conversing with them, I had experience of the general knowledge of the language".

My own research shows that today Twi-Asante is dying (but not dead), and that it serves little or no referential function. It seems never to be used spontaneously, in ordinary everyday communicative contexts. Scott's Hall and Moore Town Maroons can carry on conversations in the old language on request, but they use fixed and stylised expressions, and all creativity is lost. Most of the words and expressions that I have heard are the same as those recorded by Williams (1934).

Some of the structural changes in Twi-Asante in Jamaica are merely a continuation of changes that had already begun in Akan (the language complex of which Twi-Asante and Fante are dialects). We have already seen that in Akan the noun class system has less prefixes than in other Niger-Congo languages. According to Christaller (1875: p. 22), many Akan nouns have no prefix at all; the prefix *o-* is sometimes dropped; the prefix *e-* "is still more easily dropped while the prefix *a-* is not dropped like *o-* and *e-*." Twi-Asante as spoken by the Maroons of Jamaica has shed even more prefixes than Akan. Thus we have Maroon *paki* and (African) Twi-Asante *apaki* "small calabash; Maroon *sènsè* and Twi-Asante *asense* "type of fowl with ruffled feathers"; Maroon *kamfo* and Twi-Asante *nkamfo* "type of yam"; and Maroon *brouni* and Twi-Asante *oburoni* "European", "white man". On the other hand, the Maroon language preserves many Twi-Asante noun class prefixes, e.g. *afana* "machete", *anansi* "spider", and *abukani* "cow". It even has some prefixes that Twi-Asante has lost, e.g. *aprako* (cf. Twi-Asante *prako* "pig") and *awisa* "pepper" (cf. Twi-Asante *wisa*). The noun class system must therefore have been sufficiently vibrant and productive in Jamaica to have established prefixes where there were none in Twi-Asante or to have maintained prefixes where Twi-Asante lost them. But by and large, prefixes have worn away in the Maroon language, and had become inoperative by the end of the nineteenth century (when the language finally lost its referential function). Williams (1937: p. 464) was given a list by Colonel Rowe of Accompong of words and expressions elicited from "an old Maroon man seventy-five years of age or more". The list is full of noun-class prefixes including *aprako* "hog", which Williams picked up in Moore Town in the form *prako*, without the prefix; and *akoko*, which today survives in Scott's Hall in the plural form *nkoko*. According to Dalby (1971: p. 44), the form *òkòkò* is used in Moore Town. Today people who use these words are completely unaware of the existence of a prefix. They sometimes use the plural for the singular, e.g. Maroon *nkoko* "fowl", Twi-Asante *akoko*; and they sometimes phonologically remodel the class prefix *n* by placing a vowel before it (or lose it completely); e.g. Maroon *incheswa* "egg" (Williams 1937: p. 465), Twi-Asante *nkeswa* (plural), (but when I was in Scott's Hall I heard *keswa*, which is either the Akan singular form or the Akan plural form minus its prefix); Maroon *ishu*, Twi-Asante *nsu* "water"; and Maroon *isa*, Twi-Asante *nsa* "alcohol".

There are forms in Maroon language that either embody distinctive features of Akan phonology or can be analysed as phonological developments from an Akan base. One such archaism is the phenomenon of vowel harmony in a sequence of lax vowels, e.g. *kòtòkò*, a by-name frequently suffixed to Asante stems; *tòkòtòkò* "friend"; *apònkò* "horse" (cf. Akan *o-pònkò*); *asikèwè* "sugar" (cf. Akan *asikre*); and *òkòkò* "chicken" (cf. Akan *akòkò*). Others are the *r~l* variation (*bra~bla* "come") and the *s~sh* variation. The Jamaican Maroon language often preserves the *sh* considered by Dalby (1971: p. 44) to be obsolete in Akan. Thus Maroon *ishu* "water", modern Akan *nsu*, old Akan *nshu*; the modern form *s* appears in *asante* which in Maroon language is still *shante*. Note that modern English *Ashanti* prefers the old Akan (and Maroon) form.

The double articulation consonants, co-articulated stops (e.g. *kp, gb*) and prenasalised stops (e.g. *nd, nk*), characteristic of Akan do not generally occur in Maroon speech. But Dalby (1971: p. 45) cites *katègbè* and my own notes on Scott's Hall record an indecision in Maroon pronunciation between (i) a prenasalised stop, (ii) a syllabic nasal, and (iii) a full syllable containing vowel + *n*, for example in the word for "knife": (i) *ndepa*, (ii) *n-depa*, (iii) *indepa*. However, *indepa* clearly dominates, and the three forms taken together represent stages in the phonological evolution of Twi-Asante among the Maroons.

As we have seen, sometimes the nasal disappears altogether, e.g. Maroon *kuto*, Akan *nkutoo*. Perhaps the general loss of nasals in Saramaccan language of the Suriname Maroons (*bigi* "begin", *ma* "man") and in Jamaican *koni* "cunning" (also found among Maroons) is related to this loss of initial nasals. The Jamaican Maroon language has *piki-bo* (from *pikin(i)-bo)*; *yankipon*, Akan *nyankopo*; *akute*, Limba *kuteng*; *isu*, Akan *nsu* (by way of an earlier *insu* recorded by Williams); and *isa*, Akan *nsa* (by way of an earlier *insa*). In the last example both the nasal consonant and the nasal feature of the vowel disappear in the Maroon form. The reverse process, i.e. the appearance of a nasal, appears in words in the Jamaican Maroon language, in general Jamaican, and in Saramaccan: cf. Jamaican *sampata* (Spanish *zapato*); Maroon *enkensa* (Akan *kesua*); and Saramaccan *ain* "eye".

The Maroon Twi-Asante language, like other languages undergoing structural and functional loss as a result of contact, has become laced with importations from English and other languages, and with African words that had become "strange" and are provided with "folk etymologies" that "relate" them to English words. In many cases, the forms imported into Maroon Twi-Asante are relics of the old Jamaican language that have disappeared from contemporary Jamaican.

Williams (1937: p. 465) cites *deppa* and *entapie* as examples of English imports into Maroon Twi-Asante, and my own notes contain *ndepe* "knife". This is derived from the old Jamaican *ndefi*, a phonological adaptation of English *naif* (cf. Saramaccan *ndefi*, "knife", *wefi* "wife", *ndeti* "night"). My notes from Scott's Hall contain *agu* "pig" (see below for addition of final vowel), *suma* "someone" (cf. Saramaccan *suma*); and *chamu* "to eat" (cf. Krio *cham*).

Folk etymologies[2] include *browni* "European", derived from Twi *oburoni*[3] by association with English "brown" and *opreso* by association with English "oppressor". Williams (1938) cites the latter as *opprossoa* and Dalby (1971) ventures an Akan etymon *aberewa* "old woman" or *aboròwa* "white woman".

There is very little evidence on which to base a syntactical analysis of Twi-Asante as now used by Jamaican Maroons. What evidence there is sheds light on the historical relationship between Twi-Asante of Ghana and Twi-Asante of the Jamaican Maroons, as well as on the evolution of Jamaican Twi-Asante in contact with English. Africans in Jamaica developed what has come to be known as interlanguage, i.e. utterances that deviate from the norms of both languages in contact. Two processes with which we are already familiar combine to create this interlanguage. These are the gradual decay of the "lower" language through massive loss of structure and its replacement by importations from the "upper language" and special creations that are difficult to interpret historically; and the persistence of "lower" language forms during the acquisition of the "upper" language (that is sometimes called "interference" or "substratum influences"). We have treated these two processes as if they were discrete, but to do so is merely a methodological convenience based on a recognition of two distinct linguistic entities in Jamaica now (i.e. Twi-Asante and the general language of Jamaica). At the beginning of contact, however, when the communicative needs of and pressures on Africans were particularly great, there may have been no way of distinguishing between the transformation of Twi-Asante by loss of forms plus massive importations from English on the one hand and the persistence of Twi-Asante and other African language structures in the process of the acquisition of English on the other.[4] The utterances generated by Africans under pressure to communicate among themselves and with English speakers were not at first fixed, stable and systematic and could not easily and unequivocally be assigned to an idealised language system such as English or Twi-Asante, but rather belonged to interlanguage. Later, when slaves were more motivated to "speak English" and more aware of the English norm, either the English component in their language increased or the African continuities became more and more diluted (the net result is the same). This has culminated today in the existence of language forms that are still difficult to assign to an idealised language system and that can perhaps best be seen as differential degrees of continuity of African structures in the acquisition of English (plus some forms for which a historical interpretation is difficult).

Among Maroons the will to speak Twi-Asante (Coromantee) and an awareness of norms of Twi-Asante lingered on into the twentieth century, when the language has virtually died out in Jamaica. The few syntactical structures of the Maroon language with which we are acquainted demonstrate the nature of the interlanguage. Dalby (1971: p. 42) records several Maroon sentences that demonstrate the internal changes taking place in Twi-Asante, that were the result not of interference by another language but of loss of mastery of Twi-Asante resulting from a reduction in the functions of the language and the domains in which it was spoken. For basic Twi-Asante *me re ko a ba* "I am going to come", Dalby records the following four Maroon sentences:

1. *a me re ko oba*
2. *ame re ko aba*
3. *ame re ko obaba*
4. *mereko me ba*

The first three sentences seem to use a <u>Yoruba</u> or Ewe form of the personal pronoun (*ame*) instead of the strict Twi-Asante form *me* (which occurs only in the fourth sentence). However, it is also possible that *ame* is an instance of the generalised Jamaican topicaliser *a* ... ("it is"...), as in *a mi a go* "It is I who's going". Sentences (1) and (3) also appear to attach a third person pronoun prefix (*o-*) to the verb *ba*, which suggests a loss of mastery of the pronominal system and an inability to distinguish between pronominal prefixes. In the original Twi-Asante language it is only when the subject is a *noun* (rather than a pronoun) that the corresponding pronoun is prefixed. Such a sentence also occurs in the Maroon language: *obroni o da bra* "white man is coming". *Bra* is the imperative form of *ba* "come" in Twi-Asante, but in the Maroon language it often is used as the main verb.

As for importations from English and forms without clear historical antecedents, the Maroon language has *obroni o gaan* (and *obroni o góón*) side by side with *obroni o ko* "white man has gone", in which English *gaan* has replaced Twi-Asante *ko* in what for the rest remains a typical Twi-Asante sentence. *Da*, a Jamaican word (*mi (d)a go* "I am going") for which there is no obvious historical antecedent, replaces the Twi-Asante *re* in progressive action sentences: *obroni o da bra* "white man is coming".

3. Religion and the Need for an Esoteric Means of Communication

These are major themes of cultural marronage. Jamaica's Kumina religion has enabled the Kongo language, apparently in the form of the Kikongo dialect, to survive on the island. Warner Lewis (1977: p. 70) says of Kumina that "the control and maintenance of a proper relationship between God and/or the ancestral spirits on the one hand, and men on the other, is a knowledge of the African language (in this case Kikongo) ... This language is a powerful tool, for without it, the Kuyu i.e. the spirits or duppies, will not hear your summons or invocations."

Among Kumina adepts the African language is better preserved than among the Maroons and there is greater knowledge of its meaning. Even so, there is evidence of severe language change bordering on total language loss. As long as Kumina still has followers some African forms will persist, but they will continue to decay and will become less and less understood.

As far as form is concerned, the noun class system of Kikongo has broken down at the level of morpho-syntax or through phonological change:

Kumina	Kikongo	
zu	*nzu*	"house"
susu	*nsusu*	"chicken"
langu	*nlangu*	"water"
kombo	*ngombe*	"cow"
zambi	*nzambi*	"God"

4. Relatively Recent Migration to Jamaica

This has helped to preserve the Kikongo language in St Thomas and also explains why Kikongo has survived in Trelawny (Freeman's Hall). Kikongo in St Thomas (where it is used in the context of Kumina) is at a far less advanced state of decay than in Trelawny where it does not support the religion. The position of Kikongo in St Thomas demonstrates the role of religion in preserving a language in a situation of bilingual contact, and when St Thomas and Trelawny are compared, we get a picture of how language loss progressively occurs.

Recent migration to Jamaica also explains why fragments of the Yoruba language have survived in Westmoreland and Hanover (Whithorn, Abeokuta).

5. The Jamaican Language

African languages have played an extremely important part in the development of the mass language of Jamaica. This language is variously called "creole", "dialect", and "patois", but none of these terms is strictly appropriate. Here this language will be named according to the convention most widely followed in such matters, that is on the basis of the nationality of its speakers. I will therefore refer to the mass language of Jamaicans as "the Jamaican language", or simply "Jamaican".

The genesis and development of Jamaican is a subject that has attracted widespread interest among linguists working in "creole language studies". I will not specifically discuss these studies here since my concern is not with general theories of language change or creolisation[5] but with the evolution of African languages in Jamaica, where speakers of different African languages needed a medium of communication among themselves and between themselves and speakers of English.

The conditions of contact between English people and Africans in Jamaica inevitably led to the erosion of African languages and to what we shall call the acquisition of English. But the notion of "acquisition" is in reality no more than a descriptive convenience, for the process of language development to which it refers is an extremely complex one involving a varied set of communicative needs. This process is best viewed as a journey starting out from a West African base and moving toward an English target, even if the "target" may not have been a psychological reality for many Africans.

In what ways and to what extent were African elements preserved during the acquisition of English? The continuity of native language elements is a fundamental feature of second-language learning. The process is also called "interference", and the native language elements thus preserved are called "transfers" or "substratum" influences. Interference is both an empirically observable fact and a principle rationally deductible from a general theory of learning. It is not the only cause of change during second language learning, and, for example, current research is investigating the changes that occur "universally" in all cases of second language acquisition, regardless of the native language of the learner. (See Alleyne 1982.)

The "base" to which I referred above has the same surface diversity as religion and music, but, like religion and music, it has a common underlying structure. I discussed this in Chapter 2, and need not elaborate on it here. This common underlying structure produced identical or similar continuities in the acquisition of English by Africans of different ethnic subgroups. In the early period members of the Akan group probably set a pattern to which other groups easily accommodated and even contributed (with, for example, vocabulary items), or which they reinforced by virtue of similar or identical patterns in their own speech. Thus Jamaican forms plurals by placing the third person plural pronoun after the noun (*man dem* "men"), even though in Twi-Asante this plural formation is less common than prefixing; however, a number of other Kwa languages (such as Ewe and Yoruba) form plurals by means of the third person plural pronoun, thus reinforcing in Jamaican the less common of the two Twi-Asante plural-forming mechanisms.

The nature of the target toward which African speech in Jamaica moves is extremely complex. It would be interesting to know exactly what form of English was brought to Jamaica in the sixteenth and seventeenth centuries, but since this is not part of the main focus of this study, I shall not go further into it. The shape of the target has changed over the centuries; today it is Jamaican Standard English.

However, "target" is in many ways not a psychological reality. Military revolt by Maroons was only one form of resistance to assimilation to the English norm: there was also resistance to cultural assimilation. This cultural resistance took many forms, including both resistance to the adoption of an English language norm and the preservation of language codes incomprehensible to outsiders. Even today many Jamaicans, particularly teenagers whose native dialect is Standard Jamaican English, have turned to other forms of speech far removed from the standard English norm.

But still there has been a movement, sometimes conscious, sometimes unconscious, always inexorable, toward an English more closely approximating what is perceived as the ideal norm. In the past, during slavery, this movement could be explained almost entirely by the need for an instrument of communication between Africans and British. Since emancipation, however, the main driving force behind it has been the realisation by Blacks that command of English is a precondition for upward socioeconomic mobility. Thus two main factors influenced the development of language among the general African population of Jamaica. Both these factors moved the language toward English but at the same time prevented the complete assimilation of Africans to the existing norm of English. The main factor in this process had to do with the objective conditions of the contact situation: the different forms in which, and the different degrees to which, Africans and English interacted in Jamaica. The second important factor was more psychological in character, and had to do with the degree to which Africans were motivated to learn English (or, as the case may be, to assert their identity as Africans and to strive for their political freedom). It is only in this latter sense that the idea of English as a target – to be striven after or to be avoided – was a psychological reality for Africans.

Today this dichotomy between objective conditions of interaction among different groups of Jamaicans (in which the notion of target is not relevant) and the desire by some Jamaicans to "improve" their socioeconomic status by "improving" their English still holds. What is to a large extent new is the role played by schools in promoting an awareness of the target.

My position can therefore by summarised as follows: because Africans speaking different languages and coming from different parts of West Africa needed to communicate both among themselves and (less so) with Europeans (in this case English people, themselves speaking different dialects and coming from different parts of the United Kingdom), their language changed. It is axiomatic that during change caused by language contact of a certain sort elements of the language undergoing change will be transmitted to the new "target". No known community has ever moved from one language to another without such transmissions and continuities. Often, of course, they are eventually discarded and leave no trace whatsoever in the newly adopted language. First the vocabulary is discarded, then the morphology, then the syntax, and finally the phonology; within phonology the old intonation pattern apparently lasts longest.

These continuities and transmissions often become detached from their antecedents. They change in the course of transmission, either because of some degree of fusion with forms from other sources, or to pressures from the new environment, or to weakening of the links with antecedent forms. In the Afro-American case this is so not only for language but also for other forms of culture, including religion (see Herskovits 1947: p. 296).

The presence of African continuities in Jamaican helps to refute the theory that Jamaican is largely derived from English through processes variously described as "corruption", "pathological development", or, more recently, "pidginisation" and "creolisation". Many language forms explained as corruptions, simplifications, aberrations, pidginisations, and creolisations (whatever these terms may mean) of English can be shown to have very plausible West African antecedents.

Opponents of the theory that African elements persist in Afro-American culture often point to similar elements in cultures in areas of the world where Africans have never been. Opponents of the theory that African "substratum" influences persist in Afro-American languages ("creoles") likewise point to similar linguistic forms in languages scattered throughout the world. But there is no reason why the same linguistic form should not be explained by different factors in different places. "Substratum" influences must of course be substantiated *a fortiori* rather than merely asserted, and explanations in terms of such influences must be weighed against other possible explanations. But they cannot be ruled out just because similar forms exist elsewhere that have different histories. Thus the hypothesis that features of the Jamaican language such as vowel-final syllables and tone are West African in origin is not refuted by the presence of vowel-final syllables and tone in languages outside Africa, including in "pidgins" and "creoles" that are clearly not Africa-related. In many cases, different substrate languages underlying unrelated new languages born of cultural contact have similar structures, so that structures of the new languages also look similar even though they are unrelated. For example, Peruvian Andean Spanish, Sierra Leone Krio, and Papiamentu (spoken in the Dutch West Indian islands of Curaçao and Aruba) all have the double possessive (e.g. in Andean Spanish *el abuelo su hermano* "the grandfather's brother", i.e. "the grandfather his brother"), but whereas in Peru the source is Quechua, in the case of Krio and Papiamentu[6] it is probably West Africa (cf. Twi *Ata ne na* "Ata's mother", i.e. "Ata his mother"). The Jamaican juxtaposition of two nouns unconnected by a possessive pronoun to express possession as well as the supposed absence of copula are also features of Tok Pisin (Melanesian Pidgin English), but in both Tok Pisin and Jamaican they are adequately explained by formally similar but wholly unrelated substrate influences. Those scholars who build theories about the so-called "universals" of "creole" structure on the basis of similarities between historically unconnected "creoles" tend to ignore these influences.

That is not to deny that we need a theory of language acquisition and language shift to inform our interpretation of the emergence and development of the Jamaican language. Such a theory would have to encompass theories of language competence and language performance, theories of general learning and language learning, and theories of cultural transmission. I hope that people interested in such theories will re-examine them in the light of this study and of my earlier study (Alleyne 1980). A theory of cultural transmission is implicit in my analysis, and language theories are implicit in learning theories.

There are two basic competing theories of learning that correspond to two competing theories of language: the behavioural and the cognitive. Essentially the issue is whether deviations from the norm of a language in the speech of speakers who learn it as a second language are "errors" not determined by any factors in the input languages or transfers from the native language. And if "errors", whether they are "universal" errors. Many who support the theory that deviations from the norm are "errors" not caused by substrate interference have looked for systematic "errors" in different instances of second language acquisition, and refer to "errors" that systematically occur as "simplification universals". Some have even described "pidginisation" in terms of such "simplification errors" (cf. Schumann 1978). In other words people are trying to create a broad theoretical framework in which "pidginisation", with universal processes and forms, would be inherent in the initial stages of second-language acquisition. I welcome the search for a general framework, but I am convinced by the evidence presented here and in Alleyne 1980 that the theory of native language transfers is stronger than that of universal simplification errors in the case of Jamaican (and other Caribbean creole languages). While evidence of universal simplification errors (regardless of the nature of the input materials) is scant, numerous studies show that speakers of different languages learning the same language tend to learn it differently, and the differences (or "mistakes") are caused by differences in their mother tongues. This is why different ethnic dialects of English emerged in the United States, and why Africans speak English differently from Indians, Indians from Filipinos, West Africans from East Africans, Twi speakers from Bantu speakers, and so on. Given the current interest in language universals, the search for universal simplification errors in second-language acquisition may look more rewarding intellectually, but it flies in the face of much evidence.

The nature of the contact situation in which the Jamaican language developed, both in towns and trading stations on the West African coast and on the plantations in Jamaica placed Africans in different kinds of contact both with the English language and English culture and with Africans of other ethnic origins. Descriptions of the West African locus (e.g. Lawrence 1963) show how different groups of Africans related differently with the European traders, soldiers, and others. The situation in Jamaica was analogous. Many writers have described occupational stratification in the colonies and shown how it underlies present sociocultural and economic stratification in the West Indies and North America. Although slave society was highly homogeneous, it was also hierarchically structured in terms of occupation, privileges, and access to the culture of the masters. This meant that some slaves began to think and behave – and to speak – differently from others. The main occupational difference was between domestic and field slaves; artisans (including "drivers") occupied an intermediate position. Domestics were in close contact with Europeans; their cottages were even white-washed and located near their masters' houses (Settle 1933). The masters favoured their domestics, especially those that bore them children (i.e. mulattoes). The domestics developed forms of language and behaviour appropriate to their occupational needs and status. But though they began to behave more like the Europeans, they still had to maintain links with other slave groups. Patterson (1967: p. 54) notes that the head driver and head cooper lived only two hundred yards from the overseer while the rest of the slaves lived a half a mile away. At the end of one day the head driver got work quotas from the overseer for the following day and had to communicate them to the different classes of slaves. Most slaves worked in the fields. Field slaves were far removed from contact with Europeans, and rarely communicated or had social relations with people other than field slaves. Members of the middle group, chiefly artisans, headmen, "drivers", and perhaps also freedmen doing odd jobs in the developing urban centres and market places, met and communicated with both domestic and field slaves and their speech was therefore influenced by both groups.

During the early years of plantation slavery an important sociocultural distinction emerged between the *bozal* ("slave born in Africa") and the *creole* ("slave born in the colonies"). The *bozal*, regardless of his or her occupation in Jamaica, would pass through all the stages of acculturation: the language of the *bozal* would at first be heavily marked by native speech habits, but in time these habits would be progressively eliminated. The rate at which slaves traversed these stages depended largely on their occupational histories. The creole slaves, on the other hand, learned to speak like members of the group to which they or their parents belonged. Slaves who spent their lives among domestics spoke as domestics and their form of speech differed significantly from that of the field slaves. Many accounts of the time refer to this difference between the *bozal* and the *creole* and look particularly at language differences (cf. Alvarez 1961).

Not all domestics identified with the group of domestics (some led slave revolts); similarly, not all field slaves identified with field slaves. To the extent that slaves identified with groups to which they did not belong by occupation, they developed forms of behaviour, including speech behaviour, typical of those groups. The wider an individual's range of contacts and the more complex his or her self-image and identification, the more styles and levels of language he or she acquired.

Economic changes after emancipation brought new influences into play in Jamaica. In Barbados, most emancipated slaves stayed on the sugar plantations. The plantation as a social institution afforded little opportunity for primary social contact between master and slave or between manager and field worker. Even so, Blacks and Whites interacted more on the plantations than they did in Jamaica, where former slaves left the plantations in large numbers after emancipation and set up communities of smallholders in the remote hills.

In Jamaica Blacks have acculturated less to Whites than in Barbados. In Jamaica the form of speech – mainly rural – commonly called "creole" still shows clear links to field slave speech, of which it is the modern representative. Today there are other levels of speech alongside "creole" in Jamaica that show fewer links with the earliest period and are modern representatives of the speech of drivers, artisans, and domestics. Taken together, these levels form what is called Jamaica's linguistic continuum. Any variable – phonological, morpho-syntactical, or lexico-semantic – may appear in forms identified or identifiable with the basic "creole" variety, with the standard dialect, or with any one of a number of intermediate bands in the continuum. These intermediate variants can generally be ranged, in terms of their formal characteristics and grammatical structure and in terms of speakers' reaction to them[7], along a scale of degrees of approximation either to the "target" (Standard English) or to the base ("creole"). This scale may also be calibrated in terms of the degree of continuity (or loss) of West African features. West African features prevail at the "creole" end of the continuum and are progressively replaced by forms approximating more and more to Standard English.

The term "decreolisation" is sometimes used in connection with intermediate speech varieties in Jamaica (as well as in Antigua and in Guyana, and in connection with the non-standard English dialect of Trinidad and Barbados). Decreolisation refers to the process by which a "creole" dialect is modified in the direction of the standard dialect. Even the basic "creole" dialect of Jamaica (or of Antigua or Guyana) can therefore by analysed as an instance of decreolisation, since the contemporary "creole" form is much closer to Standard English than its seventeenth, eighteenth, and nineteenth century forms. My own argument up to now has been that what is here called creolisation (preceded, according to most of those who uphold the theory, by an initial stage of pidginisation) is in reality an initial phase (or rather, series of phases) in bilingual contact in which large numbers of West African linguistic features persist but are subsequently eliminated as contact with English grows and endures. This progressive elimination of African features and their replacement by Standard-like forms, or forms typically representing intermediate approximations to the Standard dialect, is apparently what is meant by the term "decreolisation". However, the process thus understood is not just a uniform and unilinear succession of chronological stages, but a complex reflection of different types of social and cultural relationships both among Africans and between Africans and Europeans. Intermediate varieties of speech have existed for as long as "creole" varieties, though they were at first demographically less important and less frequently used and acknowledged.

Speech variation is very intense in Jamaica, and speakers command a series of levels or registers through which they shift without any necessarily apparent motivation. Jamaican intuitions about grammaticality are based largely on prescriptive norms set by the schools or by the elite. Beryl Bailey (1966) and LePage (1960) claim to have isolated a level called "creole" in descriptive studies. But Bailey's data are very different from LePage's. LePage, who is not a native speaker of Jamaican, based his analysis exclusively on data that he collected through research. Bailey, who is Jamaican, used her knowledge as a native speaker to abstract a set of forms from actual usage and assign them to a system called "creole". What she constructs is therefore an ideal system not wholly represented by any speaker. Bailey's system may be valid as a descriptive or analytic construct to meet the demands of a certain theory, but it does not come to grips with the linguistic reality of Jamaica.

There are two ways of conceptualising the continuum: as a distribution of three codes ("creole", "intermediate", and "Standard") or as a gradual shading off from one pole to the other through a series of minimal shifts at all levels of structure. In this second case, linguistic forms and structures which can be plausibly shown to have West African historical origins are progressively replaced by forms and structures approximating in varying degrees to English. Sometimes it is not immediately obvious that one form is closer to English than another. For example, in the variation *mi ben kom ~ mi did kom ~ mi kyeem* "I came", the second form is not obviously closer to English than the first, though most people would probably think it is. The relationship to English of expressions like *mi did a kom* "I was coming" is extremely tenuous (leaving aside form of the individual words). On the other hand, in the variation *mi a kom ~ mi komin* "I am coming", the second form is obviously closer to English than the first. The following sentences will illustrate the nature of the Jamaican continuum as a gradual progression from West African to Standard English forms:

(i) *ĩ a nyam ĩ dina*   "He/she/it is eating his/her/its dinner"

(ii)	*shi a nyam shi dina*	"She is eating her dinner"
(iii)	*im a nyam im dina*	"He is eating his dinner"
(iv)	*shi a nyam ar dina*	"She is eating her dinner"
(v)	*im a iit im dina*	"He/(she) is eating his/(her) dinner"
(vi)	*(h)im iitin (h)im dina*	"He/(she) is eating his/(her) dinner"
(vii)	*(h)im iz iitin (h)im dinner*	"He is eating his dinner"
(viii)	*hi iz iitin hiz dinner*	"He is eating his dinner"

The absence of gender and case distinctions in the pronominal system in (i) has West African antecedents. The lexical root *nyam*, the nasalised phoneme $\tilde{i}$, and the reflex *a* (English *-er*) are also West African in origin. The stressed vowel of *dina* is a high front vowel, representing the use of one high vowel *i* as the reflex of both the English *i* and lower high *I*. Levels (ii) and (iii) introduce gender distinctions for the personal pronoun and level (iv) introduces case distinctions. Level (vi) accomplishes the major structural and typological shift from a verbal system based on particles preposed to the verb (*a nyam*) to an inflected suffixal system (*iitin*). Level (vii) introduces the typically English vowel ʌ, but the form *dinner* never completely conforms to British or North American Standard English in which unstressed final vowels typically become *schwa* (i.e. they become more centralised). Level (vii) also introduces an auxiliary *iz*, but at this level *iz* remains invariable – it does not change for person and number, nor does it have a contracted form.

The eight sentences are abstractions. They give the impression of an orderly shift from one pole to the other achieved by minimal changes. But the levels of Jamaican speech are not so logically ordered, and there are no clearly demarcated groups of speakers corresponding to the clearly ordered levels represented by these model sentences. Forms from different levels can be combined in a vast number of permutations. One and the same speaker will sometimes use $\tilde{i}$ for females and at other times *im*, and perhaps combine them with the inflected form *iitin* or even with *nyamin*. Thus the sentence *im nyamin im dina* "she is eating her dinner" is possible, though perhaps not now very frequently spoken. *Hi a nyam (h)im dina*, which combines the Standard form *hi* with the opposite polar forms *a nyam*, is also possible.

However, the continuum is probably not infinite: it is likely that there are limitations on the range of possible combinations, i.e. on the co-occurrence of forms at the same structural level (say syntax) and of forms at different levels (say syntax and lexicon). For example, the utterance *he iz nyaming hiz dina*, which combines ultra-Standard features like *ng* with the African-derived lexeme *nyam*, would not occur; or if it did, the speaker of it would be seeking some special effect. It seems that forms in the register to which *nyam* typically belongs cannot occur together with the grammatical and phonological feature of *iz...ing*. Sentences like *mi a iit mi dina, mi iitin mi dina, mi iz iitin mi dina, a iitin mi dina,* or *ai iitin mai dina* (all meaning "I am eating my dinner") are all possible and frequent. But *mi am iitin(g)* does not occur, perhaps because *am* belongs to one of the highest registers of standard usage and could not combine with basic creole *mi*.

These co-occurrence restrictions are probably caused by the persistence of fragments of old and dying grammars. In the past field slaves, who formed the majority of the population in Jamaica, had few if any social relations outside their own group. Their "creole" grammar remained highly homogeneous, stable, and consistent for as long as they were numerically strong, directed mainly or exclusively toward their own group, and isolated from other groups.[8] Since slaves were not socially mobile, there was no pressure on them to adopt speech behaviour typical of other groups. This changed with the emancipation of slaves and other social reforms, particularly the introduction of public education. These reforms made social mobility possible and created strong pressures on people to modify their speech in the direction of the prestige norm. This led not so much to the mixing of "creole" forms with "standard" forms as to the rejection of a number of features seen as deviating most from English and the adoption by people of speech characteristics of the social group immediately above them. First, there was a constant erosion of features such as vowel-final syllables, the genderless pronominal system, and nasalised vowels (in variation V + N), which gradually became obsolete, residual, or extinct. Second, fewer and fewer people used the most deviant speech forms, while more and more used the intermediate varieties that during slavery were used by only a small minority of slaves. The extreme variability of contemporary Jamaican speech is the result of the disappearance of forms that belonged to a relatively well constituted and homogeneous dialect; the dialect disappeared because the class of people who spoke it most consistently disappeared. There have been few phonological or syntactical innovations in the modern period; instead there have been shifts in the frequency with which intermediate forms are used, along with a great deal of variability in individual speech.

In what remains of this chapter I will give some examples of West African language continuities at the levels of phonology, morphosyntax, and lexico-semantics and show how they changed as the Jamaican language developed.

Phonology

Since language change does not affect all forms (or all speakers) simultaneously, there will always be at any point in time forms (and speakers) that do not embody changes. These "archaic" forms belong to earlier periods and stages in the language; they are relics of the past, and we must assume that the patterns they reflect were previously more widespread in the language. "Archaic" forms are therefore useful for reconstructing language history. Here are some phonological examples of such forms:

Some Jamaican words end in vowels whereas the words from which they are derived do not, e.g. *rata* "rat", *yeri* "hear", *goudi* "gourd", *ku* (from *luku* "look"), and *taki* "talk". The most plausible interpretation of this pattern is that it was once general, i.e. at first all words in the Jamaican language ended in vowels. This interpretation is supported by the fact that vowel finals are general in Saramaccan and Sranan, the languages of Suriname (cf. *rata, ye(r)i, godi, dede* "dead", *musu* "mouse", *waka* "walk"), and are more copiously documented for earlier periods of Jamaican history than for later periods. For example, Russell (1868) cites some nineteenth century forms that no longer exist today: *dari* "that" and *ala* "all". This addition of vowels can be explained as a restructuring of English syllables in line with the structure of West African syllables, which typically close not with consonants but with vowels. It was only in the course of time that Jamaican syllables acquired consonants in final position: *that, all*. This change also affected African words with final vowels. Thus in accordance with the change *rata* to *rat, poto-poto* "mud" became *pot-pot*.

Syllable restructuring also affects consonant clusters. The West African syllabic structure is *(C)V* in which a single (but not double) *C* (consonant) optionally appears before a *V* (vowel). Modern Jamaican forms that preserve this pattern include *simit* "smith", *siniek* "snake", *sumaal* "small", *worom* "worm", *panchalam* "Spanish elm", and *ferin* "fern". Note that vowel insertion affects consonant clusters whose second member is a nasal consonant. Clusters of *s* and oral consonant conform to the canonic pattern by eliminating the first of the two consonants. Thus *top* "stop", *pit* "spit", and *kip* "skip". Double consonants, usually consonant + *r* (e.g. *true*), in contemporary Jamaican were probably earlier interrupted by vowels. Russell (1868: p. 8) cites *toroo* "true"; such forms occur regularly in the Suriname languages. Today in Jamaica one still sometimes hears pronunciations such as *òròb* "herb" where the inserted vowel is only slightly prominent.

Pitch or tone is another phonological feature that survives in relic or latent form in Jamaican and that was more widespread in earlier stages of the language. Pitch today affects sound gestures such $\overset{1}{m}\overset{1}{m}$ "no", $\overset{1}{m}h\overset{3}{m}$ "yes" and $\overset{3}{m}\overset{3}{m}$ "exclamation of surprise". It also has a morphosyntactic function in the following types of expression:

di m$\overset{3}{a}$n k$\overset{1}{o}$w	"the man's cow"
di m$\overset{1}{a}$n k$\overset{3}{o}$w	"the bull"
mi$\overset{1}{e}$ri br$\overset{3}{o}$wn	"Mary Brown"
mi$\overset{3}{e}$ri br$\overset{1}{o}$wn	"Mary is brown"

$wi\ ky\overset{1}{a}n\ du\ it$ "We can do it"
$wi\ ky\overset{3}{aa}n\ du\ it$ "We can't do it"

Pitch in the early stages of the Jamaican language was – and in Saramaccan still is – a distinctive feature of the phonological shape of morphemes (words) and not merely of sound gestures and morphosyntactical constructions (as in the above examples). Pitch as a distinctive feature (for differentiating meanings) is not altogether absent from Jamaican even now, but its role is considerably reduced and may be interpreted as a predictable concomitant feature of the length of the syllable. Thus pairs like:

$ma\overset{3}{a}ta$ "mortar"
$mata$ "matter"
$bi\overset{1}{i}ta$ "beater"
$bita$ "bitter"

are distinguished both by pitch (falling on the first member of the pair, mid-even on the second) and by length. It is length that is seen as primarily distinctive; pitch is then predictable from length (but *see* Lawton 1963). It therefore seems that evolutionary tendencies in the role and structure of pitch, already evident in Niger-Congo and reaching their most advanced form in Kwa languages (Stewart 1971), continued in Jamaican.

D~R

It is likely that when Twi-Asante arrived in Jamaica, a change took place (already nearing completion in Twi-Asante) by which *d* became *r*. Christaller (1875: p. 11) makes mention of *d* and *r* as "interchanging within the same dialect or in different dialects of Akan" (thus *nera~neda* "yesterday"), with *d* as the archaic or obsolete form. Thus Twi-Asante's progressive aspect particle *re* was formerly *de*. (Cf. Jamaican *de* as in *mi de go* "I am going".) The historical alternation between *d* and *r* is present in Sranan and Saramaccan, though it is neither widespread nor regular. Thus while Sranan has *siri* "seed" and *brara* "brother", in which *d* has become *r*, *d* remains intact in most Sranan words. We may therefore conclude either that *d* regularly became *r* in Suriname but was later restored under British and Dutch influence, or that Twi-Asante was still vacillating between *d* and *r* when it reached the Caribbean. Jamaican shows some relics of this in the alternations *tada~tara* "other" and *nada~nara* "another", and in the derivation of *kasara* "cassava" from *casada*.

Perhaps the most regular and persistent Twi-Asante-derived feature of Jamaican phonology is the alternation between *v* and *b*. Here we are not dealing with relics but with modern vibrant forms like *neba* "never", *beks* "angry", and *hebi* "heavy". Some other words show a fixed (i.e. not alternating) occurrence of *b*: e.g. *bikl* "victuals" and *busha* "overseer".

Morphosyntax

The morphosyntax of Jamaican, once it was established in the sixteenth and seventeenth centuries, has changed little apart from changes connected with the various stages of the continuum. These different stages were, as we have seen, a reflection of different degrees of approximation to Standard English or of different degrees of continuity of West African language structure.

The question of the origin of the morphosyntax of Jamaican (or of that of other so-called creole languages) has provoked much controversy. Not everyone accepts the view (set out in Alleyne, 1980) that Jamaican morphosyntax (or at least certain aspects of it) can be explained as the product of native language continuities in the speech of second-language learners. However, plausible identifications can be made between a generalised West African morphosyntax (or a specific Twi-Asante morphosyntax) and the morphosyntax of Jamaican, and these identifications are unlikely to be accidental.

The main change in Jamaican syntax is that some words associated with certain grammatical rules and categories have lost or changed their functions. To put it another way, some members of classes of words that behaved syntactically in one way at the time of the formation of Jamaican (thereby creating a general grammatical "rule") later stopped behaving in that way. They dropped from the grammatical category or "rule", so that the rule became only partly applicable and had to be qualified by "exceptions".

The distinction between "adjectives" and "verbs", nebulous even in modern Jamaican, was probably even more blurred at the time that this language was formed. Welmers (1973: p. 274) writes of West African languages that:

> for non-Bantu languages the descriptions very commonly betray a great deal of confusion on the subject, usually stemming from the tacit assumption that the equivalents of English adjectives will be adjectives in other languages ... This area of analysis, at least for Niger–Congo languages, is by no means the easiest to explore. But the message derived from the discussions above is loud and clear: be suspicious of "adjectives"; some of them are not.

The same thing can be said of Jamaican, but the need for suspicion diminishes over time, as the language becomes more like English. Today, words like *strong, heavy,* and *small* behave like adjectives. But formerly they were transitive verbs that could have a subject and an object in some types of sentences. Relics of this function can still be found today in words like *mad, sick, hot, cold*, and *full*, which are first and foremost transitive verbs:

dem mad mi	"they made me mad"
dem sick mi	"they made me sick"
dem full it	"they filled it"

They are exactly parallel to other more easily recognisable transitive verbs: *dem cut it*: "they cut it"; *dem sell it*: "they sold it". Both sets of transitive verbs may be used "intransitively": *mi mad; mi sick; it full; it cut; it sell*.

This transitive feature may exist latently in many more "adjectives", and is perhaps activated by specific stimuli. Take for example this conversation that I heard on a Jamaican bus:

Passenger: *this bus late , ii*? (adjective/verb)
Conductor: *is unu late the bus* (transitive verb): "it's you all that made the bus late".

However, when these adjectives are being used as transitive verbs, there is now a tendency for them to take a suffix -*up*. Thus *nice-up, pretty-up*, and so on.

West African languages have a grammatical category called instrumental. It is rendered by a verb meaning "take" followed by an object followed by another verb. (This is an example of what is called serial verb construction.) Thus Yoruba:

Ojo fi igi na Meri
Ojo take stick beat Mary
"Ojo beat Mary with a stick"

This structure is obligatory in some languages that cannot construct a pattern such as the English phrase "beat with a stick". In other West African languages both patterns exist, though the serial verb construction is more typical and more often used. In Jamaican, the serial verb construction has become less frequent and tends only to be used in sentences that are instrumental in meaning (the Yoruba sentence cited above translates directly into Jamaican). Sentences such as: (Twi Asante) *ò de infonini kyere neba* (he take picture show his child), "he showed his child a picture"; or (Ewe) *è tsò dòme gegi yi afe* (he take empty belly go home); "he went home hungry", are no longer possible in Jamaican, or else they are used very infrequently.

At intermediate levels of the Jamaican language continuum, *and* is introduced to link the two verbs, and *use* may replace *take* to make the construction more like standard English. Thus: *He use a stick and beat Mary*. In Twi Asante and other Niger Congo languages, a verb meaning "to say" introduces a wide range of subordinate clauses. Thus: (Twi Asante) *me pe sè òko* (I want say he go), "I want him to go"; (Yoruba) *paapaa tori pe ...* (even reason say...), "even if...". The range of similar constructions is still quite wide in Jamaican, but in the past it was probably wider still: (Jamaican) *any how say ...* "if (he dares)..."; *even if say ...* "even if..."; *we believe say ...* "we believe that...".

For a more adequate list of structural identifications between Jamaican and Niger-Congo, see Alleyne 1980.

Lexico-semantics

There were obviously far more West African words in the Jamaican language in the past than there are now. Many such words have now become archaic; they are used infrequently and only by older country people. African words disappeared from Jamaican either because they came to be stigmatised in the course of the general pejoration of "folk" culture by urban culture or because they referred to West African artifacts that themselves fell out of use in Jamaica. Things like the *benta* (a musical instrument) and *dukunu* (a sort of food) no longer exist actively in Jamaican culture, so the African words that designate them have become (or are becoming) archaic or obsolete. Other African words for things still used, such as the names of various yams (*afu*, *pumpum*, *taya* and *bayere*) and words like *bankra* "basket" and *ackee* remain vibrant.

A number of African words referring to objects, actions and concepts of a very general nature, not specific to any particular culture, have also persisted in the Jamaican language, showing how tenacious are the African roots of its vocabulary. In most cases they exist side by side with English derived words, e.g. *unu* "you", *nyam* "eat", *juk* "stab", *poto-poto* "mud", *dopi* "spirit", *doti* "earth".

West African semantic structures are also present in the Jamaican language, though they have changed somewhat in the course of time. Gender and generation are expressed by affixing words meaning "male", "female", "mother", "father", or "child" to a neutral stem. Thus *man cow* means "bull", *woman cow* means "heifer", and *cow pikni* means "calf". This device is related to another that forms names by juxtaposing the names of two primary objects. A finite set of central concepts is used to form the names of an infinite set of objects. Such naming is definitional rather than arbitrary. Thus *eye water* means "tears", *mouth water* "saliva", *nose hole* "nostril", *head back* "nape", and *hand middle* "palm". Some of these words have by now given way to arbitrary names derived from English. At one time Jamaicans probably used expressions such as *bobi mofo* "nipple" (lit. "breast mouth"), *ago futu* "heel" (lit. "knot foot"), and *ago mau* "ankle" (lit. "knot hand"), still found today in Suriname. This method of labelling is common in West African languages, e.g. *ana miri* "eye water" and *òno miri* "mouth water" in Igbo and *bar bu sèt* "day clean" ("dawn") in Wolof. Jamaican has also preserved with little change a pattern of associating abstract concepts with parts of the body. Niger-Congo languages are full of lexico-semantic units such as *hard ears* "stubbornness", e.g. *ano kware* "truth" ("mouth true"), *aso oden* "disobedience" ("ear hard"), *ano yede* "flattery" ("mouth sweet") in Yoruba; and *kanga ntima* "stubbornness" ("tie heart") in Kikongo. Saramaccan (a language of Suriname) contains many such forms; and Russell (1868) cites a number (used adjectivally) in Jamaican though they are no longer used today: *pick mouth* "troublesome", *strong eye* "domineering", *strong physic* "hot-tempered", and *strong head* "stubbornness", *big eye* "greed", *dry eye* "boldness", *hard ears* "stubbornness", and *cut eye* "scorn" are the forms most often heard.

6. New Twentieth-Century Philosophies and Ideologies: Black Nationalism and Rastafarianism

It is well known that philosophical, political and intellectual movements shape languages. The lexicon of French, for example, changed greatly at the time of the French revolution. Special interest groups in a society often "create" a new "language", chiefly in the lexical field. Halliday (1978: pp. 164–5) refers to an "antisociety", i.e. "a society that is set up within another society as a conscious alternative to it. It is a mode of resistance, resistance which may take the form either of passive symbiosis or of active hostility and even destruction." Halliday also speaks of an "antilanguage" generated by the antisociety.

If we ignore the pathological connotations of Halliday's analysis, his observations about "antilanguage" and the role of philosophical and ideological movements in language evolution can be applied to the language of Rastafarianism. This language is an excellent example of the impact of social forces on cultural institutions. Even so, the form and function of Rastafari language can best be analysed in terms of a theory of African continuity.

Rastafari language differs from the "antilanguages" mentioned by Halliday in one important way. Languages of antisocial groups are strongly influenced by the need for secrecy and for an esoteric form of communication. But Rastafari language has no such motivation or intent, for Rastafarianism is universalistic. Rastafari language flows directly from Rastafari philosophy and expresses a fundamental relationship of humans to nature and the universe. The Rastafari goal is not to restrict communication but to widen it by removing internal inconsistencies in the semantic structure of the language, reducing incompatibilities between language form and function, and reducing the arbitrariness of the linguistic sign.

These aims are related to a philosophical view of language and of the word as well as to an aesthetic view of language that leads to the cultivation of various forms of verbal art. Rastas believe in the "evocative power of the word", i.e. the power of the word to evoke and, in a sense, to be the thing meant. According to Yawney (1972: p. 30), "to the Rastas, words are seals of the mind, words have power and they must not be abused but rather used with awareness." Pollard (1980: p. 6) mentions "changes in the lexicon to reflect the philosophical position of the speaker". Nettleford (1978: p. 201) talks of the "small but pointedly relevant lexicon of normative/descriptive word-symbols" and (in Owens 1976: p. ix) of "a means of communication that would faithfully reflect the specificities of [Rastafari] experience and perception of self, life and the world".

As we have seen, the Kikongo believe that personal names are mystically associated with their owners, and that a name falling into unauthorised hands can be manipulated to harm or control the name's holder. This belief in the power of names exists in different degrees throughout the Caribbean. Dalby (1970: pp. 20–1) speaks of the great importance of "verbal ability and style in Africa". The *nommo* concept discussed by Jahn is an expression of the West African belief in the mystical creative power of the word.

There is little in the historical record to prove a continuous link between the word philosophies of Africa and of modern Rastafarianism, but Barry Chevannes (cited in Pollard 1980) suggests such a link when he claims that Rastafari young men who had come together in or around 1949 under the name "Youth Black Faith" initiated the "jargon presently attributed to the Rastafari as a whole" by "carrying further" the tradition mentioned by Martha Beckwith, that is the "facility with which Jamaicans pun" and the "easy loquacity of the Jamaican peasant". True, "pre-literate" societies tend to develop high verbal skills, and the alienation of the Rastafari from Jamaican society was a main cause of the emergence of the Rastafari "antilanguage". But beyond this there is evidence that the Rastafari belief in the power of the word is an African continuity upon which Rastas successfully built.

The Rastafari language is an off-shoot from Jamaican. The main modifications have been in the lexicon, in forms of greeting and address, and in the pronominal system. Pollard (1980) divides the lexicon into four categories: (1) known items that bear new meanings; (2) words that bear the weight of their phonological implication; (3) I-words and Y-words; and (4) new items.

Categories (2) and (3) exemplify the issues that I have been discussing. In both cases, the Rastafari seek to bring the form of the word closer to the meaning and to eliminate inconsistencies between form (i.e. sound) and meaning. As far as category (2) is concerned, the point of departure is the association that has already been established in Jamaican English (and in other forms of English) between a certain sound sequence and a certain meaning. In other words, once this association is accepted, the sign loses a great deal of its arbitrariness and acquires some measure of motivation, i.e. it acquires an inherent relationship with meaning, akin to onomatopoeia and sound symbolism. Wherever the particular sound sequence occurs, it must convey the same meaning. Thus the first syllable of the word *oppressor* has the sound sequence *op* which has acquired an inherent relationship with the meaning "up". Since *oppress* (*oppressor, oppression*) means to "keep down", there is an incompatibility between form (*op*) and meaning ("down"). Thus the Rastafari language has the word *downpress* "to keep down". Similarly it has the words *overstand* "to understand"; *outformer* "informer"; *blindgaret* "cigarette" and many others constructed in the same way.

Category (3) provides us with the best examples of Rastafari word philosophy. The foundation of this philosophy, insofar as it can be put in lay terms, is a categorisation of the world into positive and negative forces, and a belief that language should reflect this categorisation. The most positive force is perception, physically realised through the eye by means of the sense of sight and leading to the metaphysical realisation of the self, the ego, the "I". Language, and especially words, have a relationship that is not accidental but necessary with these forces, therefore words *are* these forces rather than merely symbolising them. It is therefore no accident that the word "sight" contains the sound sequence *ai*, which recurs in the word "eye", instrument of perception, and in the pronoun "I". This also results in a major morphological departure from general Jamaican in the pronominal system. *I* replaces "me" and "we" in the first person forms (*I* is a singular form for subject, object, and possessive; *I and I* is the plural form and in some cases is the singular form as well, for all the cases). Second person pronoun is the *I*, which could equally well be written as "the eye". Other words that have this sound sequence are *Haile* (Selassie), *Zion* and *height* all expressing highly positive forces. The sound sequence *ai* is generalised to a number of other words, thus producing a new derivational morpheme meaning something like "positive". Examples of this derivation are *ailalu* "calalu"; *ainana* "banana"; *aipa* "pepper"; and *aital* "vital"; and most significantly *Rastafari*, pronounced with the "eye" or "I" sound at the end. It is now the most productive derivational device in the Jamaican language.

Conclusion: The Modern Period

I have examined the ways in which African culture changed in Jamaica in the fields of language, religion, and music. My main reasons for choosing these three fields are first that they have always been central to Jamaican social and cultural concerns and second that they are closely integrated both in Africa and in African Jamaica (though I have separated them for analytical convenience).

Parallels exist between language, religion, and music in Jamaica, both structurally and functionally. The distinction between deep and surface structure is useful in all three fields. In each case, deep structure is African, while surface structure is influenced by other cultures with which Africans have been in contact. This distinction enables us to go beyond the view that Jamaican culture is a mere mixing (or synthesis or syncretism) of African and European forms and to deal with it instead as a process; it enables us to explain this process rather than just list or describe objects. In religion, deep structural meaning is rendered by surface form; in language, deep structure syntax is distinguished from surface vocabulary; and in music, rhythm is distinguished from melody.

The function of religion and music in Jamaica was to draw Africans of diverse origins together, to break down barriers between them, and to allow them to communicate with one another until a common speech form crystallised. Jamaican cultural behaviour was deeply ambiguous; its range and variation allowed African Jamaicans to communicate both among themselves (and thus to consolidate their ethnic identity) and with non-Africans. This inherent structural ambiguity meant that any single cultural form or expression had one meaning for African Jamaicans and another for non-Africans.

In the twentieth century Rastafarianism merely continues along this path and integrates language, religion, and music at an even higher level. Now, as in the beginning, religion, music and language are the focal points of African Jamaican culture. For Rastafari and for followers of more generally accepted Africa-derived religions, music and worship are inseparable; for orthodox Christians music is an optional embellishment on worship, but in Africa and in African Jamaica it is an indispensable channel for communicating and interacting with God and the spirits. In Zaire, Catholic acolytes are said to dance while singing the "Glory to God" in Kikongo. It is an extraordinary fact that Rastafari language functions in similar ways to language in Africa, though we know too little about the earlier stages of language development in Jamaica to be able to reconstruct a continuous process through the seventeenth, eighteenth, and nineteenth centuries. (See p. 184 above for different types of Africanisms in Jamaica, including some that are not linear continuities.) In Africa and among the Rastafari, the magical, evocative power of the word gives it an inherent and non-arbitrary relationship to the thing meant. So the Rastafari idea of language is an expression of African culture that either remained latent throughout three centuries only to re-emerge with explosive vitality in recent times or one that persisted all along in Jamaica's Black society, unnoticed by writers and observers of the White elite.

We have reached present-day frontiers in our journey through the history of Jamaica, and must pause to reflect before we cross them. The task of analysing contemporary expressions of Black Jamaican culture is awesome. Generalities about the past are far easier to make than generalities about the present. The culture of African Jamaicans in the past was relatively homogeneous (despite some ethnic differences, especially among Jamaicans born in Africa), so that generalisations about it were often valid. Today, however, the complexity is bewildering; and things are changing so rapidly that generalisations valid today are no longer valid tomorrow. In just fifteen years four different forms of popular music (ska, blue beat, rock steady, reggae) have emerged to take their place alongside mento and other resurgent styles, and Rastafarianism is quickly becoming the main focus of Jamaican culture.

A few writers (e.g. Nettleford 1972, 1978; Norris 1962) have tried to describe contemporary Jamaican culture, but they are mainly interested in political culture and the struggle against political, economic, and cultural imperialism. They look mainly at the towns, and say very little about the lives of those African-Jamaicans who do not necessarily articulate their politics.

Today politics and political movements affect the lives of all Jamaicans and no treatment of Jamaican cultural behaviour can ignore them. But other kinds of culture of the sort discussed in these pages are also important, and should be the starting point of those who articulate militant political ideologies. Only Rastafarianism integrates the ideological, behavioural and philosophical aspects of culture. Other forms of cultural nationalism are often promoted by Jamaicans from the most Europeanised sector of the population who disregard Africa-derived aspects of Jamaican culture. But Pukumina and Revival continue to exist and even flourish; mento is a rural partner of reggae; and a variety of Jamaican continues to be spoken in the countryside that is quite distinct from the urban varieties heavily influenced by Rastafarianism.

Today we must study the interplay between urban mass culture, rural "traditional" or "folk" culture, the political culture of Afro-Jamaican ideologues, and the tremendous pull of modernisation, which creates cultural rootlessness. It is hard to say which of these is most representative of Jamaica now, but in a study of this sort, none can be neglected.

I said earlier, talking of religion, that I would emphasise exoteric aspects of religion, rather than esoteric philosophical aspects. Needless to say, esoteric aspects are crucial to an understanding of religion, but in the case of Black Jamaican culture the information necessary for a study of them is not to hand. Similarly, studies of contemporary Jamaica have failed to come to grips with two fundamental aspects of Jamaican culture: its value system(s) (or ethos) and its world view or cognitive orientations. But these are the aspects of culture that impinge most on political ideology and clash most with the culture and technology of modernisation. The term value system refers to the ways in which we classify people, things, events, and experiences as good and bad, desirable and undesirable, or right and wrong; it refers to normative and evaluative aspects of culture. The term world view refers to our assumptions (not necessarily recognisable to us) about the world and to our interpretations of the world. Cognitive orientations equip us as members of a society with basic premises that guide our behaviour. Some of these cognitive orientations are deeply buried in our subconscious, yet they determine our behaviour; there is an interesting analogy between them and the grammatical rules of language that underlie the act of speech but do not exist at the level of consciousness. Other premises are quite explicit and, if articulated into a body of ideas, constitute part of "ideology". There is much interest today in Jamaica in ideology (Rastafarianism, Black Power, Cultural Nationalism, Socialism) but little in world view. Again, the difficulty is that whereas African Jamaicans in the earlier centuries and in the first three decades of the twentieth century were relatively homogeneous – all but a few lived in the villages, and even the small number of town dwellers were closely related by kin and social contact to country people and largely shared their value system and world view – today African Jamaican society is more complex. Up to the mid-1950s when I first came to Jamaica, it was hard to find a Kingston resident over the age of twenty who was not born in the countryside and who did not frequently go back to the countryside at weekends or on holidays. Since the 1930s, the life styles, cultural behaviour, ideology, and world view of African Jamaicans have changed in different ways and to different degrees, so that Jamaican culture today is extremely varied. I will not discuss the reasons for this, but simply list some of them.

They include the centralising influence of trade unions and political parties; government policy and the idea of planned change; growing urbanisation; the monetary economy and the commercialisation of agriculture; world wars and migrations; social mobility; and the extension of formal schooling. All Jamaicans have been affected by at least some of these factors, which have greatly influenced the development of contemporary Jamaican culture. But different individuals and groups have been affected by them in different ways and to different degrees, which is why concepts such as "two Jamaicas" (Curtin 1968), "cultural pluralism", and "urban/rural dichotomy" do not adequately describe the present state of culture in Jamaica. It is better to talk of a continuum of variation, with the urban, highly Europeanised Jamaican at one pole and the Kumina worshipper at the other (see Lewis 1977 for a cultural profile of such a person).

African surface forms of culture have become progressively diluted in the behaviour of most Jamaicans; in the towns they are largely dysfunctional and are stigmatised or concealed from view. But the African heritage survives beneath the surface of distortions and dysfunctions. Jamaican culture is indeed a "degradation" or "corruption" – not so much of European culture as of African culture. The cultural history of Jamaica is one in which Black people constantly struggled to maintain their African heritage in the teeth of slavery, colonialism, neocolonialism, and imperialism in the guise of modernisation. The extended family remains, but fights to survive migration, unemployment and bad housing. Parents love and protect their children, but sometimes brutalise them to vent their frustration. Family life is still very important in the countryside. True, rural children may not spend their entire childhood in the same household, but they rarely suffer the neglect that has become a feature of the movement to cities. The affection of aunts, uncles, cousins, and grandparents creates material and psychological security that anchors the personality of the Jamaican child. On the other hand, there is evidence (Clarke 1957) that the "Jamaican family" is in severe disarray, chiefly as a result of the economic exploitation of family heads (particularly male heads). Friendship, kinship, and community come under increasing pressure from trends towards selfishness, individualism, and demeaning of others as people battle to survive.

We must stop looking solely at symptoms of alienation (laziness, irresponsibility, and so on) and examine instead the underlying qualities of popular Jamaican culture. Before I do this, I shall enumerate some of the cultural traits, practices, and beliefs inherited from Africa but preserved in diluted form and not always clearly integrated into a larger cultural structure.

Traces of West African burial customs can be detected in present-day Jamaican burial practices. One example is the "nine-night" ceremony in which the spirit of the deceased returns on the ninth night after death and – at some points closest to the rural folk end of the cultural continuum – possesses the person conducting the ceremony. At other points on the continuum, this no longer happens and the ceremony is simply an occasion on which the dead person is remembered and surviving family members meet socially. Lodges and burial societies, generally recognised as a West African continuity, assist members in the elaborate business of burying the dead. Even today infants closely related to the deceased are passed over the coffin in a ceremony that was once intended to ensure that the child's soul would not accompany that of the deceased, but which now is no more than a vague precaution against harm to the child. In another ceremony, on the birth of a child the umbilical cord is buried at the foot of a tree which is then associated with the child throughout its life. The tree was probably once thought to be the dwelling place of the child's spirit, but that belief now seems to have disappeared. People do not sweep houses late at night, throw things outside late at night without first warning the spirits, or throw away left-overs of food cooked late at night; at one time this was for fear that ancestral spirits might be about. This belief in souls and spirits is also the reason why the pockets of a dead man's suit are sewn up or cut out. (This practice is also carefully observed in middle class urban settings.) Some Jamaicans claim that this prevents the duppy from coming back with pockets full of stones to throw about and disturb the living; others say that this removes all doubt from the spirit that its corporeal abode is dead. Silence is thought to be a favourite setting for spirits. According to Lamal (1965: p. 161), "dans un groupe, durant une conversation, s'il se fait soudain un silence momentané et imprévu, un ancien dira 'Nzambi wayooki, wahiiti – C'est Nzambi qui passe.'"[1] This is also true of Jamaica.

According to Clarke (1974: p. 6), "at the graveside, in an Ashanti's funeral, the coffin is lowered three times before actually being placed in the grave." This is so that the Earth Goddess will be warned of the arrival of another body. Some Jamaicans still do this, but many simply raise and lower the body immediately after death. At the end of a burial, relatives of the deceased turn their backs on the grave and throw grave dirt between their legs to prevent the spirit of the dead person from following them home.

Ashanti believe that dreams are caused either by the visitation of spirits or by the journeying of one's soul, and attach great importance to what dreams reveal (Clarke 1974: p. 6). Many Jamaicans believe much the same and ask their religious leaders to interpret dreams. In both Akan and Jamaican cultures people who dream that dead relatives are advising them to follow a certain course of action are convinced on waking that they have actually been visited by the dead person's spirit and carry out whatever instructions they have been given. That this belief is not unique to Africa and Afro-America does not invalidate the idea that it is an African continuity, for it must be seen within the total structure of the Jamaican belief system. Certain symbols have specific meanings in dreams; for example, Ashanti and Jamaicans believe that pure water signifies prosperity, love, or peace, and that dirty water signifies a quarrel or trouble. Generally, however, dreams are interpreted antithetically, and for both peoples, someone dying in a dream means long life.

Other beliefs are associated with that other great event, birth. According to Clarke (1974: p. 4), "among the Ashanti, when the time of birth is approaching the expectant mother leaves her husband's house and returns to that of her mother, whose assistance and advice is considered necessary at this time." This practice is still alive in Jamaica today but on a much smaller scale than previously. Expectant mothers would travel great distances from one parish to another to be at their mothers' houses for the birth of their children. It is taboo among the Ashanti for a pregnant woman to look at any deformity, even a badly carved figure, lest she give birth to a child like it. In Jamaica the belief is that the woman should neither look at nor express sympathy for any deformed or dying animal for fear that her child might resemble it.

The motor patterns of Jamaicans are largely derived from African models. The Jamaican worker in the field stands with straight legs, bending almost double at the waist, to work with short-handled machetes. Jamaicans prefer to carry bundles on their heads and Jamaican children are carried in such a way that they straddle their mothers' hips. Jamaicans look away to show respect, and attenuate the grossness of laughter by placing their hands across their mouths or looking away.

Like West Africans, Jamaicans love colourful clothes; the women wrap their heads in kerchieves or pieces of cloth, and plait their hair in small designs (called cane row).

Apart from lodges and burial societies, West African social institutions preserved in Jamaica include the partner, called *susu* in Trinidad and *esusu* in Yoruba; and the "day": a group of men who assemble to work for a friend or relative (called *gayap* in Trinidad and *dokpwe* in Ewe).

World view can be inferred from religious beliefs, language structure (syntax and semantics), folk beliefs, and folk ideas expressed in the form of proverbs, sayings, folktales, songs, legends, and myths. It can also be inferred from social behaviour, e.g. child-rearing practices and recreation, and particularly from what are called "attitudes". Although people have collected Jamaican proverbs and "superstitions" (i.e. religious beliefs and folk ideas), none have distilled from them Jamaican truths about man, God, the universe, natural events, morality, and the relationships between these things.

Proverbs are used less today than they once were, but they still form – together with sayings, wise epigrams, and biblical injunctions– a very important part of Jamaican verbal communication. Some songs consist of nothing else but proverbs, strung together in verses. It should be possible to measure cultural variation within the Jamaican population in terms of the variable use of proverbs, sayings, and the like.

Although the idea of two Jamaicas does not adequately describe cultural behaviour in Jamaica, there is undeniably a conflict between the demands of modernisation and the indigenous culture of African Jamaicans: between world views that, though they may have coexisted throughout the post-Columbian history of Jamaica, are now sharply counterposed.

Lewin (1974) and Alleyne (1976) were the first to examine this conflict of world views and the dysfunctionality of some forms of African Jamaican culture in an urbanising and modernising setting. According to Alleyne (1976):

> for as long as the migrants were rural folk living in a rural setting, their culture and way of life were in harmony with the environment. The family group imparted the ethical and moral code ... [and] all the knowledge and skills that were needed to cope with the environment. The movement into cities and into metropolitan countries creates a whole series of contradictions and disruptions. Certain aspects of culture are very covert, very tenacious, and remain for generations among the migrants. They may also, in slightly different form, be reinforced in the new environment by the social conditions of *de facto* segregation (ghetto residence) creating a high density of interaction among migrants, poverty, lack of adequate educational facilities, social and cultural alienation. These aspects of culture represent disharmonies with the new environment ... The notion of time, for example, creates a disharmony. In a rural environment, time is not represented by precise points on a chronometer, but is approximate in terms of the slow gradual movement of geophysical phenomena and the behaviour of nature. According to Mbiti (1970) and Nhiwatiwa (1979), in the African world view, the time concept is based on natural events. Time is defined in terms of the events that are taking place or have taken place. Time is not an imposed mathematical formula; it is a phenomenal event. This is correlatable with structural features of the language of Jamaicans in which, in addition to tense which in some types of utterances may not be grammatically expressed, the language, perhaps with greater emphasis and significance, expresses whether an action is completed or not, whether it is in the process of unfurling, whether it is habitual, repetitive, or whether it is prospective. The system of social relations existing in the rural sector did not create a "vertical" range (i.e. hierarchies) of language variation. Although one had to learn and use different language codes, these corresponded mainly to the system of respect and authority based for the most part on kinship and age. These differences in code were not significant grammatical differences, but were mainly lexical, or pertained, for example, to the address system. In the rural sector therefore, there is no linguistic dysfunctionality, no disharmony between language structure and usage and the environment...

Once transferred to an urban industrialised modernising milieu, this language, as structure and usage, becomes dysfunctional. There is now a stratified social structure which corresponds with different levels or varieties of language. In order to gain esteem for himself and in order to carry out social transactions effectively and successfully, the migrant is now called upon to master a new grammatical system: new syntax, new phonology and to a lesser extent new lexicon with a new set of meanings. His native mode of speech is now highly stigmatised and is unable to cope adequately with all the demands of the new environment.

Time in an industrialised modern civilisation is both a mathematical formula and a commodity that can be costed, bought, and sold. Nhiwatiwa's analysis of the concept of time in Africa (see Nhiwatiwa 1979) holds also for Jamaica:

This concept of time being determined by the events and individual participation in them has puzzled many foreigners who have complained that Africans do not keep time or that Africans just waste time sitting down doing nothing. These remarks are a result of lack of understanding of the African concept of time. Time is the event that has taken place or is taking place. It does not matter how long it takes the event to finish or to start. The most important thing is the individual participation in the event taking place.

The European world view is quite different. Europeans see time as something that happens between two fixed points. They become anxious and impatient when they are "kept waiting". Jamaicans do not experience this anxiety and impatience – witness their relaxed behaviour in hospital waiting rooms and at country bus stops. (That is not to say that they will withold expressing their disgust or dissatisfaction at blatant inefficiency or at injustice.) It is not important how long you spend at (say) the barber shop: what matters is the quality of social interaction there.
  According to Lewin,

in our [Jamaican] traditional society, life is essentially communal. [When] for example someone [has] a health problem in a traditional community, the first person to be contacted, outside the immediate family, is the spiritual leader such as the Revival Mother, the Shepherd, the Kumina Queen, and if no solution springs from their mind quickly, there would be an attempt to communicate with the spirit world, the world of universal ideas. The next step most likely would be to arrange a ritual or a ceremony, and this would involve the whole group ... Note the importance of the spiritual contact, the meditative approach as contrasted with the analytical, intensely practical, materialistic approach [of Western European societies]. In all phases of life in the traditional community, there is a oneness, not only with the whole universe because we are all linked by the same creative spirit; not only in the community where each person's problems become the problems of the whole community with every member contributing to the solution through music, through cooking, through helping to prepare the setting ... but also through the 'oneness' of the individual. There is no separation between body, emotions, spirit, and the nearer one is to the spirit, the more trusted one's reactions are ... The less concrete the state of how one feels is considered to be nearer to the truth, the ultimate truth of the creative spirit, and flashes of inspiration and intuition, dreams, and the signs of nature are all accepted without question. Nature's laws are always in operation and are always the same. The weather satellite, the most advanced scientific instruments, the mind of man may err, but not the laws of nature ... It may be necessary for those who have veered towards the individualistic, the logical, the analytical, the materialistic view of the world to take a long and respectful look at the spiritual, communal, emotional, meditative approach of others. Then it may be seen that mistrust of science, the difficulty of accepting birth control schemes ... may reflect very positive attitudes and not the negative reactions they are so often assumed to be.

The reluctance of Jamaican peasants to accept modern scientific agricultural techniques, including the use of chemical fertilisers and other agents that artificially quicken growth must be seen within the philosophical framework of this oneness with nature. The Rastafarians, whose complex eating taboos reflect a belief that body, mind, and nature form an integrated whole, have developed and enriched this philosophical tradition.

West Africa possibly lives on most vigorously in the world view of contemporary Jamaicans. But since world view is subliminal and cannot be observed directly like artifacts, it would normally have escaped the attention of observers in the past. It could have been gleaned through religion, but most attention has focussed on the behavioural (ritualistic) and sociological (organisational) aspects of religions in Jamaica; their underlying philosophies have been left largely unexplored. Other forms of behaviour might, if studied, have yielded such insights, but they were either ignored or treated as obstacles to "modernisation" of the sort for which only one remedy was appropriate: excision.

We have seen that religion continues to pervade the lives of Jamaicans in a very special way, that there is no sharp distinction between the secular and the spiritual, and that spiritual beings constantly intervene in people's daily lives. It is only toward the urban middle class end of the continuum, where Christianity is, as it were, confined to Sundays, that the secular and the spiritual part company. At the other end of the continuum, nature, the supernatural, and the human closely cohere, each being an extension of the other two. Supernatural forces inhabit nature and reveal themselves to humans through nature. People and nature live in harmony together; people should not try to subdue and conquer nature, but should respect and even revere it. Jamaicans are often sceptical about reclaiming land or damming rivers; many believe that the water will eventually return to its original place. Jamaican opposition to artificial fertilisers and other agents of artificial growth is similarly inspired.

Jamaicans, especially rural Jamaicans, tend toward a collectivist or communalist view of society – here too they follow Africa (cf. Nhiwatiwa 1979). For example, in Jamaica the whole community considers itself responsible for children; it supports them, maintains them, and guides them. Children are accountable to every member of their family, their extended family, and the whole community. The extended family is one of the oldest components of African social structure. The union of a man and woman is in fact the union of two families in an extended network; this network greatly influences the new "family" and bears much responsiblity for its development and well-being. In Jamaica, the concept of extended family allows for the adoption of non-sanguinal persons as relatives: close friends easily become sisters, brothers, cousins, mothers, fathers, grandmothers, grandfathers. It is quite normal to hear someone say, in reaction for example to a physical threat being posed to a cousin, "If you touch my cousin, you touch me." A child is not free to do wrong just because his biological parents are not watching. His conduct is under supervision by every adult in the community. This notion of collectivity is at the basis of the kinship, respect and authority systems, the hospitality extended to relatives, the respect shown to elders, and the ready acceptance of destitute children into the home of relatives or other members of the community. This collectivity begins to break down in the urban sectors, but is still represented there by the "yard". The yard maintains much of the positive strengths of collectivity, but problems of space and of economic survival produce tensions and conflicts that are not normally found in the rural setting.

Brodber (1975) in a sociological study, and Roger Mais in a fictional novel (*The Hills were Joyful Together*) both refer to the collectivity principle behind the social organisation of Kingston "yards". Collective problem solving, entertainment, baby-sitting and exchange of services are some of the positive achievements of collectivity. Brodber also shows how this collectivity begins to break down in some yards (mostly government yards) in which the residents view themselves ready, as it were, to raise their socioeconomic status, and "in preparation for this life, there is little inter-household sharing. All resources, human, social and economic are needed to establish this unit as the nuclear, upward mobile family. The Government yard is a collection of families rather than a community" (p. 35). It is often said that African Jamaicans like to keep others down and do not support each other in the way that East Indians, Chinese and Jews do in Jamaica. There is some truth in this, just as there is truth in the charge that Jamaicans sometimes treat their children rather brutally. Against this, Jamaicans often extend great warmth and hospitality to strangers. They are rarely pompous, aloof, or ostentatious: to be so would be interpreted as an offence against the dignity of other people. African Jamaicans generally play down their achievements to avoid standing out from the community and alienating themselves from it. This reticence may flow from the belief that the natural and the supernatural worlds are closely linked and that the spirits or ancestral spirits of those you have offended will come to haunt you. It is not just "bad taste" but downright dangerous to laugh at someone else's misfortune, for the same thing might befall the laugher. Considerations of this sort may explain the alleged lack of ambition which some critics say is holding up the "modernisation" of Jamaica. Many African Jamaicans who could easily get rich are content to just "get by" and decline to "develop" their businesses. The pursuit of wealth as an end in itself is alien to Africans (cf. Nhiwatiwa 1979) and African Jamaicans; it offends the collectivist principle and the view of how human relations should be conducted.

Town people are less committed to collectivism than country people, and Jamaicans of all classes are less committed to it today than they once were. For example, at one time public passenger vehicles both in Kingston and in the countryside would never refuse to accept passengers simply on the grounds that they were full. This was not just to get the extra fares. On the contrary, it was the passengers themselves already aboard who insisted – even at the cost of their own comfort – on "squeezing up" to accommodate new fares. Very often the new passengers would have more room than those who had squeezed up to let them on. Later, Kingston bus drivers became rather notorious for driving past waiting people, and those with seats became less ready to call out to the driver to stop or to make room for others. At one time, passengers (and drivers) communicated totally, both verbally and physically, but lately, passengers tend to sit rigidly, gaze sternly ahead, keep themselves to themselves, and defend their individual space.

"Call and response" is one example of the extension of the collectivist principle to communication. Another is that style of preaching in which preacher and congregation are in constant and total interaction. (See p. 49 above, where the same is reported for Akan prayers.) Elsewhere in the "folk" tradition, crowds gathered around story-tellers actively participate in the performance – they respond at appropriate points in the story, join in singing the songs that punctuate the story, and collectively perform the coda. In the towns, this tradition is still not dead. For example, cinema audiences get closely caught up in the films they are watching. They interact with the dialogue and constantly respond to events on the screen. This is yet another example of the Europeanisation of the surface structure of communication: the spectators are lined up in front of the performance, whereas in the past they would have formed a circle round it, with flows in both directions. However, the deep structure (i.e. the call-and-response pattern) remains African. Even television has not completely eradicated this style. Jamaicans sitting in front of their television screens constantly talk back at the performers.

Something similar can be observed when two Jamaicans talking at (say) a bus stop are joined by a third. Even if the newcomer is a complete stranger, every effort will be made – first by looks and body language, then by direct address – to draw him or her into the conversation. The stranger normally responds as a matter of course, while tactfully maintaining the role of "stranger" by staying at a distance from the original pair.

All human societies seem to use language in a common range of functions in personal interaction. Different scholars identify and designate these functions differently, but most agree that a main common function is the referential one, vaguely and crudely defined as referring to the outside world or expressing thought. Also important in Jamaican speech and the speech of other Afro-Americans are the phatic and creative functions. The phatic function expresses sentiments of solidarity, community, and culture. It manifests itself in the constant creation of new expressions, e.g. new terms of address and greeting that help to strengthen group identity. This creative function is richly represented in the speech of Black North Americans, Trinidadians, and Jamaicans. The inherent ambiguity of Afro-American language and culture, which as we have seen serves as a barrier to the penetration of Afro-American society by the White elite, is one important aspect of this principle of creativity. Spontaneous improvisation and embellishment are highly valued forms of expression among Afro-Americans in language, music, and social behaviour. According to Sidrak (1971: p. 6):

> while the whole European tradition strives for regularity – of pitch, time, timbre, the African tradition strives for the negation of these elements. In language, the African aims at circumlocution ... The direct statement is considered crude and unimaginative, the veiling of all contents in ever-changing paraphrase is considered the criterion of intelligence and personality. In music the same tendency towards obliquity and ellipsis is noticeable: no note is attacked straight, the voice or instrument always approaches it from above or below.

The format of interaction is the circle, not the line. The circle is central to the conceptual framework of the Jamaican world view. Gardeners do not make garden beds with straight lines and angles. The corpus of dancers move in a circle (as we have seen) and the girating hips of the individual dancer carve a circular pattern. Paths blazed through the bush are never straight but curve constantly. To denote confusion Jamaicans talk not of "going round in circles" but of "up and down" or "left and right".

The creative function has been the object of some study in the United States and the Caribbean (Kochman 1972, Abrahams 1964) where it is manifested in various forms of Afro-American word art and word play. Jamaicans attribute evocative power to words and language. Language in this sense is not merely an abstract system of signs referring arbitrarily to the world of objects, actions, and ideas; the relationship between the sign and thing meant is not arbitrary but inherent and necessary. This is also the way in which language functions in African societies, witness the concept *nommo*. As we have seen, in the New World the creative function is most obviously associated with the Rastafari brethren of Jamaica, who have developed a very characteristic language.[2]

At other levels of the continuum of cultural differentiation, what Nhiwatiwa (ibid.), writing about Africa, calls "involved communication" (i.e. the sort to which all participants contribute equally and simultaneously) is either absent or degenerates into a kind of verbal adroitness of the sort that characterises musical productions called Deejay (a term presumably derived from the abbreviation for Disc Jockey). Members of the Jamaican urban middle class tend to view involved communication as "noise" or "disorderly conduct", especially when it is used not in its phatic function (to express solidarity) but for "discussion" and "serious argument". Then it is little more than "everyone talking at the same time" and "people not listening to other people's views", i.e. not accepting the speaker-audience structure of communication that is typical of modernising societies and especially of radio and television. Reisman (1971), writing about Antigua, talks of "the noisy, apparently anarchistic but actually highly patterned conversational styles of Antiguans. Sound and counter-sound are typical of many speech situations" (summarised in Reinecke 1975: p. 412).

It is ironic that British, European, and North American influence in Jamaica is now stronger than it ever was, although today the island is politically independent. The search for African roots and the campaign to "preserve the folk culture", which climaxes each year in the staging of displays of this culture at the Independence Festival, are earnestly pursued. But at the same time this culture is under relentless siege though the nature of its plight is neither understood nor perceived. European and North American culture, especially industrialisation and urbanisation which are its main institutional manifestations, is regarded extremely highly and has an extremely insidious influence. It is easy to see that natural hair is better than straightened hair, that drums are preferable to violins, and that Pukumina is more authentically Jamaican than Christianity, but other manifestations of an Africa-derived world view are less readily embraced, either because they are less visible or because they are viewed negatively and pejoratively in the towns (as a sign of "backwardness").

As we have seen, the principle of harmony with nature inclines Jamaicans against modern agricultural practices; it also inclines them against modern methods of population control. Europeans, in contrast, see nature as an object to be conquered, and plundered. Anyone who does not join in this conquering of nature is deemed "backward" and an enemy of "progress" and "development". In Jamaica production targets set within the national development programme are geared not to the requirements of ordinary people but to those of a few wealthy Jamaicans and to the export market. Against this background, opposition to artificial fertilisers and modern husbandry methods and to modern birth control techniques is seen as "ignorant" and even unpatriotic.

Adherents of this European world view believe that the unbridled exploitation of nature is the inalienable right of individuals; that individuals can claim as their personal property and boundlessly profit from however much forest, farmland, or natural wealth they conquer and stake out (Beatty and Johnson 1971). Any encroachment on this right by people who think differently is judged to be "praedial larceny" and heavily penalised, even if the thing encroached on (say a fruit tree) is growing wild.

To put it at its most abstract, traditional Jamaican collectivism is being confronted by European individualism. In the European view, individuals are responsible for their own salvation, and should be free from all restraints as long as they stay within the law and (to a lesser extent) within moral bounds. Individuals strive for personal success which they often achieve mainly at the expense of others. Those who do not strive for personal success are "lazy", "good-for-nothing", and "irresponsible".

The collectivity principle and one of its main sub-categories, involved communication, are now seriously threatened by the principle of separate (rather than integrated) and consecutive (rather than simultaneous) communication. Today people line up in queues even when there is absolutely no point in doing so (although the queues are not exactly straight lines formed by persons standing one behind the other). On the roads many drivers see only their own individual rights as set out in traffic regulations and ignore the interests of the collectivity of road users. Collectivists who refuse to yield to the principle of individualism are accused of "indiscipline", "bad behaviour", and "ignorance". Yet I once saw a clerk at the Bank of Jamaica obey the collectivity principle even while dealing with a queue of customers. She dealt with every person in the queue simultaneously, as well as with several other clerks who got caught up in the transactions. And not all car drivers in Jamaica insist rigidly on their individual right of way: many perceive the collective situation and yield even when they do not need to do so.

The industrial assembly line and other production systems that require workers to sit individually in front of whatever they produce is another manifestation of the individual principle. This conflicts with the collectivity principle which considers work to be, to a large extent, a social activity which requires some kind of social interaction. Typical examples are communal work projects accompanied by work songs and domestic work activity (pounding corn, washing clothes by the river, in the yard or by the standpipe) which bring together several persons working in unison and interacting socially. In the industrialised sector, individualised work may be frequently interrupted by conversation (involved communication), movement away from one's position to form interaction groups and visits to other work positions, all of which "slows down production".[3] The collectivity principle, communalism, and involved communication all manifest themselves in the need to be constantly relating to others (whether talking, arguing, quarrelling, working together), at the work place, at the standpipe or at the street corner.

The two world views which confront each other in Jamaica have different orderings of priorities as far as the way in which people organise their lives and set their goals is concerned. I may of course be on uncertain ground here since this interpretation is not based on any study using a method of evaluating such priorities (assuming that such a method is available or possible); but it does seem that, at a major segment of the Jamaican cultural continuum, people will forgo certain apparent comforts, convenience and economic gain in return for more fun out of life largely derived from interaction with other people. In one world view, the European, beginning with what is called Judeo-Christian ethics right up to what is called today capitalism and socialism or Marxism, a main, if not *the* main goal is to accumulate individual wealth either by exploiting land, minerals, or means of production or by working far more than is necessary. This goal depends on the notion that nature is a vast storehouse of resources that individuals or states can own, subdue, and exploit to the fullest. It is also supported by the idea of "working and saving for the future". This sort of thinking is reflected in attitudes to time and, linguistically, in an elaborate system of verbal tenses. The Jamaican concept of time is differently structured. European time is future oriented, just as Judeo-Christian religion is oriented toward a future kingdom that God will establish here on earth.[4] Individuals live their lives preparing and waiting for this to happen. Striving for personal success is often seen as part of this preparation; followers of John Calvin even believed that success in business was a sign that you were saved. The relentless striving for personal individual success (very often without regard for, and at the expense of, others) became later dissociated from salvation and now in a large measure exists as an end in itself. In this world view, the future, whether here on earth or in the hereafter, has to be carefully prepared for. This leads to an over-exploitation of nature to ensure "future" needs, an over-production of goods, the saving of money, and the acquisition of goods and property far over and above actual needs in order to ensure a secure "future". It seems, on the other hand, that this constitutes a lower priority in the world view of Africans and Afro-Jamaicans. There isn't as much over-extension of the individual in productive work activity.

A great deal of "hard work" takes place, but it is geared to the satisfaction of actual needs rather than to assuring the satisfaction of long term future needs, leaving time and nervous energy for the "enjoyment" of life. I am not saying that production in Africa has not crossed and does not cross the threshold of surplus. Particularly in Sudan savanna agriculture (in the area immediately south of the Sahara), over-production seems to have been bound up in some way with the emergence of powerful political organisations and empires like Ghana, Mali and Songhai. In the forest area where most of the slave trading took place, there was less of surplus production and a greater incidence of subsistence production, although here too granaries, for example, give evidence of the existence of a reserve supply. There is no evidence that such reserves were used for individual wealth or individual control over other members of the society, although they were probably used by kinship groups and ethnic groups to acquire and maintain political power. Ideally, work should not be divorced from pleasure, which is a product of social interaction and artistic expression. Many Jamaicans with no end of "business acumen" choose not to develop their businesses to full capacity (though some Afro-Jamaican enterprises stagnate or fail for objective structural reasons – mainly lack of capital and of so-called management "skills"). Other Jamaicans work only until they have satisfied their basic needs and then stop, much to the chagrin of their employers (though here again wages are often so low that many see little point in working hard). Some will even blow an entire week's earnings on a single day of pleasure.

In Jamaica little is done without a touch of embellishment or some panache. Jamaicans walk with style, drive cars (and buses) with style, and play with style. It is not so much scoring a goal or hitting a boundary that is important, but the way that it is done. People leaving church will admit openly that they did not understand what the preacher said, "but he sound good". Many West Indians swear that the greatest cricket innings they ever saw was sixteen runs scored by Frank Worrell, which may not have won the match but was nonetheless esteemed for its sheer beauty. In the European culture, people constantly postpone gratification, strive for "more and more", "break records", leave behind "losers" and "underdogs", and even reserve the reward for eating till the very end – the "dessert". In Afro-Jamaican culture, gratification is immediate: it is part of every activity and of every stage of it.

This is not to say that the world view of African Jamaica is unique to Africans and African Jamaicans. It can more plausibly be interpreted as a response to the ecological setting within which Africans live and work. The soil in Africa is poor, and African livestock are vulnerable to endemic tropical diseases and to the effects of droughts and other natural disasters. As a result, Africans must fight hard to survive. Their explanation of the universe, their religious beliefs, and their attitudes to nature are inevitably closely influenced by the cumulative effects of this experience. This may explain why (for example) they consume all that they produce and do not rigidly specialise: African artisans also cultivate their own fields: cf. Maquet 1972: p. 21-23. It would also explain certain features of the culture and world view of African Jamaicans; for styles, concepts, and philosophies born in one setting can migrate to new settings and determine human responses to them.

Today in Jamaica European culture pressures Jamaicans to get materially rich as individuals rather than to get spiritually rich together, and this is producing severe conflicts. Technology and modernisation are invading all quarters of the human mind and destroying links to Africa. Jamaicans are losing touch with their ancestral traditions, myths, and legends, for modernisation fosters rootlessness. Villages are giving way to towns, workshops are giving way to factories. But the collectivist principle is slow in dying. It enters the city, the factory, and the office, where it sows chaos. It is quite normal for villagers to stop and talk to each other from opposite sides of the village street, but if city people do the same, they are considered loud and uncouth, depending on the character of the area in which they do it. It is even worse if motorists driving in opposite directions along the same street stop to talk: they are considered completely irresponsible, for they halt the flow of traffic.

Modernisation also presents a systematic political and intellectual challenge to the African tradition in Jamaica. Proponents of modernisation are trying to impose new ideologies on peoples throughout the world today, including the people of Jamaica. Ideologies and culture may coexist harmoniously, or they may clash. Ideally, political and intellectual systems should flow from the collective historical experience and goals of a people. Conflicts arise when sets of ideas elaborated on the basis of the cultural experience or cultural heritage of one people (or class) are imposed on another people (or class). Hence many Africans feel that while socialist ideas may be appropriate for advancing some of the interests of African peoples, their European forms must be remodelled and adapted to African experience.

Without intellectual articulation, the culture of a people is often nothing more than a random mass of knowledge, beliefs, habits, products, and systems of production. The role of ideology is to systematise this mass and give it structured coherence. A realistic programme for the political, social, and economic development of Jamaica cannot be drawn up merely on the basis of universalist theories of human evolution like Marxism: something more is needed – an understanding of the cultural realities of Jamaica. I hope that this book will contribute to that understanding.

Notes and References

Preface

1. This is what Jamaican Maroons claim. It is also borne out by slave narratives (cf. Rawick 1970: p. 162, who writes of one such narrative, "Notice in the following example how the informant invokes memories of Africa, not as some distant unimaginable place, but as one that was culturally close at hand"), and is implicit in the high suicide rate among slaves and their belief that they would return after death to the ancestral home.
2. Note that this contradicts the view often stated but not quite substantiated that slaves were effectively mixed.

Introduction

1. An African studying in Shanghai must be considered to have a "culture". He cannot be considered to have been "stripped" of his culture or to have had his culture suspended.

Chapter 1

1. Quashee is sambo's Jamaican equivalent. Quashee connotes the following qualities: foolish, evasive, lazy, possessing a bad sense of judgement, lying, cringing, but also, contradictorily, crafty. This last quality has led some scholars to interpret the sambo personality as a form of resistance or a means of survival and self-preservation.

Chapter 2

1. Morales (1952: p. 269) mentions that a certain Pedro de Mazuelo, who in 1535 wanted to found a community on the South Coast of Jamaica, requested and got thirty Blacks from Portugal.
2. There are of course numerous toponyms in Jamaica of Spanish origin. African influences are not easily discernible here.
3. Curtin is less categorical about this later in his book (p. 96). There he claims that for the fifteenth century "we have little more than a general impression" that this was the region of origin. But two reports on Peru and Mexico for 1548–60 and 1549 respectively show that this region exported 74 per cent of the slaves in Peru and 88 per cent of those in Mexico. Cf. J. Lockhart, *Spanish Peru*, 1533–1560 (Madison 1968) and G. Aguirre Beltran, *Población Negra de México*, 1519–1810 (México D.F., 1946).
4. C(o)romantin is the name of a town that seems to have played an

important role in the export of slaves.

5. Hence, slaves from the surrounding area populated by Akan peoples were called "Coromantee", a name still used today by the Maroons of Jamaica and Suriname.

6. British colonisation of the Caribbean proceeded as follows: St Kitts 1623, Barbados 1625–6, Virgin Islands 1625, Nevis 1628, Antigua, Montserrat 1632, and Suriname 1651. From conflicting accounts of the size and recruitment of the British expeditionary force that seized Jamaica from the Spaniards, LePage (1960: p. 10) concludes that "about one-third of the total force (seems to have been) raised in the Leewards and Barbados".

7. Gardner (1873) and Bastide (1971: p. 7) are not so cautious. They claim categorically that "Negroes imported into English colonies came mostly from what used to be known as the Gold Coast".

8. It seems that the Dutch records have not yet been investigated (Curtin 1969). There is therefore a great gap in the historiography of the West Indies waiting to be filled.

9. This still does not explain Curtin's low estimate (6.3 per cent) for the Gold Coast.

10. "Angola" refers not merely to the modern republic of Angola, but to Central Africa in general.

11. This view is supported by the following authors: Parrinder, Froelich, Diop.

12. Needless to say, there have been changes everywhere that have not altered the essential structure of the religions. For example, new deities have been created, or the hierarchical ordering of deities has changed.

13. According to Froelich (1964: p. 168), "throughout all West Africa, ancestor worship, in spite of infinite variations, is the most permanent ritual nucleus, and the most solid, homogeneous and widespread."

Chapter 3

1. This statement is of course relative. Clearly Europeans also underwent acculturation, massive and rapid in the case of some individuals who found themselves in certain conditions of contact with Africans. However, as a group, Europeans at first underwent relatively little culture change.

2. Cf. Fisher (1953) for evidence that the religious songs of North American slaves may have had a private meaning for slaves, different from the meaning understood by Whites.

3. All these processes are not known to have taken place in other instances of slavery, notably in slavery carried out in Africa by Africans among themselves, in which some slaves could rise to the highest levels in society by sheer diligence, hard work and the recognition of their

potential by others. It is because of this that the qualifier "chattel" has been used to describe the special unique features of New World plantation slavery.

4. The use of talking drums was sufficiently prevalent and feared to provoke their prohibition. Cf. Gardner 1873: p. 100; Long 1774: p. 443.

5. Long (1774: p. 425) records that in 1769 "several new [Jonkunnu] masks appeared. The Ebos, the Pawpaws, etc., having their respective Connus"... This separateness and rivalry seems to have been encouraged by the Portuguese in Brazil who organised *batuques* (periodic displays of tribal drumming and dancing), playing one group against another in an attempt to create divisions and even animosity among slaves (cf. Turnbull 1976: pp. 243–44). This has not been reported for Jamaica.

Chapter 4

1. Cf. Suriname, where the coffin is also carried on the heads of two bearers and a priest is able to decipher from its movement the spirit's answers to questions about cause of death and other matters.

2. Acts of the Assembly passed in the island of Jamaica from 1681 to 1737 inclusive. London 1745, p. 55.

3. Acts of the Assembly, passed in the island of Jamaica from 1770 to 1783, inclusive. Kingston 1786, p. 256.

4. This is another of those examples of either lack of understanding of African metaphysics on the part of European writers, or else deliberate misrepresentation designed to discredit. In the metaphysics of African religion it was not the corporeal matter that returned to Africa on death but rather the eternal spirit. It is to be noted that Christianity in this sense comes close to African religious beliefs since it too believes in the survival of a spirit after death and its journey to a "kingdom of spirits". This is not to deny that lay people, both African and Christian, may believe that the body of man journeys to the Kingdom.

5. The semantic range of "pull" in Jamaican is quite different from that of English pull. The Jamaican word conveys the general idea of away from, out of; it thus means *inter alia* to "weed" and "unbutton".

6. "Pocomania" seems to be a spelling and conceptual aberration of Europeans. In their general demeaning of African culture, Europeans associated the religion of the slaves with "a little madness". As is usual in colonial systems, the colonised have largely accepted the colonisers' pejorative evaluation of them.

7. This seems to be a reference to the takeover of the Baptist and Methodist churches by Myalism.

8. This seems to be a clear recognition of the association between African religion and rebellion among the slaves.

9. Bedwardism is representative of an end-point of religious evolution in Jamaica. Bedward, like Taylor, was persecuted by the establishment,

but according to his present-day followers he broke with the Myal tradition and practised a more orthodox form of Christianity, forbidding drumming, spirit possession and the call-and-response format. However, the notion of flying, the healing stream, and the existence of "station guards" and "Mothers" in the Church hierarchy linked him to Revivalism (see Beckwith 1929: pp. 167–8).

Chapter 5

1. The origin of Jonkunu is obviously more complex than this (see Bettelheim 1976).
2. It may be argued, however, that Africans and Afro-Americans "hear" music internally when walking. This develops later into a marked tendency to grunt a vigorous rhythm while doing vigorous walking, to whistle or sing, and (more recently) to hold transistor radios to the ear. It is interesting to observe that this grunting forms part of the singing style of some performers.
3. *gumbe* has been extended in modern Jamaica and in the Bahamas to refer to a folk festival as a whole, in which drumming plays an essential part.
4. Beckford
5. Clerk
6. Clerk
7. Jahn (1968: p. 102) however says that the "blue notes" characteristic of North American blues songs go back to the middle pitch of West African tonal languages and have a modality between sharp and flat.
8. A similar kind of explosion may be observed when groups form to chat. A particularly comic remark causes participants to break out of the huddle, laugh very expressively, and then return to carry on the chat. In the modern ballroom setting dancers also periodically break away from each other to perform spins and other virtuosities before regrouping with their partners.

Chapter 6

1. There are probably gross inaccuracies in Beckwith's record of this song, including whimsical segmentation into words. The translation is also probably fanciful.
2. "Folk etymology" refers to words which the people come to associate with other better known words and meanings and which thus lose their link with their etymological source.
3. The same old Maroon who supplied Williams with a list gave the form *abrono* which shows a close relationship with Twi-Asante *oburoni*. This again supports the conclusion that the collapse of the noun class system took place at the end of the nineteenth century.
4. The same kind of dual interpretation suggests itself for other aspects of

culture: Is Pukumina an African religion with massive importations from Christianity and loss of some of its original inner form, or is it a degree of African religious continuity during the acquisition of Christianity?

5. See Alleyne 1980 (Chapter 4).
6. Colloquial Dutch, however, which has heavily influenced Papiamentu, also used the double possessive: *vader z'n hoed* "father his hat".
7. As a general rule, reactions to "creole"-like forms are the most negative. For example, *nyam* and *eat* constitute a lexical variable. The use of *nyam*, which is "creole" and West African in origin, is discouraged except when referring to animals or to grotesque or inelegant ways of eating by humans.
8. There were of course ways in which individual slaves could gain prestige and leadership within the community of slaves, and these ways would be very important to study. But they are not the same as social mobility.

Conclusions

1. "In a group, during a conversation, if there is a sudden unexpected momentary silence, an old person will say "Nzambi wayooki, wahiti – It is Nzambi passing." According to Lamal (1965: p. 173), it could also be spirits (duppies or ancestral spirits) passing.
2. Rodney (1969a: p. 67) says: "You have to listen to the Jamaican Rasta, and you have to listen to him, listen very carefully and then you will hear him tell you about the Word. And when you listen to him and go back and read Muntu, an academic text (cf. Jahn 1961) and read about Nomo, an African concept for Word, and you say, Goodness the Rastas know this, they knew this before Janheinz Jahn."
3. In 1986–87, this has been the source of a continuing labour crisis in the garment factories of the Kingston Free Zone. Chinese and Korean management have complained of poor "work ethic" and "poor worker attitudes".
4. Cf. the notion in African religions that deities, spirits, and ancestors are constantly with us here and now, and the "here and now" concept of the kingdom of God. The remarks by Bastide (1971: p. 141, citing Fernando Ortiz) about the Yoruba are very pertinent here: "His [the African's] theoanthropic economy is not one of long-term credit or enrichment, nor of capitalizing his interest by investing it in heaven, which, on the day of his death, will return eternal profits. It is a religion of immediate consumption, of barter rites, without credit or accumulated interest ... In return for sacrifices, the ancestors protected their lineages ... Later the miraculous saints were expected to help members of their fraternities in their daily lives – the only lives that

interested them – in return for immediate payment or "promises." A lighted candle or an *ex voto*, like those of the Whites, simply replaced the sacrifice of a cock or a goat. The principle remained the same – *do ut des* – but the reward was expected immediately, not in some problematic beyond."

Bibliography

Abrahams, Roger. 1964. *Deep Down in the Jungle*. Hartboro, Pa: Folklore Associates.

——and John Szwed (eds.). 1978. *Afro-American Folk Culture. Annotated Bibliography of Materials from North, Central, South America and the West Indies*. Philadelphia: Institute for the Study of Human Issues. 2 vols.

——1983. *After Africa*. New Haven: Yale University Press.

Alexandre, Pierre. 1967. *Langues et Langage en Afrique Noire*. Paris: Payot.

Alleyne, Mervyn C. 1963. "Communication and politics in Jamaica". *Caribbean Studies* 3(2): p. 22–61.

——1966. "La nature du changement phonetique". *Revue de Linguistique Romane XXX*: p. 279–303.

——1970. "Acculturation and the cultural matrix of creolisation". *Pidginization and Creolization of Languages*. Ed. Dell Hymes. Cambridge University Press, pp. 169–186.

——1971. "The linguistic continuity of Africa in the Caribbean". *Topics in Afro-American Studies*. Ed. Henry Richards. Buffalo: Black Academy Press. pp. 12–28.

——1972. "Panorama de la linguística y enseñanza de idiomas en el Caribe". *Caribbean Studies* 12: pp. 5–14.

——1975. "Some aspects of the traditional non-formal system of communication in the Caribbean". *Communication and Information for Development Purposes in the Caribbean Area*. International Broadcast Institute. pp. 11–16.

——1976. "Dimensions and varieties of West Indian English and the implications for teaching". *Black Students in Urban Canada*. Ed. V. Doyley. Ministry of Culture and Recreation, Ontario. pp. 35–62.

——1980. *Comparative Afro-American*. Ann Arbor: Karoma.

——1982. *Theoretical Issues in Caribbean Linguistics*. Kingston: U.W.I.

——and B. Hall (eds.). *The Cultural Heritage of Jamaica* (forthcoming).

Alvarez Nazario, Manuel. 1961. *Elemento Afronegroide en el Español de Puerto Rico*. San Juan: Instituto de Cultura Puertorriqueña.

Bailey, Beryl. 1966. *Jamaica Creole Syntax. A Transformational Approach*. Cambridge: Cambridge University Press.

Balandier, George. 1953. "Messianismes et nationalismes en Afrique Noire". *Cahiers Internationaux de Sociologie XIV*: pp. 41–65.

——1968. *Daily Life in the Kingdom of the Congo*. New York: Pantheon.

Banbury, Rev. R. Thomas. 1895. *Jamaica Superstitions, or the Obeah Book*. Kingston: de Souza.

Bascom, William. 1965. "La religion africaine au Nouveau Monde". *Rencontres Internationales de Bouake: Les Religions Africaines Traditionelles*. Paris: Seuil.

Bastide, Roger. 1971. *African Civilisations in the New World*. New York: Harper and Row.

Baxter, Ivy. 1970. *The Arts of an Island*. Metuchen, New Jersey: Scarecrow.

Beatty, John and Oliver Johnson. 1971. *Heritage of Western Civilisation* (3rd ed.). New Jersey: Prentice Hall.

Beckford, William. 1790. *A Descriptive Account of the Island of Jamaica*. 2 vols. London: Egerton.

Beckles, H.M. n.d. "White power and black consciousness: Slave resistance in the English West Indies during the 17th century". (Unpublished manuscript).

Beckwith, Martha. 1924. "The English ballad in Jamaica". *PMLA* 39: pp. 455–83.

——1928. *Jamaican Folklore*. New York: The American Folklore Society. (Krauss reprint, 1966).

——1929. *Black Roadways A Study of Jamaican Folk Life*. Chappel Hill: University of North Carolina Press.

Bee, Robert. 1974. *Patterns and Processes. An Introduction to Anthropological Strategies for the Study of Sociocultural Change*. New York: MacMillan.

Beet, Chris de, and Miriam Sterman. 1984. *People in Between: The Matawai Maroons of Suriname*.

Bennett, R.E. 1968. *Nigerian Studies*. London: Cass.

Bettelheim, J. 1976. "Jonkunnu Festival". *Jamaica Journal* 10: pp. 20–7.

Bilby, Kenneth. 1981. "The Kromanti dance of the Windward Maroons of Jamaica". *Nieuwe West Indische Gids* 55: pp. 52–101.

Blassingame, John. 1972. *The Slave Community: Plantation Life in the Ante-bellum South*. New York: Oxford.

Bleby, Henry. 1853. *Death Struggles of Slavery*. London: Hamilton, Adams and Co.

Bohannan, Paul. 1964. *Africa and Africans*. New York: Natural History Press.

Bradbury, R.E. 1957. *The Benin Kingdom and the Edo-speaking Peoples of South Western Nigeria*. London: International Africa Institute.

Brathwaite, Edward. 1971. *The Development of Creole Society in Jamaica, 1770–1820*. Oxford: Clarendon.

——1978. "Kumina – the spirit of Africa survival". *Jamaica Journal* 42: pp. 44–63.

——1981. *Folk Culture of the Slaves in Jamaica*. Port of Spain: New Beacon.

Brodber, Erna. 1975. *A Study of Yards in the City of Kingston*. ISER Working Papers, No.9. Kingston: U.W.I.

Bryan, P. 1984. "Towards an African aesthetic in Jamaican intuitive art". *ACIJ Research Review* 1: pp. 1–20.

Buchner, John. 1854. *The Moravians in Jamaica*. London: Longman, Brown and Co.

Busia, K. 1954. "The Ashanti". *African World*. Ed. Daryll Forde. Oxford: Oxford University Press. pp. 190–209.

Casidy, F. 1960. *Jamaica Talk*. London: MacMillan.

——and R. LePage. 1967. *Dictionary of Jamaican English*. Cambridge: Cambridge University Press.

Chaunu, Hugette and Pierre Chaunu. 1955. *Seville et l'Atlantique (1504–1650)*. 8 vols. Paris: S.E.V.P.E.N.

Chevannes, B. 1971. "Revival and black struggle". *Savacou 5*: pp. 27–40.

Christaller, Rev. J.G. 1875. *A Grammar of the Asante and Fante Language called Tshi*. Basel. (Reprint London: Greg Press, 1964).

Christensen, James Boyd. 1959. "The adaptive function of Fante priesthood". In Herskovits and Bascom 1959.

Clarke, Edith. 1957. *My Mother who Fathered Me*. London: Allen and Unwin.

Clarke, Rowena. 1974. "The influence of the Ashanti on Jamaican superstitions and religious beliefs". (Caribbean Studies Paper, Kingston: U.W.I.).

Clerk, Astley. 1914. *The Music and Musical Instruments of Jamaica*. Kingston: Courlande.

Crahan, Margaret and Franklin Knight (eds.). 1979. *Africa and the Caribbean: The Legacies of a Link*. Baltimore: Johns Hopkins University Press.

Cundall, Frank. 1915. *Historic Jamaica*. London: West India Cttee.

Curtin, Philip. 1968. *Two Jamaicas*. New York: Greenwood.

——1969. *The Atlantic Slave Trade; a Census*. Madison: University of Wisconsin Press.

Dalby, David. 1970. *Black through White: Patterns of Communication in Africa and the New World*. Bloomington: Indiana University African Studies Program.

——1971. "Ashanti survivals in the language of the Maroons". *African Language Studies XII*: pp. 31–51.

Dallas, R.C. 1803. *The History of the Maroons*. 2 vols. London: Frank Cass.

Dammann, Ernst. 1964. *Les Religions de l'Afrique*. Paris: Payot.

Deerr, Noel. 1949. *The History of Sugar*. 2 vols. London: Chapman and Hall.

Delafosse, Maurice. 1952. "Langues du Soudan et de la Guinee". *Les Langues du Monde*. Ed. M. Cohen and A. Meillet. Paris: Champion.

Delerma, D-R. 1970. *Black Music in our Culture*. Kent: Kent State University Press.

Delisser, H. 1913. *20th Century Jamaica*. Kingston: Jamaica Times.

Diop, C.A. 1962. *The Cultural Unity of Negro Africa*. Paris: Presence Africaine.

Dundes, A. (ed.). 1968. *Every Man his Way*. Englewood Cliffs: Prentice Hall.

Dunham, K. 1946. *Journey to Accompong*. New York: Holt.

Edwards, Bryan. 1793. *The History of the British Colonies in the West Indies*. 2 vols. London: J. Stockdale.

Elkins, S. 1976. *Slavery*. Chicago: University of Chicago Press.

Ellis, A.B. 1887. *The Tshi-speaking Peoples of the Gold Coast of West Africa*. London: Chapman and Hall.

——1890. *The Ewe-speaking Peoples of the Slave Coast of West Africa. Anthropological Publications*. Oosterhout N.B., the Netherlands. (1970 reprint).

Epstein, D. 1973. "African music in British and French America". *Musical Quarterly* 50: pp. 61–91.

Equiano, Olaudah. 1789. *The Interesting Narrative of the Life of Olaudah Equiano, or Gustavus Vasa, the African*. Written by himself. London.

Field, M.J. 1961. *Religion and Medicine of the Ga People*. Accra: Presbyterian Book Depot.

Fisher, Miles. 1953. *Negro Folk Songs in the United States*. Ithaca: Cornell University Press.

Forbath, P. 1977. *The River Congo*. New York: Harper & Row.

Franck, H. 1921. "Jamaica Proverbs". *Dialect Notes 5*: pp. 98–108.

Froelich, J.C. 1964. *Animismes. Les Religions Paiennes de l'Afrique de l'Ouest*. Paris: Editions de l'Orante.

Gardner, W.J. 1873. *A History of Jamaica*. London: Frank Cass.

Gbebo, P. 1954. "Music of the Gold Coast". *African Music* 1: pp. 62–4.

Gibbs, James L. (ed.). 1965. *Peoples of Africa*. New York: Holt, Rinehart and Wilson.

Greenburg, J. 1966. *Languages of West Africa*. The Hague: Mouton.

Halliday, M.A.K. 1978. *Language as Social Semiotic*. London: Arnold.

Handler, J. and C. Frisbie. 1972. "Aspects of slave life in Barbados: Music in its cultural context". *Caribbean Studies* 11: pp. 5–40.

Harris, M. 1968. *The Rise of Anthropological Theory*. New York: Crowell.

Herskovits, Melville. 1933. "On the provenience of New World Negroes". *Social Forces* 12: pp. 247–62.

——1938. *Acculturation – The Study of Culture Contact*. New York: J.J. Augustin.

——1941. *The Myth of the Negro Past*. New York: Harper & Bros.

——1947. *Trinidad Village*. New York: Octagon. and W. Bascom.

——1959. *Continuity and Change in African Cultures*. Chicago: University of Chicago Press.

——1967. *Dahomey: An Ancient West African Kingdom*. 2 vols. Evanston: Northwestern Univeristy Press.

——1973, *Cultural Relativism: Perspectives in Cultural Pluralism* (ed. F. Herskovits). New York: Random House.

Higman, B. (ed.). 1976. *Characteristic Traits of the Creolian and African Negroes in Jamaica* (1797). Mona: Caldwell Press.

Hogg, D. 1960. "The Convince cult in Jamaica". In *Papers in Caribbean Anthropology*. Ed. S. Mintz. *Yale University Publications in Anthropology*, No. 58.

——1961. "Magic and 'science' in Jamaica". *Caribbean Studies* I: pp. 1–15.

——1964. "Jamaican Religions. A Study in Variations", PhD. Dissertation, Yale University.

I.A.I. 1965. *African Systems of Thought. Studies presented and discussed at the 3rd International African Seminar.* Salisbury, 1960. London: Oxford University Press.

Inikori, J.E. (ed.). 1982. *Forced Migration: The Impact of the Export Slave Trade on African Societies.* London: Hutchinson.

Jahn, Janheinz. 1961. *Muntu: An Outline of the New African Culture.* New York: Grove Press.

——1968. "Residual element in the Blues". In *Dundes* 1968: pp. 95–103.

Jekyll, W. 1907. *Jamaican Song and Story. Publications of the Folklore Society* 55. London. (New York: Dover, 1966).

Jobson, R. 1623. *The Golden Trade.* London: Okes. (Penguin, 1932).

Johnson, Rev. S. 1921. *The History of the Yorubas.* London: Routledge.

Kochman, T. (ed.). 1972. *Rappin' and Stylin' Out: Communication in Urban Black America.* Urbana: University of Illinois Press

Lamal, F. 1965. *Basuku et Bayaka des Districts Kwango et Kwilu au Congo.* Tervuren: Musee Royale de l'Afrique Centrale.

Lawrence, Arnold. 1963. *Trade Castles and Forts of West Africa.* London: Jonathan Cape.

Lawton, David. 1963. "Suprasegmental Phenomena in Jamaican Creole", PhD. Dissertation, Michigan State University.

LePage, R. and D. DeCamp (eds.). 1960. "Jamaican Creole". *Creole Language Studies* I. London: MacMillan.

Leslie, C. 1740. *A New History of Jamaica.* London: Hodges.

Lewin, Olive. 1968. "Jamaican folk music". *Caribbean Quarterly* 14: pp. 49–56. (ed.).

——1973. *Forty Folk Songs of Jamaica.* Washington D.C.: O.A.S.

——1974. "Folk music research in Jamaica". In *Black Communication: Dimensions of Research and Instruction.* Ed. J. Daniels. New York: Speech Communication Association.

Lewis, Matthew Gregory. 1845. *Journal of Residence among the Negroes in the West Indies.* London: John Murray.

Lewis, Maureen Warner. 1977. *The Nkuyu: Spirit Messengers of the Kumina.* Savacou Publications, Mona. Pamphlet No. 3.

Lewis, Oscar. 1966. *La Vida.* New York: Random House.

Levine, L. 1978. *Black Culture and Black Consciousness: Afro-American Folk Thought from Slavery to Freedom.* New York: Oxford University Press.

Ligon, R. 1657. *A True and Exact History of the Island of Barbados*. London: Moseley

Lincoln, C. 1974. *The Black Experience in Religion*. New York: Doubleday.

Long, Edward. 1774. *The History of Jamaica*. 3 vols. London: Lowndes. (New edition: Frank Cass, London, 1970).

Luttrell, A. 1965. "Slavery and slaving in the Portuguese Atlantic (to about 1500)". In *The Transatlantic Slave Trade from West Africa*. University of Edinburgh, Centre for African Studies (mimeo).

Malinowski, B. 1945. *The Dynamics of Culture and Change*. New Haven: Yale University Press.

Maquet, J. 1972. *Africanity: The Cultural Unity of Black Africa*. New York: Oxford University Press.

Mbiti, John. 1970. *African Religions and Philosophy*. New York: Doubleday. Meillet, A. and G. Cohen. 1924. *Les Langues du Monde*. Paris: Champion.

Merriam, Allan. 1962. "Music in American culture". *American Anthropologist* 54: 1173–1181.

——1961. *Congo*. Evanston: Northwestern University Press.

Metraux, A. 1960. *Haiti: Black Peasants and Voodoo*. New York: Universe Books.

Meyerowitz, E. 1951. *The Sacred State of the Akan*. London: Faber and Faber. Mintz, S. and R. Price. 1976. *An Anthropological Approach to the Afro-American Past: A Caribbean Perspective*. Philadelphia: Institute for the Study of Human Issues.

Moore, J. 1953. *Religion of Jamaican Negroes. A Study of Afro-American Acculturation*. University Microfilm Publication 7053. Doctoral Dissertation Series, Ann Arbor.

——1965. "Religious syncretism in Jamaica", *Practical Anthropology* 12: 63-70.

Morales Padron, F. 1952. *Jamaica Espanola*. Sevilla: Escuela de Estudios Hispano-Americanos.

Morris, Katrin. 1962. *Jamaica: The Search for an Identity*. London: Oxford University Press.

Nettleford, Rex. 1972. *Identity, Race and Protest in Jamaica*. New York: Morrow.

——1978. *Caribbean Cultural Identity: The Case of Jamaica*. Kingston: Institute of Jamaica.

Nhiwatiwa, Naoim. 1979. 'International Communication between the European and the *African World Views*', PhD. Dissertation, SUNY, Buffalo, N.Y.

Nketia, J.H. Kwabena. 1962. *Unity and Diversity in African Music: A Problem of Synthesis*. Accra.

——1974. *The Music of Africa*. New York: Norton.

Nugent, Lady Maria. 1966. *Lady Nugent's Journal of her Residence in Jamaica from 1801 to 1805*. (New edition by P. Wright. Kingston: Institute of Jamaica).

Opoku, Kofi. 1974. "Aspects of Akan worship". In Lincoln 1974: pp. 286–299.

Ottenburg, Simon and Phoebe Ottenburg (eds.). 1960. *Cultures and Societies of Africa*. New York: Random House.

Owens, J. 1976. *Dread. The Rastafarians of Jamaica*. Kingston: Sangster.

Parrinder, G. 1950. *La Religion en Afrique Occidentale*. Paris: Payot.

——1953. *Religion in an African City*. London: Oxford University Press.

Patterson, Orlando H. 1967. *The Sociology of Slavery*. London: McGibbon and Kee.

Pike, Ruth. 1967. "Sevillan society in the 16th century: slaves and freedmen". *Hispanic American Historical Review* 47: pp. 344–59.

Pollard, Velma. 1980. "Dread talk, the speech of the Rastafarian in Jamaica". *Caribbean Quarterly* 26(4): pp. 32–41.

Price, Richard. 1980. *Afro-American Arts of the Rain Forest*. Berkeley: University of California Press.

Quinn, C. 1972. *Mandingo Kingdoms of the Senegambia*. Evanston: Northwestern University Press.

Raboteau, A. 1978. *Slave Rebellion*. New York: Oxford University Press.

Radcliffe-Brown, A.R. 1952. *Structure and Function in Primitive Society*. Illinois: Glencoe.

Rattray, R.S. 1916. *Ashanti Proverbs*. Oxford: Clarendon.

——1923. *Ashanti*. Oxford: Clarendon.

——1927. *Religion and Art in Ashanti*. Oxford: Clarendon.

Rawick, George. 1970. "West African culture in North American slavery: A study of culture change among American slaves in the ante-bellum South with focus on slave religions". In Spencer 1970: pp. 149–164.

Reinecke, John et al. 1975. *A Bibliography of Pidgin and Creole Languages*. Honolulu: University of Hawaii Press.

Reisman, Karl. 1970. "Cultural and linguistic ambiguity in a West Indian village". In Whitten and Szwed 1970: pp. 129–44. .

——1971."Contrapuntal conversations in an Antiguan village". Texas Working Papers in Sociolinguistics, m. 3 (mimeo).

Rencontres. 1965. *Rencontres Internationales de Bouake: Traditions et Modernisme en Afrique Noire*. Paris: Seuil.

Roberts, George. 1954. "Immigration of Africans into the British Caribbean". *Population Studies* VII: pp. 235–61.

Roberts, Helen. 1925. "A study of folksong variants based on field work in Jamaica". *Journal of American Folklore* 38: pp. 149–216.

——1926. "Possible survivals of African song in Jamaica". *Musical Quarterly* 12: pp. 340–58.

Roberts, John Storm. 1972. *Black Music of Two Worlds*. New York: Praeger.

Rodney, Walter. 1969a. *The Groundings with my Brothers*. London: Bogle-l'Ouverture.

——1969b. "Upper Guinea and the significance of the origins of Africans enslaved in the New World". *Journal of Negro History* 54: pp. 327–45.

Royes, Heather. 1978. "The politics of music and dance in the African Caribbean setting" (manuscript).

Russell, Thomas. 1868. *The Etymology of Jamaica Grammar*. Kingston: McDougall.

Schafer, D. 1974. *The Maroons of Jamaica: African Slave Rebels in the Caribbean*. Ann Arbor: University Microfilms.

Schuler, Monica. 1970. "Ethnic slave rebellions in the Caribbean and the Guianas". *Journal of Social History* 3: pp. 374–85.

——1972. "The experience of African immigrants in 19th century Jamaica". (Manuscript).

——1979a. "Afro-American slave culture". In *Roots and Branches: Current Directions in Slave Studies*. Ed. Michael Craton. Toronto: Pergamon. pp. 121–137.

——1979b. "Myalism and the African tradition". In Crahan and Knight 1979: pp. 65–79.

——1980. *Alas, Alas, Kongo, A Social History of Indentured African Immigration into Jamaica, 1841–1865*. Baltimore: Johns Hopkins University Press.

Schumann, J. 1978. *The Pidginization Process: A Model for Second Language Acquisition*. Rowles: Newbury House.

Seaga, E. 1956. "Folk music of Jamaica". Introduction and Notes to Ethnic Folkways Library Album No. P. 453.

Settle, E. Ophelia. 1933. "Social attitudes during the slave regime: Household servants versus field hands". In *Racial Contacts and Social Research. Publications of the American Sociological Society* XXVIII: pp. 95–98.

Shelton, Austin. 1971. *The Igbo-Igala Borderland*. Albany: S.U.N.Y. Press.

Sidrak, Ben. 1971. *Black Talk*. New York: Holt, Rinehart and Winston.

Simpson, George Eaton. 1954. "Jamaican cult music". Ethnic Folkways Library; Pamphlet accompanying Album No. P 461. New York.

——1955. "Culture change and re-integration found in the cults of West Kingston". *American Philosophical Society Proceedings* 99: pp. 89–92.

——1956. "Jamaica Revivalist cults". *Social and Economic Studies* 5: pp. 321–442.

——1957. The Nine-night ceremony in Jamaica". *Journal of American Folklore* 70: pp. 329–35.

——1960. "The acculturative process in Jamaica Revivalism". *Selected Papers of the Fifth International Congress of Anthropological and Ethnological Sciences, 1956*, Ed. A. Wallace. pp. 332-41.

——1970. *Religious Cults of the Caribbean: Trinidad, Jamaica and Haiti*. Puerto Rico: Institute of Caribbean Studies.

——1978. *Black Religions in the New World*. New York: Columbia University Press.

Skinner, Elliot. 1973. *Peoples and Cultures of Africa*. New York: Doubleday.

Sloane, Hans. 1707. *A Voyage to the Islands: Madeira, Barbados, Nieves, St. Christopher, and Jamaica*. London.

Smith, M.G. 1960. "The African heritage in the Caribbean". In *Caribbean Studies: A Synposium*. Ed. V. Rubin. Seattle: University of Washington Press.

Smith, R.T. 1976. "Religion in the formation of West Indian society: Guyana and Jamaica". In *The African Diaspora: Interpretive Essays*. Ed. M. Kilson and R. Rotberg. Cambridge, Mass.: Harvard University Press.

Southern, E. 1971. *Music of Black Americans. A History*. New York: Norton.

Spencer, R. (ed.). 1970. Migration and Anthropology. *Proceedings of the 1970 Annual Spring Meeting of the American Ethnological Society*. Seattle: University of Washington Press.

Stewart, James. 1823. *A View of the Present State of the Island of Jamaica*. (New York: Negro Universities Press, 1979).

Stewart, John. 1971. "Niger-Congo Kwa". In *Current Trends in Linguistics*, no. 7: *Linguistics in Sub-Saharan Africa*. Ed. Thomas Sebeok. The Hague: Mouton. pp. 179–212.

Stewart, William. 1962. "Creole languages in the Caribbean". In *Study of the Role of Second Languages in Asia, Africa and Latin America*. Ed. F. Rice. Washnigton D.C.: Center for Applied Linguistics. pp. 34–53.

Stone, C. 1973. *Class, Race and Political Behaviour in Urban Jamaica*. Mona, Jamaica: Institute of Social & Economic Research.

Taylor, Douglas. 1960. "Language shift or changing relationship". *International Journal of American Linguistics* 26: pp. 155–61.

Thomas, Mary E. 1974. *Jamaica and Voluntary Labourers from Africa 1840–1865*. Gainesville: University Presses of Florida.

Thompson, I.E. 1937. "The Maroons of Moore Town". Published as an Appendix to Williams 1938.

Thompson, Robert F. 1969. "African influence in the art of the U.S.". In *Black Studies in the University*. Ed. A. Robinson, C. Foster, and D. Ogilvie. New Haven: Yale University Press.

Thompson, R.W. 1961. "A note on some possible affinities between the creole dialects of the Old World and those of the New". *Creole Language Studies* II: pp. 107–13.

Turnbull, Colin. 1976. *Man in Africa*. New York: Doubleday.

Van der Kerken, G. 1919. *Les Societés Bantoues du Congo Belge*. Bruxelles: Bruylant.

Van Sertima, Ivan. 1976. *They Came Before Columbus*. New York: Random House.

Voorhoeve, Jan. 1970. *Sranan Syntax*. Amsterdam.

Waddell, Rev. Hope. 1863. *Twenty nine Years in the West Indies and Central Africa*. (London: Frank Cass, 1970).

Washington, Joseph. 1964. *Black Religion: The Negro and Christianity in the United States*. Boston: Beacon Press. 1972.

——*Black Sects and Cults*. New York: Doubleday.

Waterman, R.A. 1952. "African influences on the music of the Americas". In *Acculturation in the Americas*. Ed. Sol Tax. Chicago: University of Chicago Press. pp. 207–18.

Welmers, William. 1946. 'A Descriptive Grammar of Fante'. Dissertation Abstracts, no. 39.

——1973. *African Language Structures*. Berkeley: University of California Press.

Westermann, D. and M. Bryan. 1970. *The Languages of West Africa. Handbook of African Languages*, Part II. Folkestone: International African Institute.

Whitten, N. and J. Szwed. 1970. *Afro-American Anthropology. Contemporary Perspectives*. New York: Free Press of Macmillan.

Williams, Joseph. 1932. *Voodoos and Obeahs: Phases of West Indian Witchcraft*. New York: Dial.

——1938. *The Maroons of Jamaica*. Chestnut Hill, Mass.: Boston College Press.

Wolfson, Freda. 1958. *Pageant of Ghana*. London: Oxford University Press.

Wright, Richardson. 1937. *Revels in Jamaica*. New York: Dodd, Mead & Co.

Wyndham, H.A. 1935. *The Atlantic and Slavery*. London: Oxford University Press.

Yawney, Carole. 1979. *Lions in Babylon: The Rastafarians of Jamaica as a Divisionary Movement*. PhD. Dissertation, University of McGill.

Index